D1881335

# NOTES ON NEPAL

# NOTES ON NEPAL

CAPTAIN EDEN VANSITTART, capt.,
2/5TH GURKHA RIFLES,
(LATE DISTRICT RECRUITING OFFICER.)

WITH AN INTRODUCTION

BY

H. H. RISLEY

INDIAN CIVIL SERVICE; COMPANION OF THE INDIAN EMPIRE; OFFICIER OF THE FRENCH ACADEMY; CORRESPONDING MEMBER OF THE ANTHROPOLOGICAL SOCIETY OF BERLIN

GYAN

*Published by*

Gyan Publishing House
5, Ansari Road
Daryaganj, New Delhi-110002
Phone: 011-47034999, 9811692060
E-mail: books@gyanbooks.com

*Distribution Network*
gyanbooks.com
India, USA, Canada, UK, Australia, France

© **Publisher**
All rights reserved. No part of this work may be reproduced, stored, adapted, or transmitted in any form or by any means, electronic, mechanical, photocopying, micro-filming, recording or otherwise, or translated in any language, without the prior written permission of the copyright owner and the publisher.

ISBN : 978-81-212-3833-5 (PB)
First Published, 1896

2nd Impression 2020

*Printed at:* Gyan Press, Delhi.

The book is sold subject to the condition that it shall not, by way of trade or otherwise, be lent, resold, hired out, or otherwise circulated without the prior publisher's written consent.

The book at your disposal is the edition of an old book originally published long back. The Text quality of this book may not be at par as compared to our other books but many readers approached us to reprint this important book so that it could satiate their hunger. We request all the readers of this book to help us to improve its quality by providing the necessary text of those pages which are not properly visible. Your valuable support in this case will be highly appreciated and acknowledged and our future readers will be benefitted immensely.

# NOTES ON NEPÁL

CAPTAIN EDEN VANSITTART, *Capt.*,

2/5TH GURKHÁ RIFLES,

(LATE DISTRICT RECRUITING OFFICER.)

WITH AN INTRODUCTION

BY

H. H. RISLEY,

INDIAN CIVIL SERVICE, COMPANION OF THE INDIAN EMPIRE; OFFICIER OF THE FRENCH ACADEMY; CORRESPONDING MEMBER OF THE ANTHROPOLOGICAL SOCIETY OF BERLIN.

CALCUTTA:

OFFICE OF THE SUPERINTENDENT OF GOVERNMENT PRINTING, INDIA.

1896.

THIS book is dedicated by kind permission to Field Marshal the Right Honourable Frederick Sleigh, Baron Roberts of Kandahar and Waterford, G.C.B., G.C.S.I., G.C.I.E., V.C., R.A., late Commander-in-Chief in India, as a token of gratitude for the great interest invariably shown by him in all Gurkhá Regiments.

EDEN VANSITTART, *Capt.*,
*2/5th Gurkha Rifles*,
(*Late District Recruiting Officer.*)

ABBOTTABAD;
*The 16th Dec. 1895.*

# PREFACE.

THIS book is an enlarged copy of my "Notes on Gurkhás" written in 1889.

In compiling this book I have borrowed most freely from every author that I know of who has written on Népál or its inhabitants.

As probably nearly one-half of this book consists of extracts from various authors strung together, often with alterations and additions of my own, I am unable to put between inverted commas every borrowed paragraph, but where feasible I have generally done so, and quoted the name of the author from whose book the extract has been taken.

The Chapter on Ancient History of Népál is mostly taken from Wright, Bendall, and Pandit Bhagvánlál Indraji Dass.

From Oldfield, Brian Hodgson, Wright, and Hamilton I have borrowed most heavily.

I have also to thank Dr. Rudolph Hœrnle for directing my attention to useful books, of the existence of which I was unaware. Mr. Vincent Smith, B.C.S., has also very kindly given me the benefit of his great experience, and assisted me with advice.

In my search after and classification of tribes and clans of Eastern Népál, I have been very much assisted by Havildar Purandhoj Limbu of 2/4th Gurkhá Rifles.

It was only after very much trouble that I was able to obtain a copy (and then only of a portion) of a Limbú Vancávali.

I give my translation of the same (seepage 139), as in my opinion it throws some interesting light on Eastern Népál generally and Limbús especially.

The classification of the various races of Népál is almost entirely my own.

The Magars, Gurungs and Thákurs, I believe, are fairly complete and correct.

The lists given regarding the Khas, Limbús, Rais, Sunuwárs and Murmis are undoubtedly incomplete, and perhaps in parts incorrect, but to give a full and true list of their tribes and subdivisons can only be done after years of incessantly putting down on paper each fresh tribe, and each fresh clan of the same, at such time as a member belonging to it presents himself for enlistment, and then by checking its accuracy over and over again.

My classification of "Gurkhás"—*viz.*, Magars, Gurungs, Thákurs and Khas—will be found to be almost identically the same as Chapter IV of the Blue Book on Népál, but this is owing to the fact that I wrote Chapter IV for the Intelligence Branch of the Quarter Master General's Department.

The following is a list of such books as I have had access to :—

Colonel Kirkpatrick's Mission to Népál, 1793.

Doctor F. Hamilton's account of Népál, 1819.

Captain T. Smith's Five Years' Residence in Népál, from 1841 to 1845.

Captain O. Cavenagh's Account of the Kingdom of Népál, 1851.

Brian Hodgson's Essays of the Language, etc., of Népál, etc., 1874.

Doctor Oldfield's Sketches of Népál, 1880.

Quarter Master General's No. 18 of 1883.

Confidential Report, 1884.

Lieutenant-General R. Sale Hill's Notes, with addenda by General Sir C. Reid, K.C.B., dated 1874.

Lieutenant-Colonel E. Molloy's Memorandum dated Abbottabad, 1885.

Doctor Wright's History of Népál, 1877.

Bendall's Catalogue, Buddhist and Sanskrit MSS., 1883.

Bendall's journey in Népál, 1886.

Pandit Bhagvánlál Indraji Dass's Inscription of Népál, 1885.

H. H. Risley's Tribes and Castes of Bengal, 1891.

Sarat Chandra Dass's Journey to Lhása.

Doctor Rudolph Hœrnle's Inscribed Seal of Gupta, 1889.

I also received many vernacular papers from Népál which, after translating, I embodied in my book.

I gathered much information from many sources at Gorakhpur and Darjeeling, and have especially to thank Captain J. G. Robinson, 2/2nd Gurkhá Rifles, for the careful way he checked my manuscript in regard to Eastern Népál tribes.

Jemadar Assaram Burathoki, 2/1st Gurkhá Rifles, also assisted me very much in translating vernacular papers, in verifying many points on which I was uncertain, and in obtaining information for me.

The interest which I take in Gurkhás and in everything connected with Népál and its inhabitants, must be my excuse for writing this book; and although I am well aware that it is faulty in many respects, as it represents the results of the patient labour of many years, I venture to submit it as it stands, hoping that it may prove of some use, and in parts perhaps of interest, and that through its pages the public may be made better acquainted with a race whose country, considering its size, provides the Native Army of India with perhaps a greater proportion of gallant soldiers than any other of the many martial races of India.

# INTRODUCTION.

IN a well-known passage of his work on *Village Communities* the late Sir Henry Maine drew attention to the great value which the records of settlement and revenue operations in India possess for the student of early law and custom. His remarks are equally applicable to Captain Vansittart's *Notes on Nepal* and for much the same reasons. Like a settlement officer the writer has a purely official object in view—in this case, I believe, the promotion of recruiting for Gurkha regiments and the instruction of the younger officers who serve in them. But his minute knowledge of his subject and his keen sympathy with the Gurkhas themselves have led him, as similar motives lead so many revenue officials, to extend the range of his inquiries and to touch upon questions which belong rather to the province of the ethnologist than to that of the practical soldier. Here it will naturally be asked what is the province of ethnology and what light is likely to be thrown upon it by recording the traditions and usages of the Nepalese tribes from whom our recruits are drawn? The answer is best given in the words of M. Elisée Reclus, to whom we owe the following definition of two terms the promiscuous use of which, especially by English writers, has given rise to much confusion. "Ethnography," he says, "embraces the descriptive details, and ethnology the rational exposition, of the human aggregates and organisations known as hordes, clans, tribes, and nations, especially in the earlier, the savage, and barbarous stages of their progress." In other words, ethnography collects and arranges the facts, ethnology analyses, compares and seeks to draw conclusions. To ascertain the facts and record them accurately is the harder task, and unless that is properly done no conclusions worth having are ever likely to be drawn. The facts which the ethnologist wants to get hold of, and for which he must depend in the main upon those who, having had Captain Vansittart's opportunities, have known how to use them, are of two kinds,—physical characteristics and social rules or usages. Both admit of being recorded in a more or less systematic fashion, and we may sometimes observe a curious correspondence between the two sets of data.

Physical characteristics are recorded for ethnographic purposes by the processes known collectively as anthropometry—an uncouth term of which much has been heard of late years in connexion with the identification of criminals. In its relation to ethnology anthropometry may be defined as the science which seeks by measuring certain leading physical characters, such as the stature and the proportions of the head, features, and limbs, to define and classify the chief types of mankind, and eventually by analysing their points of agreement and difference to frame some hypothesis as to the probable origin of the various race-stocks now traceable. In respect of this object, of its endeavour to discover and define types, the method is one of the oldest in the world. It dates from the days of Egyptian sculpture, and has held a prominent place in the literature of ideal art down to modern times. Fifty years ago a Swedish naturalist applied it to the classification, for scientific purposes, of the different forms of the skull and it has since been greatly extended and developed by anthropologists. Its use for police purposes is a modern adaptation which approaches the subject from a very different point of view. The artist and ethnologist care nothing for the individual and endeavour only to determine the type. The detective is indifferent to types and seeks only to identify the particular criminal he is in search of.

The record of custom is more difficult to construct. With well designed instruments, a good method, careful observers, and a large number of subjects, anthropometry conducted under modern conditions can be relied upon to turn out fairly accurate results. But usage, whether social or religious, is a Proteus whom it is less easy to seize. No one can have studied any of the standard books on ethnology without acquiring a vivid impression of the extreme difficulty of entering into primitive modes of thought, of the imperfection and untrustworthiness of testimony and of the extraordinary fluidity and mutability of custom itself. All that can be done is to work on a system, to ask every one the same set of questions, to repeat them as often as possible with different sets of men, to collate the answers diligently, and to endeavour to follow the same usage through all the different forms in which it appears. In this way, to take a simple instance, the common practice of smearing vermilion on a bride's forehead and the parting of her hair may be traced, through the mixture of blood and vermilion used by the Kharwars in Chota Nagpur, to the more archaic usage, in vogue among the Birhors and Rautias, of marking the forehead of the bride with a drop of blood drawn from the little finger of the bridegroom and *vice versá.* Here the analysis of a familiar custom brings us into touch with primitive superstitions as to blood kinship which some authorities believe to have played an important part in the earlier stages of social evolution. By methods such as these results of considerable interest may be arrived at, but it may be doubted whether the mere investigation of usage is likely to throw much light upon the origin of any particular tribe or group of tribes. An exception must however be made in favour of one set of facts, in which Captain Vansittart's book is particularly rich. Such experience as I have of the ways of primitive people rather goes to show that the least variable portion of their social arrangements is their system of exogamous groups—in other words, the subdivisions of the tribe or caste within which its members may not marry. Not only are the names of such groups often very curious in themselves, but where their meaning can be ascertained they often throw considerable light upon the antecedents of the tribe or of portions of it. Thus a tribe with Tibetan group-names may be presumed to have come from Tibet, though none of its members are now acquainted with Tibetan; and where, as is more common, the group-names refer to villages, localities or tracts of country, which admit of being identified, or which figure in the tribal traditions of origin, it may even be possible to recover the history of earlier wanderings from a study of the names. This line of inquiry, which Captain Vansittart has followed to some extent, seems to me to offer considerable prospects in the hands of an observer who knows the language and the geography of Nepal as well as he does. It is hardly an exaggeration to say that almost all the history that tribes of the Gurkha type can boast of is wrapped up in the long lists of their group-names.

Some years ago I ventured to publish in England[1] a tentative description of the Mongoloid type as found along the Northern and Eastern Frontiers of Bengal. The description was based upon certain measurements, taken under my instructions and supervision,[2] of a number of subjects comprising representatives of the Gurung, Khambu, Mangar, Murmi, and Newar tribes. It is much to be regretted that the series was not more extensive and that it included no members of the higher castes of Nepal. The definition of the type which is based upon the measurements has, however, been accepted by anthropological authorities in Europe,[3] and so far as it goes it appears to me to give a fairly correct idea of the average Gurkha. As originally published it runs thus: "A mesorhine, platyopic, brachycephalic type of low or medium stature, sturdy build, yellowish complexion, broad face and low facial angle." Translated into ordinary language that means merely that the most prominent characters of the Gurkha type are a head much broader in relation to its length than that of the average native of India; a broad face; a short wide nose, not so wide as is common among the black races of Chota

(1) Journal of the Anthropological Institute, February 1891.

(2) Tribes and Castes of Bengal: Anthropometric Data, Vol. I, pp. i—xxxvii and 232 to 273.

(3) L'Anthropologie aux Indes, par Paul Topinard. *L'Anthropologie*, Tome II., pp. 351—357.

L'Anthropologie du Bengal ou étude des documents anthropométriques recueillés par M. Risley, par Paul Topinard. *L'Anthropologie* Tome III., pp. 282—316.

Anthropometry in India. By John Beddoe, M.D., LL.D., F.R.S. *Science Progress*, November 1895, pp. 188—203.

Nagpur and the Central Provinces, but very low in the bridge, and in extreme cases almost bridgeless; high and projecting cheek-bones, and eyelids so formed as to give the impression that the eyes are obliquely set in the head. In the form of vague personal impressions these facts are familiar to any one who has had to do with Gurkhas, but measurements systematically conducted enable such impressions to be accurately recorded and reduced to statistical formulas, and it is this process which brings out the most interesting and curious results. For example, a certain method of measurement devised by Mr. Oldfield Thomas and described in his paper(1) on some skulls from Torres Straits enables us to gauge with considerable accuracy the comparative projection or depression of the base of the nose in different individuals in relation to the outer edge of the orbit and thence to construct a formula, called the naso-malar index, which expresses in any particular group the relative preponderance of a Mongolian or Caucasian element. The lower the index the greater is the proportion of Mongolian blood and *vice versâ*. Thus the naso-malar index of the Biloch is 117·9 and that of the Pathan 117·1, an average not differing materially from that of European races, while the same index ranges among the Nepal tribes from 106·9 in the Limbu to 110·2 in the Newar. Similar results follow from the cephalic index showing the relation of the maximum breadth of the head to its maximum length, the latter being taken to be one hundred. In this case the higher indices—not the lower—denote Mongolian affinities. The figures vary from 78·5 in the Murmi to 84·3 in the Limbu, an index which compares fairly with those recorded by

(1) Journal of the Anthropological Institute, May 1885.

Welcker[1] for the Calmucks and Siamese. A third formula combines the recorded height and weight of the specimens observed so as to show the number of grammes per centimetre of height, and thus serves to distinguish certain types of figure. Selecting extreme cases in illustration of the working of the method we find that the Munda tribe of Chota Nagpur have an average index of 372·6 and the Sikkimese Tibetans of 370·7, while the trading Khatri caste of the North-Western Provinces have the low average of 290·7. The Sikh index is 320·2, while the index in the case of the Nepalese races is 350·5 for the Lepcha, 334·7 for the Limbu, 331 6 for the Gurung, and 317·9 for the Murmi. The average stature ranges from 166·9 centimetres in the Murmi to 157·0 in the Lepcha, the average for the group being 116·2 as compared with 168·4 for nine Panjab groups and 163·5 the average of 23 castes of the North-Western Provinces and Oudh.

The interesting point about these dry figures is not merely that they give a statistical form to our general impressions as to different types and enable us to trace gradations of physical characters, but also that there is a distinct correspondence between them and certain facts of the social order. In Nepal, for example, so far as these observations go, it may be said in a general way that the social status of a particular tribe varies inversely as the average width of the head and directly as the average naso-malar index. In other words, the tribes in which Mongolian characteristics are most marked stand at the bottom of the social scale,

(1) Schädelmessungen (Archiv für Anthropologie. Bd. 16, quoted by Peschel, *Volkerkunde*, p. 561, Sixth Edition, Leipzig, 1885.

and the tendency is for these characteristics to become less and less prominent as we pass from the lower to the higher group. These indices therefore point in the same direction as the nasal index in Western Bengal and Chota Nagpur and lend further support to the opinion that race sentiment rather than community of occupation was the motive principle which in the first instance gave rise to the caste system. Other factors no doubt entered in as the system grew, but they all rest upon the fiction that men who speak another language, who live in another place, who observe other customs, worship other gods, or follow another occupation must belong to a fundamentally different race. A country like Nepal, forming a sort of debateable land between Aryan and Mongolian territory, drawing the rank and file of its population from Tibet, and the leaders, intellectual and social, from India ought, one would think, to be peculiarly rich in survivals of archaic usage which may enable us to reconstruct the earlier stages of the evolution of caste. Such survivals will in my opinion most probably be found among the customs relating to marriages and in particular among the rules which govern alliances between members of different castes and define the social status of the offspring. Much interesting information on these matters is contained in Captain Vansittart's book, but I doubt whether the subject has been exhausted, and it is possible that further researches would yield even more valuable results. At first sight one is tempted to wonder whether the intermarriage of different castes, described in the tenth chapter of Manu, may not have survived in the remote valleys of Nepal long after it had fallen into disuse in the plains of India. But the more probable explanation is that the immigrant Aryans brought no women with them and were compelled by sheer necessity to adopt practices at variance with their own strict rules of endogamy.

In conclusion I may say that if any officers attached to Gurkha regiments are disposed to pursue further the lines of inquiry which I have indicated, it will give me much pleasure to furnish them with full particulars as to the best methods to adopt. The study is fascinating in itself; the material is abundant; and of Gurkhas it may certainly be said, what is true in a measure of most of the Indian races, that the more a man knows of their customs and beliefs, the deeper he penetrates into their inner life, the better will he like the people themselves, and the more of their sympathy will he command.

H. H. RISLEY.

# CONTENTS.

# NOTES ON NÉPÁL.

## CHAPTER I.

## GEOGRAPHY.

### NÉPÁL.

THE word "Népál"* is said to be derived from "Né,"* the name of a certain ascetic, and "pálá," cherished, and therefore means "cherished by Né."

General description.

Népál is a narrow tract of country extending for about 520 miles along the southern slopes of the central portion of the Himalayas, between the 80th and 88th degree of East Longitude.

Its breadth nowhere exceeds 140 miles, and averages between 90 and 100 miles.

Its general direction is from west to east, the most southern and eastern corner at the Michi River reaches as low as the 26th, whilst its most northern and western angle extends up to the 30th degree of North Latitude.

It is bounded on the north by Thibet; on the east by Sikkim and the River Michi; on the south by Bengal and the North-West Provinces; and on the west by Kumáon and the River Káli (Sárdah).

Previous to 1815 the kingdom of Népál was much more extensive, and included Kumáon and the hill country up to the River Sutlej. This territory was ceded to the British by the treaty of Segowli.

* It is said that Né Muni performed his devotions at the junction of the Bágmati and Késávati, and by the blessing of Swayambhú and Bajra Jogini he instructed the people in the true path of religion. He also ruled over the country. Kesárati is the same river as Vishnumati.

Character of country.

The country consists of four distinct zones running east and west:—

(1) *The Terái.*—A belt of grass or sâl jungle, varying in breadth from 10 to 30 miles, and skirting the British frontier from the Sárdah to the Michi.

(2) *Dhúns or Máris.*—Beyond the sâl forest and separating it from the second zone, *viz.*, the Dhúns, is the sandstone range.

This range runs in a more or less pronounced form along the whole frontier, and does not rise more than from 300 to 600 feet above its immediate base, and is from 2,000 to 3,000 feet above the level of the sea.

The "Dhúns" or "Máris" are valleys lying behind and below the sandstone ridge, generally at about 2,500 feet above the sea, and between the sandstone and the second range of hills.

Dehra Dhún was one of the Dhúns.

(3) *Hill country.* — From the northern extremity of the "Dhúns," the main range of the Himalayas rises to the north; hill succeeding hill until they culminate in the snowy range. This hill region up to an elevation of 10,000 feet may be taken as the third zone.

(4) The fourth zone is formed by the alpine region above that altitude.

Passes.

The Népál Himalayas are traversed by several passes leading into Thibet, but which, owing to their great elevation, are only open to travellers during the warmer months of the year:—

(1) The Takla Khar Pass, midway between Nunda Devi and Dewalgiri. The Karnáli branch of the Gogra river quits Thibet and enters Népál by this pass.

(2) The Mastang Pass is about 40 miles to the east of Dewalgiri and leads to a small principality of the same name at the foot of Dewalgiri, but on its northern or Thibetian side. On the northern side of the pass, on the high-road to Mastang, is a large village called Muktinath, which is much visited by pilgrims as well as by traders in Thibetian salt. Muktinath is eight days' journey from Mastang and four from Bini Shaher, the capital of Malibam.

(3) The Kerong Pass to the west, and

(4) The Kuti Pass to the east of Gosainthan. These two passes being nearest to the capital are most frequented by Thibetian

pilgrims. The former, *viz.*, the Kerong, is passable for ponies; the latter, the Kuti, is very dangerous and difficult for ponies. The Kuti road is shorter than the Kerong.

The high-road to Lhássa runs through the Kuti Pass and the traffic is greater on this than on any other pass.

(5) The Hatia Pass, about 40 or 50 miles east of Kuti. The Áran, by far the largest of the seven streams whose union forms the Kosi river, quits Thibet and enters Népál through the Hatia Pass.

(6) The Wállang or Wallanchen Pass is situated quite in the eastern extremity of the Népál Himalayas, a little to the west of Kinchinjanga. This Pass was very extensively repaired during the last scare with Thibet about 1885.

River basins.

The territory of Népál, within the hills, from Kumáon on the west to Sikkim on the east, is divided into to three large natural divisions, by four very lofty and massive ridges, which respectively are given off from the high peaks of Nunda Devi (25,700′), Dewalgiri (26,826), Gosainthan (26,305′), and Kinchinjanga (28,156′).

(Mount Everest lies about midway between the two last, and is 29,000 feet, but throws off no main ridges.)

These four enormous ridges stand out at right angles from the central axis of the Himalayas, and run parallel to each other nearly due south towards the plains. Each of these three natural divisions into which Népál is divided by these lofty ridges is walled in on all four sides by mountain barriers—on the north by the snowy range, on the south by the chain of sandstone hills, and on the east and west by one of the above ridges.

Each of these districts thus walled in forms a large mountain basin, sloping gradually to the south, and furrowed by numerous streams which rise in the surrounding amphitheatre of mountains. All these flow towards the plains of India, and all converge towards each other in their course through the hills, so decidedly, that they unite into one large river in two out of three districts, before they reach even the sandstone range of hills.

Each of these three mountain basins derives its name from the river by which it is drained. Thus—

*1st.*—Western division, or mountain basin of the Karnáli or Gogra.

*2nd.*—Central division, or mountain basin of the Gandak.

*3rd.*—Eastern Division, or mountain basin of the Kosi.

Besides these three grand geographical divisions, there are a fourth and fifth, *viz.*—

*4th.*—The Népál Valley.

*5th.*—The Terái.

The Népál Valley is formed by the bifurcation of the ridge running south from Gosainthan, thus forming an isolated triangle; it is watered by the Bhágmati, which drains the whole of this district.

The valleys formed by the numerous streams running down from the snowy watershed, are, in the lower portion, thickly inhabited and well cultivated. The most populous valleys are a an elevation of about 4,000 feet, but cultivation is carried on in the interior up to 13,000 feet.*

The principal rivers of Népál from west to east come as follows:—

The Káli (or Sárdah), the Karnáli, the Rapti, the Gandak, the Bhágmati, the Kosi, and the Michi.

As already explained, Népál is divided into five divisions, *viz.*—

| | |
|---|---|
| 1. The Western. | 3. The Eastern. |
| 2. The Central. | 4. The Népál Valley. |

5. The Terái.

Western Division.

The western division is inhabited by Doti and other non-Gurkhá tribes, and until the close of the last century was divided into twenty-two separate principalities, which were collectively called the Baisi Ráj and were all tributary to the Rájá of "Yumila"—Júmla.

Baisi is derived from Bais (twenty-two). The names of these principalities were—

| | | |
|---|---|---|
| Jumla. | Mallijanta. | Jehari. |
| Jagwikot. | Balhang. | Kálágaon. |
| Chain. | Dailek. | Goriakot. |
| Acham. | Darimeka. | Gutam. |
| Rugham. | Doti. | Gajur. |
| Musikot. | Sallian. | Jajarkot. |
| Roalpa. | Bamphi. | Bilaspur. |
| | Mellianta. | |

* Sarat Chandra Dass says: "The part of the village Yangma where we sat was nearly 14,000 feet high. Buckwheat, barley, sweet turnips, radishes and potatoes grow here."

The central division has been called from time immemorial by the Népálese, the Sápt Gandaki, or "country of the seven Gandaks," and lies among the seven main streams which, uniting, form the Gandak River; by these the whole hill country between Dewalgiri and Gosainthan is drained.

Central Division.

These seven rivers, known collectively as Sápt Gandaki, are, taking them successively from west to east,—

(1) The Barijai; (2) the Narayani; (3) the Sweti Gandakī; (4) the Marsiangdi; (5) the Daramdi; (6) the Gandi; and (7) the Trisulganga.

The central division is the home of the Magars and Gurungs, and it is practically from this portion of Népál that all recruits for the British service are enlisted.

Towards the close of the last century the central division included in its limits, besides the kingdom of Gurkhá proper, twenty-four other independent principalities, collectively called the Chaobisi Ráj, or country of the twenty-four kings.

These principalities were called—

| | | | |
|---|---|---|---|
| Lámzúng. | Rising. | Botwál. | Músikot. |
| Tanahúng. | Ghiring. | Gúlmi. | Argha. |
| Galkot. | Dhoar. | Nayạkot. | Pyúng. |
| Malibam. | Pálpá. | Khách̄i. | Latahúng. |
| Sathúng. | Pokra. | Isma. | Kaikho. |
| Garhúng. | Bhirkot. | Dharkot. | Piuthan, |

Previous to the conquest of the western hills by the Gurkhás, Júmla was the chief of the 46 principalities into which the country between the Káli and the province of Gurkhá proper was divided, and all of which were nominally tributary to the Rájá of Júmla.

These 46 principalities, 22 of the western and 24 of the central division, were all conquered and annexed to Népál by Bahádur Sah towards the close of last century.

The Rájá of Júmla was confined in Khátmandu, and the allegiance of all tributary chieftains, all of whom were Rájputs, was secured by hostages at the capital, or by marriages between them and the royal family of the Gurkhás.

The descendants of the different Rájás of both Chaobisia and Baisi are still recognised as of royal blood.

The central division was divided by the Gurkhás into five provinces called (1) Malibam (north-west); (2) Khánchi (south-west); (3) Palpa (south); (4) Gurkhá (east); (5) Pokra (north).

Eastern Division.

The eastern of the three great natural divisions of Népál includes the whole of the region watered by the mountain tributaries of the Kosi river. In consequence of its containing within its limits and having the whole of its waters drained off by the seven branches of the Kosi river, it is called the Sápt Sosi Kosiki.

The seven Kosi rivers are the following, taking them successively from west to east: (1) Milamchi; (2) Sún Kosi; (3) Támba Kosi; (4) Likkhu; (5) Dúd Kosi; (6) Áran; (7) Tambar.

These streams all rise in the neighbourhood of the snows, and run nearly parallel to each other; but as they approach the lower range, they suddenly converge towards a common point of confluence at Várshá Kshattra or Bára Chattra, from which place these united waters roll in one large river which is called the Kosi, and eventually falls into the Ganges, a little below Bagalpúr. The Áran river is by far the biggest of the seven rivers.

The hill country constituting the basin of the Kosi river, is divided into two provinces or districts by the Áran river. The

NOTE.—The original seat of the Magars is most of the central and lower parts of the mountains between the Jingrak (Rapti of Gorakhpur) and the Marsiangdi rivers.

The original seat of the Gurungs is in a line parallel to that occupied by the Magars and to the north of it, and extending to the snows in that direction. Modern events, however, have spread both the Magars and Gurungs over most part of the Kingdom of Népál.

The Trisulganga previous to the conquest of Népál by Prithwi Narain separated the territories of the Gurkháli and Newár Princes, the western limit of Gurkhá being marked by the Marsiangdi.

Kirkpatrick writing in 1793 says:—

"This tract contains besides a pretty numerous peasantry, several Rájput families and some Newárs, but the tribes by whom it is chiefly occupied are of the Brahminical and Chattri orders, and as these last constituted the principal strength of Prithwi Narain's Government, and continue to form the main support of the present one, they rank very high among its subjects, no description of whom possess such considerable credit and authority as their leaders enjoy.

"They consist for the most part of the Khas and Magar tribes of the Chattri class.*

"Amongst these classes (with the exception of a few individuals deriving their descent from the same† stock as the reigning Prince, and who are consequently Rájputs) are to be found by far the greatest part of those who conduct the affairs of this State."

* By this is most evidently meant such Magar tribes as were converted by the Brahmins and invested with the sacred thread.

† Reference is here made to Thákurs.

district lying on the right bank of the A'ran (on the west) and extending between it and the Dúd Kosi, is the country of the Kirántis (Rais), a hill tribe of low-caste Hindus, who once possessed considerable power in territory, but were speedily reduced to submission by Prithwi Narain after his conquest of Népál.

The district lying on the left (or eastern) bank of the A'ran, and extending from it to Sikkim, is Limbúána, or the country of the Limbus, another tribe of low-caste Hindus. It formerly belonged to Sikkim, but was conquered and permanently annexed to Népál by Prithwi Narain.

Previous to the Gurkhá conquest of the Valley of Népál, the territories of the Newár kings of Bhátgáon extended eastward to the Dúd Kosi river, which formed the boundary between the country of the Newárs and the country of the Kirántis.

The Terái.

The Terái consists of that portion of lowland which intervenes between the outermost hills of Népál and the British frontier.

It is a long narrow slip of forest and grass jungle, with here and there patches of cultivation and stretches of swamp. This Terái extends from the Sárdah river on the west to the Michi river on the east. In its greatest breadth it nowhere exceeds 30 miles.

The valley of Népál, or Népál proper, is completely surrounded by mountains which vary in altitude from 5,000 to 8,000 feet above the level of the sea.

It is of an oval shape, with an average length of 15 miles, and an average breadth of 13 miles. The area is about 250 square miles. The British Residency is 4,700 feet above the sea.

The Népál Valley is densely populated and is supposed to contain nearly 300,000 souls, most of whom are Newárs and Murmis.

It is well supplied with water by numberless streams, which all converge towards the central long axis and join the Bhágmati river.

Kátmandu,* the capital of Népál, is an immense city, and here live in different palaces the King, the Prime Minister, and all great officials.

Area.

It is impossible to calculate with any accuracy the area of Népál, but it is supposed to be about 54,000 square miles.

* Kátmandu is derived from *kát*, wood; *mander*, palace.

The population of Népál is estimated by the Népálese at from 5,200,000 to 5,600,000, and by most writers at about 4,000,000. It is impossible to form any correct estimate of the population, but it is probably about 4,000,000.

Population.

The revenue of Népál is supposed to be about ten lakhs of rupees, but the writer thinks it must be nearer one hundred lakhs.

Revenue.

The grains produced in the lowlands of Népál are indian-corn, rice, wheat, barley, millet, pulses of various kinds, and an enormous amount of red pepper.

Crops and minerals.

Of fruits the chief are the pine-apple, orange, guava, plantain, and pomegranate. Of vegetables the principal are garlic, cabbages, peas, turnips, ginger, and sugarcane.

In the mountain regions the peach, apricot, walnut, raspberry, and wild strawberry are found. These parts also are rich in mines of iron, lead, and copper, and it is said that gold mines also exist.

There are some coal mines not far from Botwál, and also close to Tribeni, as the writer of this obtained some specimen bits, through some recruiters, in 1889. He submitted the same for examination to the Chief Agent of the Bengal and North-western Railway, who pronounced them to be very good coal.

An enormous amount of sál wood is annually cut in the Terái, and this forms one of the principal sources of income to the Népál Government.

The Thibetans bring down for sale in Népál blankets of various kinds, and other woollen manufactures; also ponies, watch-dogs,—large hairy beasts, about the size of an ordinary Newfoundland dog,—goats, sheep, agate, turquoise, yák-tails, gold-dust, gold and silver ore, and quantities of rock-salt.

Trade.

The salt is packed in bags forming loads of about 15lb each which are brought across the snows fastened to the backs of sheep.

All mines in Népál are worked by the Agrái tribe, who must find it a paying business, as a proverb exists in Népál which says, *Kanipút o Ránipút* (a miner's son and a prince's son).

There are three principal eras in use in Népál—

| | | |
|---|---|---|
| Samvat Vikrámáditya—Commences | | 57 B. C. |
| Sáká Saliváhana | „ | 78 A. D. |
| Samvat of Népál | „ | 880 A. D. |

The Kaligat era is also sometimes used ; it begins B. C. 3101.

The era by which Népálese MSS. are almost invariably dated is the Népálese Samvat still used in Népál, and which commences A. D. 880, the year beginning on 1st of October.

The Sriharsha era was also used and commences 606 A. D. Sriharsha conquered all India from Gujerat to Assam—*vide* Bendal, page 41. Excursus on two MSS.

*List of months.*

The Népálese month commences about the middle of the corresponding one of ours. Practically therefore half of two of their months complete each of our months. The following list will, however, answer all practical purposes :—

| | | | |
|---|---|---|---|
| January | . Mágh. | July | . Sáun. |
| February | . Phághun. | August | . Bhado. |
| March | . Chait. | September | . Assojh. |
| April | . Baisákh. | October | . Khátic. |
| May | . Jheth. | November | . Mangsir. |
| June | . Asar. | December | . Pús. |

*Days of the week.*

| | | | |
|---|---|---|---|
| Monday | . Sombár. | Friday | . Sukhbár. |
| Tuesday | . Mangalbar. | Saturday | . Sansarbár. |
| Wednesday | . Búdhbár. | Sunday | . Aitabár. |
| Thursday | . Bihibár. | | |

A "Jágir" is a grant of land for a term, which may be resumed by the doncr. No rent is paid for it. Soldiers and officials are usually paid in this way, the grant terminating with the service. From this is derived the term "Jágirdár" for a soldier.

On retirement into private life he becomes a Dákria, but is able under certain conditions to be called out for service into the "Jágirdárs" again.

A "Guthi" is land assigned for a religious purpose, which cannot be resumed by its donor nor seized by creditors. Rent may or may not be paid for it.

A "Birtha" is a grant of land in perpetuity for which rent is paid.

# CHAPTER II.

## HISTORY OF NÉPÁL VALLEY.

### UP TO CONQUEST BY PRITHWI NARAYAN (KING OF GURKHÁ).

THE Népál Valley was in early days called "Nág Hrád," *viz.*, the "Tank of the Serpent." That the Népál Valley was once upon a time a huge lake would appear by ancient Hindu writings to be a fact, and is, geologically speaking, most highly probable.

Its present name of Népál is said to be derived from the famous ascetic and patron saint of Népál "Ne Muni."

To Manjusri (by the Buddhists) and to Vishnu (by the Hindus) is given the credit of transforming the lake into a fertile plain by cutting a pass through the mountains with his sword. The pass is called Kotbár, Kotwál, or Kotpál.

The legends of the country recorded by Wright and Oldfield may be summarized as follows, but it should be understood that very little is really known concerning the history of the country before A. D. 500 or 600, and that the legends professing to give early history are pure mythology.

It is said that Manjusri* came from China, and that, prior to returning, he established a King in Népál by name Dharmakar,† who, having no issue, appointed as his successor one Dharmapál.†

The next King heard of is one called "Sudhanwa" who is described as a descendant of "Dharmapál."

* Dr. W. Hoey, B.C.S., suggests that Manjusri is merely the "Sri" or "venerable one" from Manchu or Manchuria, a Tartar Province, and not the name of the person alluded to.

† The name Dharmakár is merely the "doer of dharma" and "Dharmapál" the "protector of dharma," and as "Dharma" is the Buddhist religion, this passage regarding Manjusri and these two successors seems merely to be an invention to cover the period when Buddhism entered Népál.

Dharmapál is said to have come to Népál with a saint called "Krakuchand," who evidently was a famous Hindu apostle, as he "permitted 700 of his disciples of the Brahman and Chattri castes to live as Bhiksús."

Krakuchand went to Gunjeswari and saw in the wood planted by Manjusri the three gods of "Brahma," "Vishnú," and "Maheswara" (Siva).

In the earliest of all writings mention is made of "the four castes," *viz.*, Hindus, as existing in the Népál Valley.

Sudhanwa apparently went to Janakpúr to compete in feats of strength for the hand of Sítá, the daughter of the King of Janakpúr.

King Janak for some unknown reason murdered Sudhanwa and sent his brother Kushdwaj to reign instead.

Kushdwaj's descendants ruled the country for some years, after which the dynasty became extinct.

After this Kanak Muni Buddh came from Sobhárati, and after him Kasyapa Buddh from Benares, who sent Prachand Deva, King of Bengal, to Népál as King; after this many Rájás came.

It is stated in the Népálese "Vancávali" that the Kiránties came and conquered Népál at some far back period and that after them came their gods.

The Kiránties, who dwelt originally to the eastward, but had removed to the city of Suprabhá (now Thankot) came and conquered Népál and ruled over the country for some immense period.

They were conquered and driven out by Rájá Dharma Datta of Conjeveram, near Madras, who peopled the country with the four castes—Hindus.

He built the temple of Pashupati.

After this came Vikramádita, who was succeeded by his son Vikramá Kesári, who caused his son Mándeva to sacrifice him by becoming a parricide.

Mándeva built a Buddhist temple, which exists to this day, and is now called Bodhnath, which the Bhutias hold in great veneration.

Né Muni, the patron saint of Népál, installed the son of a pious cowherd as king, and thus started the cowherd (Gópála) dynasty.

Gopál Dynasty.

[NOTE —Kirkpatrick says at page 148:—

Sumbhunath is a very ancient edifice, having, it would seem, been erected at a period when Népál was ruled by a race of Thibetans who, being subsequently expelled by the Newárs, obtained the name of Kát Bhutias (or Bhutias of Kátmandu), which they preserve to this day, occupying at present the mountains of the Kuchái, but principally that part of the range situated in the Koote quarter.

The possession of this temple has always been claimed by the Dalai Lamá (or sovereign Pontiff of Lhássa), and this pretension appears to have been usually yielded to by the existing Government of Nepál, until 1792, when the rupture took place between Népál and Thibet.

Sumbhu is one of the appellations of Mahadeo, and the word, signifying self-existing or self-created, is applied to a stone image of the god supposed to be the spontaneous production of nature.

There were eight kings of this dynasty, the first being Bhutamana and the last Yaksha Gupta.

Ahir Dynasty from India.

Yaksha Gupta having no issue, an Ahir from the plains of Hindustan came and ruled over the country. His name was Bara Simha. There were only three kings of this dynasty, the last of whom, Bhurana Simha, was conquered by the Kirántis, who came from the east.

Kiránti Dynasty.

There were 29 Rájás of the Kiránti Dynasty, beginning with Yalambar.

During the reign of the seventh king, by name Jitedasti, Sakya Simha (Buddha) came to Népál.

Jitedasti assisted the Pándevas in the great war and was killed.

During the reign of Stunko, fourteenth king of this dynasty,* Asoká, King of Pataliputra (Patna), came to Népál. Asoká's daughter, Charumati, was married to a Kshatriya called Devapála, settled in Népál and founded Devapátan (near Pasupati).

The 28th of the Kiránti kings, by name Patuka, was attacked by the Somavansi Rajputs, and built a new Fort at Sankhamulatirtha.

The last of the Kiránti kings, by name Gasti, was defeated by, and lost his kingdom to, the Somavansis.

Somavansi Dynasty.

This dynasty was founded by Nimikha, a Hindu by religion, who conquered Gasti.

There were only five generations of the Somavansis, the last of whose kings was called Bháskara Varman, and figures as a very powerful and wealthy king, and as the conquerer of the whole world up to the seas, *viz.*, the whole of India.

He enlarged the village of Devapátan into a town.

---

After all it is highly probable that the sanctity of this spot might be safely referred to a period very anterior both to the Newár and Khat Bhutia dynasties of Népál, since the sacred books of the Hindus scarcely leave any room to doubt that the religion of Brahma has been established from the most remote antiquity in this secluded valley, where, in truth, there are nearly as many temples as houses, and as many idols as inhabitants.]

* Asoka, King of Patna, reigned from 256 to 219 B. C., over the whole of Northern India, including Kashmir. He was a jealous Buddhist, and he is famous through his rock edicts, one of which is to be seen at Khálsi, Dehra Dún. He belonged to the Maurya Dynasty. He conquered the mountainous regions of Népál.

The grandfather of Asoka, by name Chandra Gupta, drove the Greeks from the Punjab in 316 B. C.

Having no issue he appointed as his successor one Bhumi Varman, a Chattri of the Solar Race (Surajvansi) of the Rájputs, and of the Gotama gotra.

Surajvansi or Suriavansi Dynasty.

He was a descendant of one of the followers of Sakya Simha Buddha who had remained in Népál.

There were thirty-one kings of this line.

During the reign of the eighteenth king, Rudra Deva, 653 to 656 A. D., one Sankara Achárya, a bigoted Brahman, induced a most furious persecution against all persons of every age and rank, and of either sex, who professed or protected the religion of Buddha. He destroyed their literature, burned their temples, and butchered their priests and sages, but failed to overthrow their religion.

Up to this reign no corn had been grown in Népál.

Sivadeva Varman, the twenty-seventh king, made Devapátan a large town, and transferred his seat of government thither.

Visvadeva Varman, the thirty-first and last of the Solar Dynasty, had no male issue, so he gave his daughter in marriage to a Thákur, or legitimate Rájput, named Amsu Varman.

At this time Vikramáditya (see note) a very powerful monarch of Hindustan, came to Népál, and by clearing off all the debts of the country he introduced his new era.

After this Vikramájit obtained salvation, and being a stranger he left no son, so that Amsu Varman, who had married the daughter of Visvadeva, ascended the throne (about A. D. 634, according to the latest authorities).

Thákur Dynasty.

Amsu Varman * founded the Thákur Dynasty, which consisted of eighteen kings.

[NOTE.—The Népálese historian in his anxiety to make the Népálese ancestors go back to a very famous and ancient origin here drags in Vikramáditya, although he had already appeared once, just before the Gópála Dynasty.

Vikramáditya was King of Ujjain, and his coronation is usually put by the Hindus at 57 B. C. He therefore could not possibly reappear in the seventh century A. D.

The real truth would appear to be that between 630 and 635 A. D. a powerful ndian king, by name Sriharsha, conquered Népál, and forced the adoption of his era on to the humbled princes of Népál. The Sriharsha era according to Abiruni began in 606 or 607 A. D. *See* Paudit Bhagvánlál Indraji's "Inscriptions from Népál," from page 43.

It is highly probable that Sriharsha returned to India leaving some one to rule in his stead in Népál, and that this ruler was driven out of the country, and Amsu Varman made king.]

* As the date of the famous Chinese traveller Hiuen Tsang is fixed beyond any doubt, and as his visit to Northern India most probably falls in the year

He reigned from 635 to 650 A. D. (*vide* Fleet) according to inscriptions.

Rájá Bir Deva, the fifth of this dynasty, founded Lalitpur, naming it after a grass-seller, whose ugliness was changed into beauty by washing in a tank close by the spot where the city was afterwards built.

The sixth king, Chadraketu Deva, was sorely oppressed by his enemies and plundered.

During his reign the existence of Khátmandu village is mentioned under the name of Kántipur.

During the reign of the seventh king, Narendra Deva, the "Khas" nation is mentioned as having been relieved from a water famine through their obtaining the god Makindranatha.

The 8th king, Vava Deva, removed the seat of government to Lalitpattana.

Sankára Achárya † came to Népál at this time and persecuted the Buddhists.

Guna Káma Deva, fifteenth king of the Thákur Dynasty, built "Kántipura," the modern Kátmandu, at the junction of the

---

637 A. D. (Cunningham, Geography, page 565), it follows that Amsu Varman must have reigned within the first half of the seventh century of our era

Hiuen Tsang, according to M. Stanislas Julien's translation, says the following:—

"Dans ces dernier temps, il y avait un roi appelé Yang-chou-fa-mo (Chinese way of pronouncing and writing Amsu Varman) qui se distinguait par la solidité de son savoir et la sagacité de son esprit. Il avait composé lui-même un traité sur la connaissance des sons; il estimait la science et respectait la vertu. Sa répu, tation s'était répandue en tous lieux."

It would appear that, however great a king Amsu Varman became eventually, he was originally a Samanta or feudatory of the King of Népál. In his own early inscriptions he assumes no higher title than "the great feudal baron." Later on he appears as Máharájá dhirájá (great King of kings).

† It would seem possible that the Thákur Dynasty did not follow as a sequence of the Suriavansi Dynasty, but that from the time of the sixteenth king of the latter, *viz.* Shiva Varman, there were two kings existing, one of each dynasty.

According to Mr. Fleet there can be no doubt from inscriptions that Shiva Varman reigned from 635 A. D., as the first inscription of his son, *viz.*, Rudra Deva Varman, as King of Nepal, is dated 653. According to Mr. Fleet, also, Amsu Varman's reign is placed by inscriptions as having lasted from 635 to 650.

I would also point another reason for believing in two dynasties as existing at the same time, *viz.*, that in the reign of Rudra Deva Varman, seventeenth king of the Suriavansi Dynasty, mention is made of Sankára Acharya as oppressing Buddhists, *viz.*, in 655 A. D. But Sankára also appears during the reign of Vava Deva, eighth king of the Thákur Dynasty. This would seem to prove the existence at the same time of two dynasties, but it should also be noted that Professor Bühler has recently shown good reasons for believing this view to be mistaken.

Bágmati and Vishnumati rivers, and removed his court here from Patan, but he ruled over both cities.

Jayakáma Deva, the last of the dynasty, having had no issue, the Thákurs of the Navakot mountains came and elected a Rájá from among themselves.

Navakót Thákur Dynasty.

Bhaskara Deva was the first king of this line, and there were only five altogether.

During the reign of the last king, Sankara Deva, cruelties were practised by Brahmans and Buddhists upon each other.

Second Thákur Dynasty of Amsu Varman.

Váma Deva, a collateral descendant of Amsu Varman's family, assisted by the Chiefs in Lalitapattana and Kántipur, expelled the Navakot Thákurs and drove them back to their original home.

Váma Deva founded the second Thákur Dynasty which gave twelve kings.

Sadásiva Deva, the third king of this line, built Kirtipur on a hill south-west of Kátmandu. He introduced copper coins alloyed with iron, marked with the figure of a lion.

Ari Deva, the ninth king, had a son born to him whilst engaged in wrestling, and he therefore gave the child the title of Malla "the wrestler."

Jaya Deva Malla, the eleventh king, established the Nevári era, beginning A. D. 880. He ruled over Lalitapattana whilst his younger brother Ananda Malla founded Bhaktapura or Bhátgáon and ruled there.

Ananda Malla is the last king of the second Thakúr Dynasty and reigned from 1286 to 1302 A. D. (*vide* Bendall).

During his reign many Khassias (a western tribe) migrated to (or conquered) Népál and settled there. A considerable number of Tirhut families also planted themselves there.

Kárnataki Dynasty.

In the Sáká year 811, and Népál Sambat 9 (A. D. 889), on the 7th Srávana Sudi, a Saturday, Nánya Deva Rájá came from the South Kárnataki country and entered Népál. He brought with him the Sáká

[NOTE.—After Ananda Malla's death much confusion arises regarding dynasties. Ananda Malla died about 1302 A. D., yet the Népálese historian now drags in several dynasties beginning with the Kárnataki Dynasty, which, according to him, came under Nanya Deva in the Sáká year 811 and Népál Sambat 9 (A. D. 889), and having defeated the Malla Rájás (Ananda Malla and his brother Jaya Deva Malla) seized the country of Népál.

Sahkála era, and introduced it. Amongst the troops that were with him were Newárs, from a country called Náyéva, who were Brahmaputra Chattris and Achárs.

He defeated the Malla Rájás, and having established his court at *Bhaktapúr* or Bhátgáon, he ruled over it as well as over Lalitapattan (present Pátan), and Kántipur or Kátmandu, and established a dynasty, which lasted about 220 years and gave six kings.

The sixth and last king of this dynasty, by name Hari Deva, had at this time (about 1100 A. D.) a Magar in his service, who, through the machinations of the ministers, was dismissed.

---

The "Vancávali" gives the following dynasties after Ananda Malla's death:—

(1) Karnataki Dynasty (6 kings).
(2) Invasion and conquest by Makunda Sena, the Magar King of Nepal.
(3) Vaishya Thákur Dynasty (reigned 225 years).
(4) Ajodhya Dynasty (4 kings).

Now, we know through history that Harisimha Deva, the first king of the Ajodhya Dynasty, actually did invade and conquer either all or a portion of the Népál Valley in 1324, and it therefore follows that there was only a matter of 22 years between the death of Ananda Malla and the arrival of Harisimha Deva, which would not be sufficient time for two complete dynasties besides an invasion to take place in.

Bendall makes no mention of the Kárnataki or Vaishya Thákur Dynasty as having ever existed.

This confusion may be due, perhaps, to the fact that there were several kingdoms in Népál. The Bhátgaon king seems generally to have been the most powerful of all, and hence to have been called the King of Népál. It may be that the Kàrnataki and Vaishya Thákur Dynasties were co-existent (from some period or other) with the second Thákur Dynasty of Amsu Varman, and that after Ananda Malla's death, either the Khas nation, the Kárnataki Dynasty, or the Vaishya Thákurs asserted their supremacy, or arrogated to themselves the title of King of Népál either at the same time or at different periods.

Whether these dynasties ever did or did not exist, I give them in the next few pages, as Wright produces them in his translation of the "Vancávali," and because there is some interesting matter about the Newárs, and the Magars of Pálpá.

The twenty odd years of uncertainty which exists from date of Ananda Malla's death, *viz.*, 1302, to arrival of Hari Simha Deva, *viz.*, 1324, might well be accounted for by the invasion and conquest of the Népál Valley by the Magar nation under Makúnda Sena, King of Pálpá.

It is interesting also to note that, in the reign of Narendra Deva, the seventh king of the Thákur Dynasty, mention is made of the Khas nation (who certainly were close to the Magar nation, if not already identical with them) being relieved from a famine, by obtaining (probably by right of conquest), the god Machindranatha from Népál.

In Makunda Sena's invasion, we hear that "the victorious soldiers sent the Bhairava in front of Machindranatha to their own country." Can Makúnda Sena's invasion have taken place during Narendra Devá's reign? If so, it would admit the possibility of the Karnataki and Vaishya Thákur Dynasties having actualy existed, but as separate and independent states in some portion or other of Népál.]

This man returned to his home and praised Népál as having houses with golden roofs and golden pranális (or dharas).

Magar King of Pálpá.

The Magar Rájá, by name Makúnda Sena, a brave and powerful monarch, having heard of this, came to Népál from the west with a large number of mounted troops, and subdued Hari Deva, the son of Rama Singha Deva.

Of the Népálese troops some were slain and others fled. Great confusion reigned in the three cities. The victorious soldiers broke and disfigured the images of the gods and sent the Bhairava in front of Machindranatha to their own country, Pălpá and Botwál.

With this Rájá the Khas and Magar castes came to Népál. These men having no mercy, committed great sins, and the southern face of Pashupati showed its frightful teeth, and sent a goddess named Mahá-mári (pestilence), who, within a fortnight, cleared the country of the troops of Mukúnda Sena. The Rájá alone escaped to the east in disguise. On his way back to his own country he arrived at Devighat* and died there.

From this time the Khas and Magars came into the country and sinki and hakuwa† were made.

As Népál had been completely devastated, an interregnum of seven or eight years followed.

The Vaish (or Baish) Thákurs of Navákot came back and occupied the country. In Lalitapattana every "tol" or ward had its own, king, and in Kántipura twelve kings ruled at once. Bhátgáon, too, was held by a Thakúr king.

Vaish Thákur Dynasty.

The Thákurs ruled the country 225 years, after which Hari Simha Deva, King of Simraun,‡ conquered Népál and founded the Ajodhya Dynasty.

Ajodhya Dynasty.

* Devighat is at the junction of the Taddi and Trisulganga rivers in Navakot Valley.

† Sinki is radishes buried in the ground till they ferment. They are then taken out, dried, and eaten: the smell is atrocious and utterly abominable.

Hakuwa is made by stacking the rice when not perfectly ripe, covering it with earth, and allowing it to heat and become slightly malted. It is then dried. It is considered very light and wholesome.

‡ The ruins of Simraun are 15 miles west of the Bhágmati river, and the same distance from the foot of the hills.

Simraun was the ancient and fortified capital of the powerful Hindu kingdom of Mithila (modern Tirhut) which extended from the Gandak to the Kosi, and from

Hari Simha came to Népál in 1324.

The third king of this dynasty, Sakti Simha Deva, received a letter from the Emperor of China, with a seal bearing the inscription Sakti Simharáma in the Chinese year 535.

The fourth and last king of this line was called Shyama Simha Deva. His daughter was married to a descendant of the Mallas, who fled to Tirhut on the invasion of Nánya Deva, and thus after the king's death arose the third Thákur Dynasty, which lasted until displaced by Prithwi Narayan.

Third Thakúr Dynasty. The Thákur Dynasty was as follows :—

1. Jaya Badra Malla.
2. Nága Malla.
3. Jaya Jagat Malla.
4. Nagendra Malla.
5. Ugra Malla.
6. Asoka Malla.—This king drove the Vais Thákurs out of Pátana.
7. Jayasthiti Malla (1385—1429 A. D.) made laws for castes and families, dedicated many images and built temples. An inscription of his exists on a stone near Lalitapattana. He died in 1429.
8. Yaksha Malla (1429—1460 A. D.) is said to have annexed Morang, Tirhut and Gaya to his dominions, and to have conquered Gurkhá to the westward and Shikarjang of Thibet to the north. He likewise completely subdued the refractory Rájás of Pátan and Kátmandu.

He had three sons, the eldest and youngest of whom founded two separate dynasties at Bhátgaon and Kátmandu, while the second held the town of Banepa but founded no dynasty.

To follow history clearly it must be remembered that after Yaksha Malla's death there is no further king of Népál, but a

---

the Ganges to the hills of Népál. Simraun, it is said, was built A. D. 1097 by Rájá Nanynpa Deva, and his descendants occupied the throne for several generations.

The last of his dynasty, Rájá Hari Simha Deva, was conquered and driven into the hills A. D. 1322 by Ghaias-ud-din Toghlak Shah, Emperor of Delhi. The kingdom of Methila was annexed as a province to the Mahomedam dominions, and its capital, Simraun, was reduced to ruins. On retiring to the hills Hari Simha Deva conquered Népál, and his descendants continued on the throne of Népál till they were displaced by Prithwi Narayan.

The descendants of the Newárs, who came from Náyera, were not molested and still occupied the country.

king of Bhátgáon (descendants of Raya Malla, eldest son of Yaksha), and a king of Kátmandu (descendant of the youngest son of Yaksha).

Bhátgáon Dynasty.

9. Raya Malla.
10. Suvarna Malla.
11. Prána Malla.
12. Biswa Malla.
13. Trailokya Malla, 1572 A. D.
14. Jagatjyola Malla, 1628 A. D.
15. Narendra Malla.
16. Jagat Prakása Malla built a temple to Bhimasena inscribing the date A. D. 1655 on a stone lion. In 1662 A.D. he incised five hymns on a stone. In 1665 he incised another hymn on a stone, and in 1667 A. D. dedicated a temple to Bhavánisánkara.
17. Jita Mitra Malla dedicated an image to Harisánkara near the Darbar in 1682 A. D. Incised an inscription in 1683.
18. Bhúpatindra Malla. The dated inscriptions of his reign are A. D. 1703—1707, 1707—1718, and 1721.
19. Ranjit Malla dedicated a bull to Annapurna Devi, A. D. 1737. Defeated, and his kingdom taken from him by Prithwi Narayan, the Gurkhá, A. D. 1769. With him the dynasty of Bhátgáon became extinct.

Kátmandu Dynasty.

1. Ratna Malla, youngest son of Yaksha Malla, and younger brother of Raya Malla, King of Bhátgáon, seized Kántipur (Kátmandu) and established himself as king of the same and founded the Kátmandu Dynasty.

In 1491 A. D. he defeated the Thákurs of Navakot, and later on, being hard pressed by Bhutias (Thibetans) called Kuku, he obtained troops from Sena, the Magar King of Pálpá, and with their assistance defeated the Bhutias at a place which has ever after been called "Kuku Syáná jor."

At this period Yavanas (Mohamedans) first entered Népál as traders, etc.

Ratna Malla conciliated the people of Kátmandu and Pátan, and having brought copper from Támba Khâni (in Chitlong Valley at the foot of the Sisaghari hills) he introduced pice into currency instead of sukichás (an ancient coin worth 8 pice).

2. Amara Malla ruled over 26 towns, including Kirtipúr, Thánkot, and Pátan, but his capital remained Kátmandu.

3. Surya Malla took two towns from the King of Bhátgáon.

4. Narendra Malla.

5. Mahendra Malla received from the Emperor of China permission to issue silver coinage called the Mohar and became a friend of Trailokya of Bhátgáon in 1572 A. D. In his reign Purandara Rajvansi built a temple of Náráyana close to the palace in Lalitapattana (A. D. 1566).

6. Sadasiva Malla, owing to his licentiousness, was expelled by his people and fled to Bhátgáon, where he was imprisoned—1576.

7. Siva Simha Malla (brother of Sadasiva) according to an inscription repaired the temple of Swayambhu in 1594. He had two sons, and at his death in 1639 these two sons divided the kingdom of Kátmandu: the elder, Lakshminar Simha, retaining Kátmandu; the younger, Haribara Simha, starting a kingdom at Pátan and founding a dynasty there. From this time there are three kingdoms within the Népál Valley: (1) Bhátgáon; (2) Kátmandu; (3) Pátan.

8. Lákshminar Simha Malla, eldest son of Siva Simha, ruled at Kátmandu. During his reign, 1595 A. D., the wooden temple of Gorakhnáth called "Kát Mauder" was built, after which the town of Kántipura was called Kátmandu.

He became insane, was dethroned by his son, and kept in confinement during sixteen years.

9. Pratapa Malla ruled from 1639. He was a poet. The inscriptions of his reign date 1640, 1650, 1654, and 1657 A. D.

He allowed his four sons to reign by turns each for one year, during his lifetime. He died in 1689 A. D. He waged war with Sri Nivasa, third king of Pátan.

10. Mahindra Malla, third son of above, died in 1694.

11. Bháskara Malla died of a plague after ruling till 1702, leaving no children, and in him the Solar Dynasty of Kátmandu became extinct.

12. Jagat Jaya Malla, a distant relative, was placed on the throne. He kept Khas sepoys in his employ. He heard that the Gurkháli King Narbupal Sáh had extended his rule as far as Navakot, which grieved him much. He died in 1732.

13. Jayaprakása Malla, second son of Jagat Jaya, expelled his brother Rájyaprakása. In 1736 he drove Narbupal Sáh, King of the Gurkhás, out of Navakot, and forced the Gurkhá back to his own country.

In 1744 he put to death a Gurkháli by name Kasirám Thápá, and Prithwi Náráyan having heard of this came to Navakot and took possession of the land belonging to thirty-two Tirhutia Brahmans. Jayaprakása was deposed by Prithwi Náráyan in 1768.

Pátan Dynasty.

1. Harihara Simha, younger son of Siva Simha of Kátmandu, and younger brother of Harihara Simha, 8th king of Kátmandu, seizes Pátan as his capital, start in his kingdom and founds a dynasty.

2. Siddhinar Simha Malla built a palace at Lalitpúr in 1620. Consecrated an image in 1637, made a water-course in 1647, became an ascetic in 1657.

3. Sri Nivasa Malla reigned from 1657; had war with Pratápa Malla of Kátmandu 1658 to 1662. His latest inscription is 1701 A. D.

4. Yoga Narendra Mal lost his son and became an ascetic.

5. Mahindra Malla died in 1722.

6. Jaya Yoga Pakrása Malla. An inscription of his reign is dated 1723 A. D.

7. Vishnu Malla dedicated a bell, 1737 A. D., and died shortly afterwards leaving no issue.

8. Rájyaprakása, distant relative, appointed king by Vishnu Malla, made blind by the Pradháns and expelled after one year.

9. Gaya Prakása, thirteenth king of Kátmandu, ruled two years over Pátan, when the Pradháns expelled him.

10. Visvajit Malla, son of a daughter of Vishnu Malla, reigned four years, murdered by Pradháns.

11. Dalmardan Sáh of Navakot (brother of Prithwi Naráyan) made king by Pradháns, and expelled after four years' reign in 1765.

12. Tejnar Simha Malla, a descendant of Visvajit Malla, reigns ıree years. Then the country is conquered by Prithwi Naráyan.

---

## APPENDIX.

### List of the Rájás of Népál Valley from the time of "Né Muni."

*A. Gupta Dynasty.*

1. Bhutamána.
2. Jaya Gupta.
3. Parama Gupta.
4. Harsha Gupta.
5. Bhima Gupta.
6. Mani Gupta.
7. Vishnu Gupta.
8. Yaksha Gupta.

## APPENDIX.

### *B. Ahir Dynasty.*

1. Vava Sinha.
2. Jayamati Sinha.
3. Bhuvana Sinha.

### *C. Kiránti Dynasty.*

1. Yalambara.
2. Pavi.
3. Skandhará.
4. Valamba.
5. Hriti.
6. Humati.
7. Jitedasti. (About 600 B. C.)
8. Gali.
9. Pushka.
10. Suyarma.
11. Parba.
12. Thunka.
13. Swananda.
14. Sthunko. (226 B. C.)
15. Gighri.
16. Nane.
17. Luk.
18. Thora.
19. Thoko.
20. Varma.
21. Guja.
22. Pushkara.
23. Kesu.
24. Sunsa or Suga.
25. Samma or Sansa.
26. Gunan.
27. Shimbu.
28. Patuka.
29. Gásti.

### *D. Soma Vansi Dynasty.*

1. Nimisha.
2. Matáksha or Manáksha.
3. Kákha Varman.
4. Pashupresha-Deva.
5. Bháskara Varman *

### *E. Surja or Surya Vansi Dynasty.*

| No. | Name | | About A. D. |
|---|---|---|---|
| 1. | Bhumi | Varman. | |
| 2. | Chandra | „ | |
| 3. | Jaya | „ | 330—335 |
| 4. | Varsha | „ | Names not recorded in inscriptions A. D. 335—630. |
| 5. | Saiva | „ | |
| 6. | Prithwi | „ | |
| 7. | Jyeshtha | „ | |
| 8. | Hari | „ | |
| 9. | Kubéra | „ | |
| 10. | Siddhi | „ | |
| 11. | Haridatta | „ | |
| 12. | Vasudatta | „ | |
| 13. | Pati | „ | |
| 14. | Shivavriddi | „ | |
| 15. | Vasanta | „ | |
| 16. | Shiva | „ | 635—645 |
| 17. | Rudradeva | Varman | 653—655 |
| 18. | Vrikshadeva | „ | 655—670 |
| 19. | Shankaradeva | „ | 670—685 |
| 20. | Dharmadeva | „ | 685—704 |
| 21. | Mánadeva | „ | 705—732 |
| 22. | Mahádeva | „ | 733—750 |
| 23. | Vasantadeva | „ | 754 |
| 24. | Udayadeva | „ | 675 to 724 |
| 25. | Mánadeva | „ | |
| 26. | Guna Kamadeva | „ | |
| 27. | Shivadeva II. | „ | 725—748 |
| 28. | Narendradeva | „ | |
| 29. | Bhimadeva | „ | |
| 30. | Vishnudeva | „ | |
| 31. | Vishwadeva | „ | |

* Existed after 222 B. C.

## APPENDIX—*contd.*

### *F. Thákuri Dynasty.*

1. Anshu Varman 635—650 A. D.
2. Krita „
3. Bhimarjuna Varman.
4. Nanda Deva.
5. Vira Deva.
6. Chandraketu Deva.
7. Narendra „ 700–724 Khas nation mentioned.
8. Vara Deva
9. Shankara Deva.
10. Vardhamán „
11. Bali „
12. Jaya „ 750—758
13. Bálárjuna „
14. Vikráma „
15. Gunakáma „
16. Bhoja „ 1015 A. D.
17. Lakshmikáma „ 1039 A. D.
18. Jayakáma „

### *G. Vaisa or Baisa Thákuri Dynasty from Navakot.*

1. Bháskara Deva.
2. Bala „
3. Padma „ . A. D. 1065
4. Nágárjuna Deva.
5. Shankara „ 1071 A. D.

### *H. Second Thákuri Dynasty (Amsu Varman Dynasty).*

1. Váma Deva 1083 A. D.
2. Harsha „ 1093 „
3. Sadáshiva „
4. Mána „ 1139 „
5. Narsinha „ 1141 „
6. Nanda „ 1165 „
7. Rudra „
8. Mitra „
9. Ari Deva.
10. Abhaya Malla (Népál era introduced, beginning in October) A. D. 1224
11. Jaya Deva Malla 1257
12. Ananda Malla 1286 to 1302

### **I. Karnataki Dynasty about 1302.*

1. Nanya Deva.
2. Ganga „
3. Narasinha „
4. Shakti Deva.
5. Ramasinha „
6. Hari „

### **J. Makúnda Sena, the Magar King of Botwal and Pálpá, invades and conquers the country, A. D. 1100.* (?)

### **K. After Makúnda Sena's expulsion various Vaishya Thákuri dynasties for 225 years.* (?)

### **L. Ajodhya Dynasty.*

1. Harisinha Deva (from Simraungarh, A. D. 1324).
2. Matisinha Deva.
3. Shaktisinha Deva.
4. Shyámasinha „

* Not mentioned in Bendall.

## APPENDIX—*contd.*

### *M. The Malla Rájás (third Thákuri dynasty) descendants of Abhaya Malla.*

1. Jayabhadra Malla.
2. Nága „
3. Jayajagat „
4. Nagendra „
5. Ugra „
6. Ashoka Malla.
7. Jyasthiti „
8. Yaksha Malla (division of the kingdom) . 1429—1460

### (*a*) *Rájás of Bhaktapur or Bhátgáon.*

9. Raya Malla (eldest son of Yaksha Malla).
10. Suvarna Malla.
11. Prána Malla.
12. Vishwa Malla.
13. Trailokya Malla . 1572
14. Jagajoyti Malla . 1628
15. Narendra „
16. Jagatprakása „ . 1642
17. Jitámitra „ . 1663
18. Bhupatindra „ . 1695
19. Ranajit „ . 1722—68

### (*b*) *Rájas of Kántipur or Kátmandu.*

9. Ratna Malla (youngest son of Yaksha Malla)
10. Amava Malla.
11. Surya „
12. Narendra „
13. Mahindra „
14. Sadáshiva „ . 1576
15. Shivasinha „ . 1600
16. Lakshmi Narsinha Malla (eldest son of Shivasinha) . 1631
17. Pratápa Malla . 1665
18. Mahindra (Bhupálendra) Malla.
19. Sri Bháskara . 1701
20. Jagajjaya Malla . 1722
21. Jaya Prakása „ .1736—1769

### (*c*) *Rájás of Lalittapur or Pátan.*

1. Harihara Sinha Malla (younger son of Shivasinha, 15th king of Kátmandu).
2. Shiddi Narsinha Malla . . 1631—54
3. Sri Nivasa Malla 1655—1678
4. Yoga Narendra Malla . . 1686—1705
5. Mahindra (Mahipatindra) Sinha Malla of Kátmandu . . 1722
6. Jaya Yoga Prakása Malla . . . 1722
7. Sri Vishnu Malla . 1729
8. Rájya Prakása . . 1742
9. Jaya Prakása (of Bhátgáon).
10. Jaya Prakása Malla (of Kátmandu).
11. Vishwajit Malla.
12. Dalmandan Sah (a Gurkháli).
13. Teja Nar Sinha Malla. 1769

### (*d*) *Gurkháli Rájás of Népál.*

1. Prithvi Narayna Sáh.
2. Pratápa Sinha „
3. Rana Bahádur „
4. Girvána Yuddha Vikrama Sáh.
5. Rajendra Vikráma Sáh.
6. Surendra Vikráma „
7. Prithwi Vira Vikráma Sáh.

*Rájás of Népál (Valley) 1008—1457 A. D., with dates from manuscripts and other sources.*

| Name of King. | Dates derived from manuscripts. | Reign according to Kirkpatrick, Prinsep, and Hodgson's papers. | |
|---|---|---|---|
| | | Years. | |
| Nirbhya . . | | | |
| Rudra . . . | 1008 | 7 | |
| Bhoja . . . | | | |
| Rudra . . . | 1015 | 8 | |
| Lakshmi Káma . . | | | |
| Lakshmi Káma . . | 1039 | 22 | |
| Jayadeva . . . | ... | 20 | |
| Udaya . . . | ... | 8 | |
| Bháskara . . . | ... | 7 | According to Kirkpatrick Bháskara was a refractory tributary of Pátan; according to the "Vancávali," the founder of a new dynasty. Clearly the succession was broken here, some of these kings being contemporary rivals. |
| Bál Deva . . . | ... | 11 | |
| Pradyumna Káma Deva . | 1065 | 7 | |
| Nagarjuna Deva . . | ... | 3 | |
| Cankara Deva . . | 1071-72 | 17 | |
| Vána or Váma Deva . | 1083 | 2 | |
| Rama Harsa Deva . . | 1093 | 16 | |
| Sadáciva Deva . . | ... | 28 | |
| Indra Deva . . . | ... | 12 | |
| Mána Deva . . . | 1139 | 5 | |
| Narendra . . . | 1141 | 7 | Mention is made of the Khas nation in this reign. |
| Ananda (Nanda) . . | 1165-66 | 20 | |
| Rudra Deva . . . | ... | 80 | |
| Mitra or Amrita . . | ... | 4 | |

*Rájás of Népál (Valley) 1008—1457 A. D., etc.*—contd.

| Name of King. | Dates derived from manuscripts. | Reign according to Kirkpatrick, Prinsep, and Hodgson's papers. | |
|---|---|---|---|
| | | Years. | |
| Ari Deva . . . | (Date uncertain.) | 31 | |
| Ranacura . . . | 1222 | Not named | |
| Sumesar Deva . . | ... | 6 | |
| Raz Káma . . . | ... | Year not given. | |
| Anya Malla . . . | | 32 | |
| Abhaya Malla . . | 1242(?) | 48 | |
| Jaya Deva . . . | 1257 | 2 | |
| Ananta Malla . . | 1286<br>1302 | 34 | Kirkpatrick tells us that in this reign an immigration took place, in 1288. |
| Kings uncertain for 60 years. | ... | ... | |
| Jayárjuna Malla . . | 1364<br>1374<br>1384 | ... | Not named in any history, geneology or inscription. |
| Jayasthiti Malla . . | 1358<br>1386<br>1389<br>1391<br>1392 | No years given for reign by Kirkpatrick. | For this King see the histories and inscriptions in Indian Antiquary for August 1880. |
| Ratnajyoti Malla . . | 1392 | Not named. | |
| Joint regency . . . | 1400 | Ditto | |
| Regency of Jayadharma Malla. | 1403 | ... | |

*Rájás of Népál (Valley) 1008—1457 A. D., etc.*—contd.

| Name of King. | Dates derived from manuscripts. | Reign according to Kirkpatrick, Prinsep, and Hodgson's papers. | |
|---|---|---|---|
| | | Years. | |
| Jayajyoti Malla . . | 1412 | Years not given. | |
| Yaksha Malla . . | 1429<br>1454<br>1457 | Ditto | After this the Népál Valley is no longer one kingdom only. |

After Yaksha Malla the Népál Valley ceased to exist as a kingdom under one king—and we find two kings in 1460, one by name Raya (or Rámá) reigning at Bhátgáon, and the other Ratna, King of Kátmandu.

*Table of the Kings in Népál Valley from division of the Kingdom of Népál down to the Gurkhá conquest.*

YAKSHA-MALLA (KING OF NÉPÁL).

Became King 1429, died A. D. 1460.

Kings of Bhátgáon.

(9) Raya.
(10) Suvarna.
(11) Prana.
(12) Biswa.
(13) Trailokya, A. D. 1572.
(14) Jagatjoyla, 1628.
(15) Narendra, 1633.
(16) Jatgat Prakasa, 1642.
(17) Jita Mitra, 1663.
(18) Bhupatindra, 1695.
(19) Ranjit, 1722—1768.
Deposed by Prithwi Narayan).

Kings of Kátmandu.

(1) Ratna.
(2) Amara malla.
(3) Surya.
(4) Narendra.
(5) Mahindra.
(6) Sadasiva, 1576.
(7) Siva Sinha, 1600.

Kings of Kátmandu—continued.

(8) Lakshmi.
1649—59 (9) Pratapa.
1669 (10) Mahindra.
1701 (11) Sri Bhaskara.
1722—26 (12) Jagatjaya.
1736—68 (13) Jaya Prakása.
(Deposed by Prithwi Narnyan.)

Line of Pátan founded.

(1) Harihara.
(2) Siddhi, 1631—54.
(3) Nivasa, 1665—78.
(4) Narendra.
(5) Mahindra.
(6) Jayayoga, 1686—1701.
(7) Vishnu, 1729—31.
(8) Raiya, 1742—53.
(9) Jaya Prakása.
(10) Viswajit } no dates.
*(11) Dalmandar } no dates.
(12) Tejnar, 1768.
(Deposed by Prithwi Narayan.)

* Brother of Prithwi Narayan, King of Gurkhá.

After this Prithwi Narayan of Gurkhá assumes title of King of Népál.

# CHAPTER III.
# GURKHÁ HISTORY.

## HISTORY OF GURKHÁ DYNASTY.

FORMERLY Suryabansi and Chandrabansi Rájás (*viz.*, Kings of the Solar and Lunar dynasties) ruled over the people, until their kingdoms were taken from them by the Yavanas (Musalmans).

Sri Vikramáditya* and Sáliváhna† were two powerful kings of the Solar dynasty, and they sought out the Rájás of the two dynasties and allotted them kingdoms, according to their abilities, wisdom and power, and placed them on the thrones. They installed in this way eight hundred Rájás.

Amongst these was one Rishi Raj Ránáji of the Lunar dynasty, who was made Rájá of Chitaurghar and received the title of Bhattárak.

Rishi Ráj Ráná and his descendants ruled their country through thirteen generations, when their last Rájá, Deva Sarma Bhattárak, was subjugated by the Mahomedans, who, after establishing their authority over him, left the country.

Deva Sarma had a son named Ayutabam, who, disgusted at the loss of his independence, gave up the name of Bhattárak and retained only his original caste surname of Ráná.

The Rájás, who retained the title of Ráná, were (14) Ayutabam Ráná, (15) Barábubam Ráná, (16) Kanakbam Ráná, (17) Yasobam.

* Vikramáditya is generally said by Hindu authorities to have been installed B. C. 57.

† The Saliváhna era being A. D. 78, it is presumed he reigned at that time.

The irruption of the Hans (a Scythian race) into India took place in the fifth century, and their power was finally broken by the great victory obtained over them by Yasodharman (or Yásovarman), A. D. 530.

The irruption of the Hans into Europe is said to have begun in A. D. 375 under their leader Balamir, and was most successful under their leader Attila, A. D. 445—458.

Their power in Europe was broken in the great battle on the Catrlonian field, A. D. 451 (near village of Moirey in Champagne).

See Bradley's history of the Goths, page 112.

The people commonly called Indo-Scythians were a Scythic race that conquered India about three centuries before the irruption of Hans, and gave several famous rulers to Northern India (*e. g.*, Kaniskka, in the first century A. D., who is probably the real founder of the so-called Saliváhana era, A. D. 78).

The son of the last, named Audambar Ráuá, pleased the Mahomedan emperor by his skill in sword exercise and had the title of Rává (Ráo) conferred on him. The Rájás, who held the title of Rává in addition to their caste surname of Ráuá, were—

| | | |
|---|---|---|
| 18. Audambar | Ránáji | Rává. |
| 19. Bhattárak | „ | „ |
| 20. Bir Vikramjit | „ | „ |
| 21. Jilla | „ | „ |
| 22. Ajilla | „ | „ |
| 23. Atal | „ | „ |
| 24. Tutha | „ | „ |
| 25. Bimiki | „ | „ |
| 26. Hari | „ | „ |
| 27. Brahmá | „ | „ |
| 28. Bakbán | „ | „ |
| 29. Manoratha | „ | „ |
| 30. Jaya | „ | „ |
| 31. Jagatra | „ | „ |
| 32. Bhoj | „ | „ |
| 33. Bhupati | „ | „ |

This Rájá had three sons—

| | | |
|---|---|---|
| Udayabam | Ránáji | Rává. |
| Fatte Simha | „ | „ |
| 34. Manmath | „ | „ |

Fatte Simha had a daughter named Sadal, who was unrivalled in beauty.

The Mahomedan Emperor asked that Sadal should be given to him, but this having been refused, he attacked Chitaur and a bloody battle was fought.

King Bhupati, Fatte Simha and a great many Rájputs were killed, and thirteen hundred Ránis immolated themselves as Satis. Sadal killed herself by leaping into a pan of boiling oil.

The survivors under Udayabam Ráná Rává founded Udayapúr and settled there.

Manmath Ráná Rává went to Ujain. He had two sons—

| | | |
|---|---|---|
| Brahmánika | Ráná | Rává. |
| 35. Bhupál | „ | „ |

These two brothers being on bad terms separated, the elder remaining at Ujain, the younger going to the northern hill (Népál).

The latter arrived at Riri or Ridi. In 1495 he set out from Riri and reached Sargha, from whence he went to Khilum, a place in Bhirkot, and brought waste land under cultivation. In this place he had two sons born to him—Khancha and Mincha.

The former went to Dhor, conquered Mangránt and reigned over Garhung, Sathung, Bhirkot and Dhor.

Mincha went to Nayakot* and ruled over it.

In 1802 Doctor F. Hamilton writes: "The first person of the Gurkhá family, of whom I have heard, were two brothers, named Khancha and Mincha,† words altogether barbarous, denoting their descent from a Magar family, and not from the Pamars, as they pretend."

Khancha was the founder of the imperial branch of the family, *viz.*, they remained Magars. Mincha was the Chief of Nayakot, and adopted the Hindu rules of purity, and his descendants intermarried with the best families, although not without creating disgust.

The Khancha family possessed Bhirkot, Garhung, and Dhor.

Bhirkot seems to have been the head of the whole, as its chief was at the head of a league containing Nayakot.

Mincha, the Rájá of Nayakot, and the chiefs of this place, although they lived pure, continued to the last to follow in war the impure representatives of Khancha.

A branch of the Mincha family ruled at Káski. The Chief of Lámzúng was descended from a younger son of the Káski ruler, and in time became very powerful, and he was followed in war not only by his kinsman, the Chief of Káski, but by the Rájá of Tanahung.

The Rájás who ruled over Nayakot were—

36. Mincha.
37. Jayan.
38. Surya.
39. Micha.
40. Bichitra.
41. Jagdvea.

Kulmandan, the són of Jagdeva, obtained sovereignty over Káski, and having pleased the Mahomedan Emperor in something,

* Not the Nayakot near Kátmandu, but another far to the west, close to Bhirkot.
† "Khancha" is the Khas Kura for "younger brother."
‡ In Rajputána, in Mewár district.

received from him the title of Sáh. He had seven sons; the eldest succeeded him in the government of Káski.

The second, Kálu Sáh, was asked for by the people of Lámzúng (Gurungs) and was made their king.

Kálu Sáh was murdered.

For some time after this Lámzúug remained without a Rájá, but at last the people, unable to manage without one, again went to ask Kulmandan Sáh for another son to become their Rájá. After a solemn promise that they would not murder their next king, Kulmandan allowed them to chose any of his six other sons, excepting the eldest.

These five sons were sleeping in one room, and it was noticed that the four elder had their heads, just in the place where they first laid them, but that the head of the youngest had moved upwards a long way. They therefore considering this a very fortunate man selected the youngest and made him their Rájá. His name was Yasobam.

42. Kulmandan Sáh (King of Káski).
43. Yasobam Sáh (King of Lámzúng).

Yasobam had two sons. The elder, Narhari Sáh, ruled over Lámzúng. The younger, Drabya Sáh (or Sáhi), rebelled and took to himself Gurkhá, which then formed the southern part of the principality. The capital Gurkhá is situated on a very high hill and contains the temple of Gurákhánát. From this we may infer that the proper name of the place is Gurákhá, and that previous to having adopted the doctrines of the Brahmans, this family had received the "jogis," or priest, of Gurákhánát as their spiritual guides.

The taking of Gurkhá is described as follows:—

The younger brother Drabya Sáh went to Gurkhá, and gained over the subjects of that town, the Rájá of which was of the Khándka tribe of the Khas race.

On Wednesday, the 23rd September 1559, Drabya Sáh, aided by Bhagiráth Panth, Gánesa Pánde, Gangaram Ráná, Busál Arjyal, Kanál Bohra, and Múrli Khawás of Gurkhá, concealed himself in a hut. When Gánesa Pánde had collected all the people of Gurkhá such as the Thápás, Busáls, Ránás, and Máski Ránás of the Magar tribe, they went by the Dábyá Gaudá route and attacked the Durbar

Drabya Sáh killed the Khándka Rájá with his own hand with a sword during the battle that ensued.

At the same auspicious moment Drabya Sáh took his seat on the throne amidst the clash of music.

| | | | | |
|---|---|---|---|---|
| 44. Sri Drabya, Sáh, King of Gurkhá, from A. D. | | | | 1559 to 1570. |
| 45. Sri Purandar Sáh | „ | „ | „ | 1570 to 1605. |
| 46. Sri Chatra Sáh became | „ | „ | „ | 1605 to 1606. |
| 47. Sri Rámá Sáh became | „ | „ | „ | 1606 to 1633. |

Chatra Sáh reigned only seven months, and having no issue his brother Sri Rámá Sáh succeeded him.

Rámá Sáh introduced the measures manu = 1 lb, páthi = 8 lb, and muri = 160 lb, and the use of scales and weights.

He also made laws for debtors and creditors fixing the rate of interest at 10 per cent. for money, and one-fourth of the quantity of grain.

He made many other laws.

| | | | |
|---|---|---|---|
| 48. Sri Dambar Sáh reigned from | | | 1633 to 1642. |
| 49. Sri Krishna Sáh | „ | „ | 1642 to 1653. |
| 50. Sri Rudra Sáh | „ | „ | 1653 to 1669. |
| 51. Prithwipati Sáh | „ | „ | 1669 to 1716. |

His son Birbhadra Sáh died before the close of his father's reign.

52. Narbhúpál Sáh reigned from 1716 to 1742.

Of the senior Ráni of Prithwipati Sáh was born Birbhadra Sáh, who was the eldest son. He married the daughter of the Rájá of Tanahung.

She was pregnant, but no one knew of her state, except Birbhadra Sáh, when she went away to her father's home, being on bad terms with her mother-in-law.

Birbhadra Sáh being very ill called his youngest brother Chandrarup Sáh, told him of his wife's condition, and begged him to make enquiries as to the result of her pregnancy, and give her his support.

A few days after Birbhadra Sáh died.

The Ráni in time gave birth to Narbhupál Sáh. Chandrarup Sáh succeeded in having the boy brought to his house in Gurkhá where he kept him carefully.

After the death of Prithwipati, Narbupal Sáh was installed King. He invaded Nepál and had a pitched battle with Jayaprakása Malla, thirteenth king of Kátmandu, in A. D. 1736.

Narbupal was defeated and had to return to his own country.

In 1730 A. D. Narbupal had a son, Prithwi Narayan Sáhi, born to him, who, on his father's death, became King in A. D. 1742 at the age of 12.

51. Prithwi Narayan Sáhi.

Prithwi Narayan Sáhi was a person of insatiable ambition, sound judgment, great courage, and unceasing activity. He is practically the great founder of the house of Gurkhá. It would appear that, in the earlier days of Prithwi Narayan's reign, the inhabitants of the district of Gurkhá were almost entirely Magars, Gurungs, Thákurs, and Khas, with a sprinkling of the menial classes.

Directly on his accession to the throne Prithwi Narayan determined to take Nayakot,* and in 1749 A.D. he invaded Népál and attacked Kirtipur, and a great battle was fought between his troops and those of Jayaprakása.

On the Gurkhá side Surpatráp (brother of Prithwi Narayan) lost an eye and Kálu Panre was killed. The battle lasted nearly five hours (twelve gharis) and both sides lost many men. On the Népálese side twelve thousand sepoys brought from the plains of India were killed. Prithwi Narayan had a narrow escape of being killed. Jayaprakása now made great rejoicings, thinking the Gurkháli were annihilated. He enlisted Nágá sepoys to fight the Gurkháli. Prithwi Narayan returned to his own country, burning the bridge over the Gandak.

In the year 1749 one of the princes in the Népál Valley, who was King of Bhátgáon, was ill-advised enough to apply for assistance to Prithwi Narayan against his enemies, rival princes, who were pressing him hard.

Ranjit Mal soon found out his mistake, and was obliged to come to terms with the neighbouring kings, with a view to resist the encroachments of the Gurkhás.

From 1749 to 1765 Prithwi Narayan had been extending his own dominions on all sides, and had occupied the hills round the valley, and established a series of forts on them, the ruins of which exist to this day.

In 1765 Prithwi Narayan again invaded Népál and laid siege to Kirtipur, which was a dependency of the King of Pátan.

* Close to Kirtipur in Népál Valley.

Gainprejas of Kirtipur offered battle to Prithwi Narayan and defeated him in two pitched battles.

An assault which was tried upon Kirtipur was also repulsed with great slaughter.

Prithwi Narayan then tried to starve out the city by posting troops all round the neighbouring hills. In 1767 Prithwi Narayan obtained possession of Kirtipur through treachery.

In 1768 Prithwi Narayan fought for six months with the people of Chaukot, who under Mohindra Rai made a most gallant defence, defeating him on many occasions. On 21st June 1768 a hardly contested battle was fought in which Mahindra Rai was killed, seeing which the Chaukotiyas fled.

On 29th September 1768 Prithwi Narayan entered Kátmandu by treachery. Jayaprakása's troops fought for an hour or two,* when Jayaprakása fled first to Pátan and thence, taking Tejnar Simha with him, to Bhátgáon.

Tularám Thápá (a General) and a number of Gurkháli troops were blown up in the Teleju temple, where a mine had been laid by order of Jayaprakása, and which was exploded when Kátmundu was lost.

After the fall of Kátmandu, Pátan surrendered to Prithwi Narayan.

The Gurkhá historian states that in 1766 Nawáb Kásim Ali Khan of Murshidabad, having been defeated by the British, had taken refuge in Népál for some time, and that in return for the hospitality shown him, he sent 60,000† troops to help the Népálese by the route of Makwánpur, but they were cut to pieces by only 400 scouts of Prithwi Narayan Sah! After this 5,000 Nágás were coming to the assistance of the Népálese, but they shared the same fate at Panávati.

In May 1769 Prithwi Narayan came to attack Bhátgáon, where he had previously gained over the Sátbábályás (seven illegitimate sons of Ranjit Malla) by promising to leave to them the throne and revenue, and to content himself with a nominal

* (1) Chaukot lies to the east of Bhátgáon.
(2) The troops and most of the people were drunk, as is the custom during the Indrajatra festival.

† It need hardly be said that this is very gross exaggeration, but evidence exists that soldiers from the plains of India were obtained by kings of Népál to fight the Gurkhás.

sovereignty over the country. The Gurkhá troops were accordingly admitted within the fortified walls, and Bhátgáon was taken.

Prithwi Narayan now entered the Durbar and found the Rájás of the three towns Bhátgáon, Kátmandu, and Pátan sitting together, whereat he and his companions began to laugh.

Jayaprákasa was offended at this, and said: "O Gurkhális! this has come to pass through the treachery of our servants, or else you would have had no cause for mirth."

Prithwi Narayan, mindful of the days of his early youth, when for three years he lived at Bhátgáon as Ranjit Malla's guest and received much kindness from him, now paid his respects to Ranjit Malla, and respectfully asked him to continue to rule as he had done hitherto, although he (Prithwi Narayan) had conquered the country. Ranjit Malla refused this and begged for permission to go to Benares. Prithwi Narayan gave him this permission and also provided for his expenses on the road.

Jayaprakása Malla, late King of Kátmandu, was, at his own request, allowed to go to Pashupati, where he shortly afterwards died.

Tej Nar Sinha, the Rájá of Lalitpur (or Pátan) was sent to Lakshmipur to be kept in confinement, and there he died.

After some time Prithwi Narayan returned from Bhátgáon to Kátmandu and began to rule over the three towns.

Because Surpratáp Sáh (his brother) had lost one of his eyes in the war with the people of Kirtipur, Prithwi Narayan ordered the nose of every male in that town, above the age of 12 years, to be cut off. The people thus mutilated were 865 of those who had fought valiantly and kept the Gurkhális out of the town.

The conquest of the valley of Népál, from the first siege of Kirtipur in 1765, till the fall of Bhátgáon in the commencement of 1769, occupied four years.

We are quite ignorant of the details connected with the several sieges and engagements, nor are we informed of the number of troops engaged either on the Népálese or the Gurkhá side, but no one can deny to the Newárs, and especially to the men of Kirtipur, the credit of having displayed the most heroic bravery in the defence of their capital, while the Gurkhás have earned eternal disgrace by the savage barbarity with which they signalized all their triumphs.

Nothing can detract from the gallant patriotic spirit shown by the Newárs under the high-spirited and heroic Gainprejas.

This Gainprejas is said to have been a deposed king of Pátan. He certainly was a nobleman by birth and displayed great bravery.

After the fall of Kirtipur he fled to Kátmandu, where he made a gallant defence after the city had been betrayed. From Kátmandu he fled to Pátan, but being unable to keep up the courage of his troops he fled to Bhátgáon.

On Prithwi Narayan obtaining possession of Bhátgáon (through treachery as usual), Gainprejas, with a few followers, made a gallant attempt to escape, but was wounded in the foot and died a few days afterwards.

After the conquest of Népál, Prithwi Narayan established Kátmándu as his capital and consolidated his power. He next sent Káje Kahar Simha (a Thákur) with an army, with which was subdued the whole of the country lying between Bijayapur on the east, the Sápt Gandaki on the west, Kirong and Kuti on the north, and Makwánpur and the Terái on the south.

Between 1770 and 1772 Prithwi Narayan employed himself attacking such of the Chaobisia Rájás as had not joined him in his invasion of Népál. For some time he had rapid success, but in an engagement with the Tanahúng Rájá (in 1772) he was so roughly handled that he was compelled to relinquish these conquests.

No chief resisted with such gallantry and effect the rising power of Prithwi Narayan of Gurkhá as the Rájá of Tanahúng.

Prithwi Narayan died at Mohan Tirtha on the Gandaki in 1775, having ruled the Gurkhás for 33 years.

He left behind him two sons, Pratab Simha Sáh and Bahádar Sáh.

54. Pratab Simha Sáh was made King in 1775. He threatened an invasion of Sikkim, but failed in his attempt.

The war was, however, waged with varying success for several years.

During this war a Lepcha General, by name Athingpoi, *alias* Changzed Karwang, *alias* Satrajit, greatly distinguished himself.

This last name is said to have been given to him to commemorate his seventeen victories over the Gurkhás in the Terái and Morang.

A military colleague of Satrajit, by name Deba Takarpos, *alias* Jorden, carried on the war against the Gurkhás successfully for a time, and drove the Gurkhás back; but he was defeated and slain, and his army dispersed in a battle fought at Chainpur about 1776.

In consequence of this defeat Satrajit had also to retire from the Morang.

In 1778 Pratab Simha Sáh died leaving one legitimate son, Ran Bahádar Sáh, who, at the time of his father's death, was but an infant.

55. Ran Bahádar Sáh elected King from 1778 to 1807.

Bahádar Sáh, brother of Pratab Sáh, and uncle of Ran Bahádar Sáh, became Regent. The mother of the infant King opposed him, and after a struggle of some years Bahádur Sáh had to fly to Bettiah, where he remained until 1795, when the Ráni died, and he again became Regent.

The Gurkhá family had hitherto failed in all their attempts to extend their dominions to the west, and if Pálpá had continued to assist the neighbouring Chaobisia Rájás, it is probable that their resistance to the Gurkhás might have been continued with success. Mahadatta, King of Pálpá, however, agreed with the Regent Bahádur Sáh to make common cause against the rest of the Chaobisia Rájás and to divide the spoil.

About 1786.

This scheme completely succeeded, and Damodar Páure, a Khas by birth, but representative of one of the chief families in Gurkhá, and a most gallant officer, was sent in command of the Regent's forces. After the conquest Damodar took the lion's share for his master, but allowed Mahadatta to retain Gúlmi, Arghá, and Káchi.

Lámzúng, Tanahúng, and the rest of the Chaobisia principalities were kept by the Gurkhás.

Sarup Simha, a Gurkhá General, conquered the whole of the Kiránti country (Rais and Limbús) and extended the Gurkhá conquests as far as Sumbeswára in the east.

About 1787.

A Gurkhá force penetrated into Sikkim and overran and held possession of all Sikkim south and west of the Teesta.

In 1788-89.

In 1790. Troops sent in 1790 to Shikárjung invaded Thibet and plundered Digarchá.

In 1792 a Chinese army 70,000 strong, under a General called Dhurin, and a minister called Thumthám, invaded Népál by the Kirong route, and after some desperate fights overcame the Népálese, and dictated terms to the Gurkhá King at Nayakot, some 25 miles from Kátmandu.

War with China.

Treaty with the British. In March 1792 Lord Cornwallis entered into a commercial treaty with the Gurkhás.

In consequence of this, a mission under Colonel Kirkpatrick was despatched to Népál the same year. In 1793 Colonel Kirkpatrick quitted Népál, as he found the Népálese determined to avoid a closer alliance.

Kumáon* conquered. In 1793 the Gurkhás under Jagajit conquered Kumáon.

In 1794 the Gurkhás under Amar Sing Thápá conquered and annexed Gharwál. They next fought the Gharwális in the Dún near Gúrúdhána, utterly defeated them, killed their Rájá, and annexed the Dún, which had belonged to the Gharwális.

Gharwál conquered.

By this time the Gurkhá territories extended from Bhútán to Kashmir, and from the borders of Thibet to the British provinces.

In 1795 Ran Bahádar Sah removed his uncle from the regency and assumed the reins of government: two years subsequently he put him to death.

From this time till 1800 Népál was the scene of most barbarous outrages perpetrated by the king.

In 1800 Ran Bahádar Sah was expelled from the country and obliged to abdicate in favour of his illegitimate son, who was still an infant.

56. Girbán Juddha Vikram Sáh, elected King in 1800 A. D. (in place of his father, exiled), ruled till 1816. The second Mábáráni Mahilla ruled the country for her infant son.

In October 1801 a treaty was signed by the British and Népálese authorities, and in consequence Captain W. D. Knox was appointed Resi-

First British Resident of Népál.

* Kumáon and Gharwál remained subject to the Gurkhás until 1816, when they were ceded to the British by the treaty of Segowli.

dent at the Court of Népál, and he reached the capital in April 1802.

Becoming dissatisfied with the political conduct of the Népálese, who evaded the fulfilment of their engagements, he withdrew in March 1803. In January 1804 Lord Wellesley formally dissolved alliance with the Durbar.

In 1804 Ran Bahádar Sáh returned from Benares to Népál, and put to death Dámodár Káji and others of his enemies. He made new laws, and issued many orders, stopped the main roads, confiscated all the birta* lands from the Brahmans in the country, raised money by re-assessing the lands, and from fear of small-pox ordered all the children to be taken out of the city.

He was the first Rájá who introduced gold asharfis into currency.

In 1807 he was cut down with a sword and killed by his step-brother, Sher Bahádar, who in turn was killed by Bal Nar Simha, father of Sir Jang Bahadar.

Girbán Juddha, as above mentioned, was elected King in 1800 on the banishment of his father, and, although Ran Bahádar returned in 1804, and actually ruled (though but jointly with Mahilla and with Girban Juddha) for a few years, nevertheless the actual king must be regarded as Girban Juddha from 1800 to date of his death in 1816.

Girban Juddha appointed Bhima Sena Thápá to be Prime Minister and Protector of the whole country.

In 1805 Prithwi Pal, Rájá of Pálpá, was allured to Kátmandu by Ran Bahádar Sáh, the most solemn promises for his safety and well-being having been made; but no sooner was he in Kátmandu than he was made a state prisoner.

In 1807 immediately after Ran Bahadur's death Prithwi Pal was put to death, and General Amar Sing Thápá (father of Bhim Sen Thápá) marched with a considerable force upon Pálpá, and within a month took possession of it without any resistance.

This puts an end to the last of the Chaobisia kingdoms, and with the fall of Pálpá one and all of the Chaobisia principalities came under the sway of the King of Népál.

In 1810 a violent earthquake occurred by which many lives were lost in Bhátgáon.

* Birta is a grant of land in perpetuity for which rent is paid.

A powder magazine was built at Thambahil Khel, and "Dhyak" or double pice brought into currency.

From 1804 to 1814 the Népálese carried on a system of outrage and encroachment on the British frontier.

War with Népál.

On the 1st November 1814, Lord Hastings declared war against Népál, on account of these continual outrages and encroachments, which culminated in the treacherous attack and murder of all our police in the Botwál district.

The Gurkhá army consisted of 12,000 men, equipped and disciplined in imitation of Company's sepoys.

When war was determined on, 30,000 British troops with 60 guns were told off in four divisions.

The war, though ultimately brought to a successful termination by the brilliant operations of Ochterlony, was one very discreditable to the military abilities of our Generals; yet it reflected the highest credit on the troops employed, being perhaps the most arduous campaign in which the Company's army had ever been engaged in India.

Throughout the war the Gurkhás displayed the most conspicuous gallantry.

Operations of General Gillespie's Division.

Major-General Gillespie, advancing from Meerut, seized the Keeri pass over the Sewalíks and occupied Debra without opposition. Five miles from Debra is a hill 500 to 600 feet high, surmounted with a fort called Nálápáni or Kalanga, of no great size or strength.

Kalanga.

The defence of this post against General Gillespie was most creditable to the Gurkhás, though exhibiting extreme rashness on his part, as he had been directed to avoid strong works which required to be reduced by artillery.

In this defence Balbhadar and 600* Gurkhás repulsed two assaults, inflicting on the British division a loss of 31 officers and 718 men killed, wounded, and missing, including General Gillespie, who was killed when leading the first assault; and when ultimately three days' incessant shelling compelled them to abandon the

* These 600 men belonged mostly to the regiment known as the Purána Gúrakh which consists entirely of Magars.

place, Balbhadar and the survivors, reduced to 90 in number, cut their way through our posts, and escaped.

The defence of this fort retarded a whole division for over one month.

On the fall of the fort it was at once occupied by the British troops, and there indeed the desperate courage and bloody resistance the Gurkhás had opposed to means so overwhelming were mournfully and horribly apparent. The whole area of the fort was a slaughter-house strewed with the bodies of the dead and wounded.

Gallantry of the defenders.

The determined resolution of the little party that held this small post must surely claim universal admiration.

The men of Nálápáni (or Kalanga) will for ever be marked for their unsubdued courage, and the generous spirit of courtesy with which they treated their enemy.

Anecdote.

They fought us in fair conflict like men, and in the intervals of actual combat showed us a liberal courtesy worthy of a more enlightened people; so far from insulting the bodies of the dead and wounded, they permitted them to remain untouched till carried away, and none were stripped even. The following story illustrates their confidence in British officers. One day, whilst the batteries were playing, a man was perceived on the breach advancing and waving his hand. The guns ceased for a while, and a man came, who proved to be a Gurkhá, whose lower jaw had been shattered by a round shot, and who came thus frankly to solicit assistance from his enemy. It is unnecessary to add that it was instantly afforded. He recovered, and when discharged from the hospital, signified his desire to return to his corps to fight us again, exhibiting thus through the whole a strong sense of the value of generosity and courtesy in warfare, and also of his duty to his country, separating completely in his own mind private and national feeling from each other.

Bravery of women.

During the assaults on the fort, women were seen hurling stones, and undauntedly exposing themselves; and several of their dead bodies, and one wounded, were subsequently found amidst the ruins of the fort.

Balbhadar with the survivors retreated to a hill a few miles distant, and was there joined by 300 fresh Gurkhás, and subsequently he formed a part of the garrison of Jythak.

On General Gillespie's death, General Martindell was given the command of the division.

He left a detachment in the Dún, and entered the valley below Náhan by the Kolápári pass on 19th December 1814.

General Martindell advances.

Náhan was found evacuated and was thereupon occupied by the British. Colonel Kesar Sing, who had been in Náhan with 2,300 of the *élite* of the Gurkhá army, had retired to Jythak, in accordance with General Amar Sing's orders.

General Martindell sent two detachments, one of 738 men under Major Richards, and the other of 1,000 men under Major Ludlow, to occupy two ridges on the flanks of the enemy's main position.

Jythak.

The detachment under Major Ludlow attacked the enemy and drove them off with some loss; but being flushed with success he pursued too far, and on seeing a stockade in front of him, he attempted to seize the same and failed. This stockade was afterwards always known as the second stockade.

The officer commanding the stockade seeing the disordered state of our troops, and how few of them there were together, sallied out with no great number of men, bore down the leading troops, and put the rest to flight. Reinforced by fresh troops, the enemy followed up the charge, and our men, out of breath and panic-struck, could not be rallied. Major Ludlow and other officers three times attempted to rally the troops at favourable points, but as often the Gurkhás charged and dispersed them, and followed cutting them up with their kúkries.

Defeat of Major Ludlow's detachment.

In the meanwhile the other detachment under Major Richards made good its object, but, owing to the failure of Major Ludlow's column, they were ordered to retreat.

Success of Major Richards, but subsequent retreat.

Lieutenant Thackeray, with a company of the 1st Battalion, 26th Native Infantry, made a gallant charge to cover the retreat; but the enemy breaking their way in on all sides, and using their kúkries, committed terrible havoc. The British loss was

12 officers and 450 men killed and wounded. In February 1815 Ranjit Sing with 200 Gurkhás attacked and defeated 2,000 irregulars under Lieutenant Young.

The fall of Jythak was only brought about by the successes of General Ochterlony and the surrender of Amar Sing.

Operations under General J. S. Wood.

General J. S. Wood, who commanded a division at Gorakhpur, having heard that the enemy under Colonel Wajir Sing held a stockade called Jitghar close to Botwál, determined to attack the same.

Jitghar stockade.

He advanced for this purpose on the 3rd of January 1815. The route led for the last seven miles through sál forests. General Wood had been told to expect an open space in front of the stockade, but whilst still in the thick of the forest, he suddenly found himself in front of the stockade, and within 50 yards of it. A destructive fire was opened on the British troops. The stockade was merely a hollow one, and a position was gained round the left flank completely commanding the stockade: the carrying of the work was certain, and the enemy were already reatreating from it, when General Wood ordered the retreat to be sounded. The British lost 5 officers and 128 men killed and wounded. General Wood did nothing from this date until 17th of April, when he made a useless demonstration against Botwál, with no results.

Operations under General Marley.

General Marley was expected to attempt the Bichiakoh and Hetounda pass, and, if successful, from thence straight on to Kátmandu. He occupied several posts in the Terái and kept his main army at Parsa. One post, held by Captain Sibley, was 20 miles to the left of Parsa, and another under Captain Blackney at Samanpur, about as far again to the right.

Captain Sibley and Captain Blackney both surprised.

The main army of the Gurkhás was at Makwanpur under Colonel Randhar Sing, who gave orders that both these posts should be attacked on the 1st January 1815.

Captain Blackney was completely surprised, and he and Lieutenant Duncan were killed, and in ten minutes his sepoys broke and fled in every direction. Captain Sibley was more on his guard, and made a good fight of it, but was surrounded and overpowered.

Our loss out of 500 men was 123 killed, 187 wounded, and 73 missing.

*Lieutenant Pickersgill suprises the enemy.*

General Marley was superseded for incompetence, and General George Wood took command in his stead. The very day before he assumed command, Lieutenant Pickersgill, with a body of cavalry, surprised a body of 500 Gurkhás and cut nearly all up.

General George Wood had a fine army of 13,400 men, but being of opinion that the fever season had commenced, he refused to risk penetrating the forest, and accordingly he did nothing.

*Operations in Kumáon.*

In December 1814 Lord Hastings, considering that a diversion from Kumáon might have a good effect, gave orders to Colonel Gardner and Major Hearsey to raise two levies composed of Rohillas.

*Success of Colonel Gardner.*

Colonel Gardner advanced on the 11th February from Kashipur in the Moradabad district, and after some skirmishing established himself on 20th February 1815 on a ridge immediately facing Almorah.

*Defeat of Major Hearsey.*

About the same time Major Hearsey advanced through Pilibhit and moved on towards Almorah, with the intention of co-operating with Colonel Gardner, but on 31st March he was defeated in an engagement, and he himself was wounded and taken prisoner.

*Success of Colonel Nichols.*

Towards the end of March, Colonel Jasper Nicolls was sent with 2,500 infantry and 10 guns to support Colonel Gardner. After the junction was effected a good deal of fighting took place round Almorah. By 25th April guns had been put up in a position within 70 yards of the fort. The Governor of the province thereupon proposed an armistice. On the 27th a formal convention was signed, in which the whole Kumáon province was surrendered, and Major Hearsey was released.

*Operations under General Ochterlony.*

General Ochterlony, who took the field in the middle of October, had 7,000 troops under him, and was opposed by General Amár Sing, who never had more than from 2,800 to 3,000 Gurkhás under him.

General Ochterlony determined to act with the utmost caution, and by his perseverance and skilful operations he was enabled to out-manœuvre Amar Sing from position to position. Up till the middle of February nothing of much importance was done.

Between this and the 14th April a number of small forts were reduced. On the 15th April, after some very hard fighting, the British troops seized a peak called Deothal, in the very heart of the enemy's position, and therein placed two whole battalions with two field-pieces, and threw up earth-works all round the same.

Success at Deothal.

Amar Sing, seeing the absolute necessity of dislodging the British from Deothal, attacked the same on the 16th with 2,000 Gurkhás, led by Bhagti Thápá.*

Bhagti Thápá's attack on British.

The attack took place from all sides with furious intrepidity, but the enemy were repulsed with a loss of 500 men, Bhagti Thápá being killed. The British lost 4 officers and 209 men killed and wounded.

The Gurkhás now concentrated round Maláon, but news of the the fall of Almorah having arrived, Amar Sing's sirdars urged him to accept terms for himself and his son Ranjit at Jythak. This he refused to do, and as the chiefs began to desert him, he retired into Maláon with 200 men, and there held out as long as any hope remained, after which he capitulated on highly honourable terms to General Ochterlony.

Fall of Maláon.

The gallant defence of Fort Maláon by Amar Sing elicited the admiration of General Ochterlony, who allowed him to march out with his arms, accoutrements, colours, two guns, and all his personal property, "in consideration of the bravery, skill, and fidelity with which he had defended the country entrusted to his charge:" the same honourable terms were granted to his son, who had defended Jythak against General Martindell.

The fall of Maláon brought the campaign of 1814-15 to an end.

Negociations for peace were now opened in May 1815, but the refusal of the Népálese to submit to Lord Hastings' demands led to the campaign of 1816.

General Ochterlony advanced with 20,000 troops early in February against the Bichakoh pass, which he found impregnable. Fortunately he was able to turn this position, on 14th February 1816, by means of a very rugged road, which was unknown to the enemy, and was shown to him by some smugglers.

Second campaign.

* Famous amongst Gurkhás even to this day for his bravery.

On the 27th an advance was made upon, and a position taken up in front of, Makwánpur. On the 28th 2,000 Gurkhás attacked a post called Sekhar Khatri, situated on a hill to the left of the camp. The village was obstinately and gallantly defended by the small detachment there. General Ochterlony successively detached one European and three Native battalions in support, and after a most obstinate fight the enemy was beaten off. The British casualties were 2 officers and 220 men, but the loss of the enemy was over 800.

Battle of Sekhar Khatri (or Makwánpur).

On the 1st March a strong point, 800 yards from the Gurkhá stockade on the hill on which Harihárpur stands, was surprised, and the Gurkhá picquet driven off.

Defeat of Gurkhás at Harihárpur.

The Gurkhás, in considerable numbers, made a most desperate and obstinate attempt to recover this position. It was impossible, owing to the nature of the ground, to use the bayonet, and the musketry fire lasted from 3 A.M. till 11-30, when the arrival of some guns at last drove the enemy away, after several hours of hard fighting. British loss 5 officers and 56 men.

After the war of 1816, Sir D. Ochterlony expressed an opinion confidentially to Lord Hastings that "the Company's soldiers, then Hindustanis, could never be brought to resist the shock of these energetic mountaineers on their own ground."

The intelligence of their reverses at Sekha Khatri and Harihárpur spread consternation at Kátmandu, and the Durbar immediately tendered unqualified submission; and thus was ended the second war in a short and brilliant campaign.

Gurkhás submit.

On the 4th March the treaty of Segowli was signed, by which Népál was reduced to the country lying between the River Michi on the east and the River Kali on the west, and by this treaty they also ceded nearly the whole Terái west of the Gandak river to the British.

Treaty of Segowli.

In fulfilment of the terms of this treaty, a British Resident was appointed, Mr. Gardner being selected. The King was at this time still young, and Bhim Sen Thápá held the reins of government.

Mr. Gardner appointed Resident.

In 1816, the King Girbhán Juddhra Vikrám Sáh died at the

age of 18, and shortly after Mr. Gardner's arrival. He was succeeded by his infant son aged two years.

57. Rajendra Vikrám Sáh reigned from 1816 to 1847, when he was deposed, being insane.

Bhim Sena Thápá continued in complete power as Prime Minister.

In 1823-24 a bad epidemic of cholera swept over Népál.

In 1829 a month* was lost in the year, which is very unlucky, and consequently many beasts, birds, and fishes died.

In 1830 the powder magazine at Nawakot was struck by lightning and 62 men were killed. In the same year the Thambahil magazine was struck by lightning and exploded, and 18 men were killed.

In 1833 terrible damage and loss of life occurred through four shocks of earthquake.

In 1833 the King, instigated by the Queen, endeavoured, but without success, to free himself from the rule of Bhim Sen Thápá.

The attempt was renewed in 1836, and in 1837 Bhim Sen Thápá was removed from office and imprisoned. He was, however, soon released, but never regained his former position, and in 1839 he was again put in irons. Threats were made that his wife and female relatives would be shamefully treated in public, and preferring to die rather than witness the disgrace, Bhim Sen Thápá committed suicide† in prison. So ended the life of a gallant old chief, who had ruled the country for twenty-six years.

Death of Bhim Sen Thápá.

In 1843 Matbar Sing Thápá, the nephew of Bhim Sen Thápá, who was in exile in the Punjab, was recalled and made Prime Minister.

In 1845 he was murdered at the instigation of one Gagan Sing, a great favourite of the Máharáni.

The murder of Gagan Sing and thirty-one of the most influential chiefs, in 1846, paved the way for the rise of Sir Jang Bahádar.

Sir Jang Bahádar.

* In Népál the astrologers sometimes increase or decrease the number of months in the year, so as to keep the lunar months by which the time of the festivals is fixed at the same period. Otherwise the months and festivals would fall at various times of the year, as is the case in the Mahomedan calendar.

† This suicide (or murder) took place on the 29th of July 1839.

Finding that Sir Jang Bahádar was not so subservient to her purposes as she expected, the Máharáni endeavoured to compass his death, but failing, she was expelled with her two sons from the country, and was accompanied to Benares by the Máharájá, who returned to Népál the following year, only to abdicate in favour of the heir-apparent, Surendra Vikram.

In 1847, on the 12th May, (58) Surendra Vikram Sáh was proclaimed King and reigned from 1847 to 1881, the date of his death.

In September of this year (1847) the deposed King Rajendar Vikram Sáh made an attempt to recover his throne, assisted by a large party of discontented exiles. At 3 A.M. of 20th September, Captain Kanak Sing Adikári surprised the King's camp at Alu or Ulu, killing about 50 or 60 and taking the *ex* King prisoner.

Rajendar Vikram Sáh, *ex* King of Népál, was from this time until date of his death, kept under strict surveillance as a state prisoner in Bhátgáon.

In 1848 an offer was made to the British Government to assist in the war with the Sikhs, but the offer was declined.

On the 15th of January 1850 Sir Jang Bahádar started to visit England.

Second war with Thibet.

In 1854 the Népálese entered into a war with Thibet, which lasted two years, and terminated favourably for Népál. Dr. Oldfield gives the following details :—

The first week in April about 1,000 Gurkhás under General Dher Sham Sher (the father of the present Prime Minister, Máharájá Sir Bir Sham Sher Rana Bahádar) attacked a body of about from 3,000 to 5,000 Thibetans and defeated them.

On the 26th news arrived of a victory gained by the Gurkhás. It would appear that a large body of Thibetans occupied a post called Ganta, about eight miles from Jhanga. For nine days the Thibetans repulsed with considerable loss the successive attacks of the Gurkhás, but at length they were driven out of the post, which was occupied at once by the Gurkhás.

On the 4th May news arrived that the Gurkhás had captured the post of Jhanga.

In November news arrived that a very large force of Thibetans and Tartars had surprised the Gurkhá position at Kuti, to which place they had retired at the commencement of the rains. The Gurkhás were, after several hours' hard fighting, utterly routed and lost 700 men killed and nine guns.

Only 1,300 Gurkhás escaped.

On the 19th November the Thibetans attacked Jhanga at night and entered the position, but after some hours' fighting they were driven out and defeated, leaving 1,200 dead behind them.

On the 25th November news arrived that General Dher Sham Sher with 5,000 to 6,000 Gurkhás, divided into nine regiments, advanced against Kuti. The Thibetans were in an entrenched camp, and numbered about 10,000. After some good hard fighting they were defeated with a loss of 1,100 killed. The Gurkhás here recovered two of the guns they had lost.

Colonel Sanak Sing with five regiments attacked the Thibetans near Jhanga and killed over 1,100, chiefly with the kúkri.

The force in Jhanga killed 559 Thibetans; after these reverses the Thibetans submitted.

In 1857, when the Mutiny broke out, the Népálese offered the assistance of their troops to the British Government, and the same was accepted on the 26th June.

On the 2nd July, 3,000 troops were sent off to the plains of India, and 1,000 more followed on the 13th and 14th August. On the 10th December, Sir Jang Bahádar himself went down with a force of 8,000. This force was joined by Colonel Macgregor as Military Commissioner, and assisted in the campaign of 1857 and 1858.

Early in 1858 numbers of fugitive rebels took refuge in the Népálese Terái. In 1859 the Népálese organized an expedition and swept the remnant of the mutineers out of the country.

In return for the above services, Sir Jang Bahádar was created a G.C.B., and under a treaty concluded on 1st November 1860, the tract of country on the Oudh frontier, which had been ceded to the British Government in 1816, was restored to Népál.

In 1878 Sir Jang Bahádar died, some say of fever, others from the effects of injuries received from a wounded tiger.

Ranodhip Sing, a brother of Sir Jang Bahádar, then became Prime Minister.

In 1881 Surendra Vikram Sáh died and was succeeded by his grandson Prithwi Viri Vikram Sáh, who was born in 1875, and is the present reigning King of Népál (Máharáj Dhiráj).

On 22nd of November 1885 Ranodhip Sing* was assassinated and his nephew Sir Bir Sham Sher Rana Bahádar, the present Prime Minister, took up the reins of government.

In 1886 Sir Bir Sham Sher discovered the existence of a plot whereby his brother Kharak Sham Sher intended to displace him and take over the office of Prime Minister.

Kharak Sham Sher was banished to Pálpá and made Governor of that important district.

When Sir Bir Sham Sher became Prime Minister of Népál, he exiled such relations of his own as he deemed likely to prove a source of danger to him.

Amongst the exiles was one Ranbir Jang, son of Sir Jang Bahádar.

Early in 1888 Ranbir Jang attempted to seize Népál by a *coup-de-main*, and an insurrection broke out in the Terái and Hanumannagar was sacked.

An action took place (I believe somewhere in the Botwál direction) in which the Ranbir Jang faction got beaten.

In February 1888 Sir Bir Sham Sher proceeded to Calcutta to have an interview with Lord Dufferin, the then Viceroy of India. The writer accompanied Sir Bir Sham Sher to Calcutta and thence to Kátmandu. Whilst marching through the Terái, north of Segowlie, numbers of prisoners, who had been concerned in the Ranbir Jang insurrection, were brought in tied up hand and foot in carts.

Each case was tried by those whose duty it was to hear the cases, and the next morning Sir Bir Sham Sher himself pronounced sentence on each man, hearing each man's case first.

Early in 1888 a plot was discovered to assassinate Sir Bir Sham Sher on his return to Kátmandu, but owing to the rapidity with which he reached Kátmandu, doing three long marches without drawing rein, he escaped, and the conspirators were apprehended and put to death.

In February 1889, the writer travelled with Sir Bir Sham Sher from Botwál to Philibit. During this trip the Sandstone ridge was

---

* Sir Jang Bahádar died in 1876, and in accordance with the laws of succession, his eldest existing brother, Ranodhip Sing, succeeded to Prime Ministership.

Although Népál is nominally ruled by a king, excepting in the constant use of his name, and the occasional trotting him out for state ceremonies, his actual power is *nil*. The real ruler of the country is the Prime Minister.

Political revolutions in Népál are almost invariably caused by struggles for the Prime Ministership.

crossed, and for several days the camp travelled through the Dang Sallian Valley. Many tigers and much sport was obtained.

In March 1890 H.R.H. Prince Albert Victor of Wales proceeded to Philibit, and thence into the Népálese jungle to the north, on a shooting expedition, which Sir Bir Sham Sher had got up on his account.

The writer was detailed as assistant to Major E. L. Durand* (now Sir Edward Durand). Ten tigers, eight leopards, five bears, and numbers of deer and other game were obtained.

In 1892 Sir Bir Sham Sher provided Kátmandu with a full supply of pure spring water,—a measure which must have cost him much money, as the water had to be carried in pipes from a long distance, but which speaks well for the enlightened policy he has introduced.

In 1893 Sir Bir Sham Sher was knighted, and during the cold weather of 1893-94 was a guest of Lord Roberts, V.C., Commander-in-Chief in India, at the various camps of exercise being held.

The moderation with which Sir Bir Sham Sher acted when first he took over the Prime Ministership of Népál, stands in marked contrast with former action in like cases.

He has permitted the free enlistment of Gurkhá recruits for the Native Army in India.

Sir Bir Sham Sher has proved himself to be an able man, and by his liberality, his moderation, and his impartiality, he is rapidly making himself famous in his own land, respected by all, and loved by his own countrymen.

Népál Army.

The Népálese Army is said to consist of 30,000 drilled soldiers including artillery, who are almost all paid in land. They are drilled according to the English drill book and with English words of command.

At a parade held in Kátmandu on 6th March 1888, 108 guns marched past the Prime Minister, and it is therefore only natural to conclude that the Népálese are strong in this branch.

Several regiments are armed with Martini-Henrys manufactured in the country. More are being daily manufactured,

* Major Durand was Resident in Nepal at this time, and it was owing to his kindness that the writer of this book was continually meeting Népálese officials of high rank, whereby much useful information was gathered, whilst friendly relations were established which proved of great value to recruiting.

and it would appear the whole army is to receive them. There are also a number of Népálese-made sniders, and some thousands of Enfields, either captured from the mutineers in 1859, or given by the British Government.

Besides the regular army of 30,000 there is a large force of men who have served for several years and taken their discharge.

These men (called Dákrias), after staying a few years at home, may again enter the ranks, and take the place of others who in turn lie by for a year or two.

Thus the Népálese could with very little trouble raise a force of from 60,000 to 70,000 men who have been trained to arms.

The usual dress of the army is a blue cotton tunic and pyjamas of the same colour.

Some few regiments have red cloth tunics and dark trousers with red stripes.

The artillery uniform is blue.

The head-dress of all consists of a kind of skull-cap, with a thick tightly rolled coil or rim, which is in most cases adorned with silver or brass wire.

On the head-dress each soldier, as a distinctive mark of his regiment, wears a silver badge, the property of Government. Some of these are crescent-shaped (The Rifle Regiment), others oval, and so on.

The officers wear gold badges, which are jewelled, or jewelled and plumed, according to their rank.

All regiments are now armed with either Martini-Henrys (manufactured in Népál), sniders, or muzzle-loading percussion-cap Enfield rifles. Every soldier carries a kukri in addition to his bayonet.

Cavalry.

The Népálese cavalry all told is about 70 strong. These men are used as orderlies.

As regards the efficiency of the army, there is no doubt that the material is good, and for defensive purposes in their own hills and forest, the soldiers would fight well and be formidable foes. The weak point in the army are the officers, who are generally either very old men long past doing work, or very young lads.

The home-made rifles, too, are very inferior, whilst their ammunition is distinctly bad. They have not yet succeeded in learning how to make good powder.

Musketry practice, if any at all, is much too insufficient for the men to be skilled shots, even admitting the rifles to be capable of carrying true for any distance.

Regarding throwing open the country to Europeans, the Gurkhás have a saying " with the merchant comes the musket, and with the Bible comes the bayonet. " They have always shown the strongest objection to admitting any European into Népál, and they seem to consider that, were they to relax this rule, their independence, of which they are intensely proud, would shortly be lost.

Perhaps they are right ?

## GENEALOGY OF SIR JANG BAHÁDAR.

*Genealogy of Swasti Srimad Ati-Prachand Bhujdandetyadi Sri Sri Sri Mhárája Sir Jang Bahádar Ráná, G.C.B. and G.C.S.I., Thong-Lin-Pim-Má-Ko-Káng-Váng-Syán, Prime Minister and Commander-in-Chief of Népál.*

Táta Ráná was Rájá of Chitaur. His nephew had a son named Rámá Sinha Ráná, who, when Chitaur was taken (1324), came to the hills with four of his followers, and entered and remained for some time in the service of a hill Rájá.

The Rájá treated him with much kindness and gave him in marriage the daughter of the Rájá of Bináti, a Bagáli Kshattri.

By her he had six sons.

One of these six sons showed much bravery in a battle which was fought between the hill Rájá and the Rájá of Satán Kot, for which he had the title of Konwár* Khandka conferred on him, by which title his descendants are known to this day.

Rámá Sinha had a son called Ráut Konwár, who was made a nobleman by the hill Rájá, and Commandant of troops.

Ráut Konwár had a son named Ahiráma Konwár, who was invited by the Rájá of Káski, who made him a nobleman.

Ahiráma had a daughter of great beauty, whom the Rájá of Káski wished to marry by "Kalaspuja."† Ahiráma replied that he would only give his daughter in lawful marriage, and in no other way.

The Rájá then wanted to take her by force, and brought troops to the village, but Ahiráma was assisted by the people of the village, of the Parajuli Thápá‡ caste, and an affray took place in which persons on both sides were wounded.

The same day Ahiráma took his family and went to Gurkhá and took service under Máharája Prithwi Narayan, who gave him the village of Konwár Khola to live in and made him a nobleman.

His son Ráma Krishna Konwár was made a nobleman at 14 years of age, and having given proof of great bravery in one or two battles, which he fought and gained against hill Rájás, was made

* Konwár is a tribe of Khas. Khandka is a "pad" of the Konwár, as well as a separate tribe.

† This ceremony does not admit to the full standing of a lawfully married wife.

‡ Khas Thapa. *See* chapter on Tribes under "Khas Thapa."

Commander-in-Chief (Sardár) of the army, and selected to subjugate Népál.

After taking Pátan and Bhátgáon, Máharája Prithwi Narayan sent him to the East along with three or four other Sardárs and after some fighting he conquered as far as Méchi.

After his return he was sent to Pyuthan, where he established a magazine, and where he died at the age of 59.

His son Ranjit Konwár, when 21 years old, obtained the post of Subáh of Júmla. The country had only been recently conquered.

The Júmliyas fled to Homlá, whence they brought troops to retake the country, but were repulsed by Ranjit Kunwár. He was then ordered to conquer Kangra, and having captured Jhapahesar in Kumáon, he attacked and took it by storm after a severe encounter with Sausár Singh.

During the attack, as Ranjit was scaling the wall by a bamboo ladder, he received a bullet in the right breast and fell down. He died from the effects of this wound at the age of 58.

His son Balnar Sinha Konwár was then 22 years old and was made the principal among the four Kájis (muktár).

He was present when Máharájá Ran Bahádar Sáh was struck with a sword by his step-brother Sher Bahádar. The Máharájá called for help and Balnar Sinha killed Sher Bahádar.

Kaji Balnar Sinha died a natural death at the age of 59.

His eldest son was Sri Máharáj Sir Jang Bahádar Ráná, G.C.B., G.C.S.I., and Thong-lin-Pim-Ma-Ko-Káng-Váng-Syán.

Sir Jang Bahádar died in 1878 from effects of injuries he received from a wounded tiger, so it is rumoured, although it is always said he died of fever.

He was succeeded by his younger brother Ranodhip Sinha, who was assassinated on 22nd November 1885.

Ranodhip Sinha was succeeded by Sir Bir Sham Sher, eldest son of Dher Sham Sher, a brother of Sir Jang Bahádar.

Sir Bir Sham Sher was knighted in 1893.

# CHAPTER IV.

## ABORIGINAL TRIBES OF NEPÁL, AND MILITARY TRIBES OF NÉPÁL.

### ABORIGINAL TRIBES.

NÉPÁL, a name celebrated in Hindu legend, in a strict sense ought to be applied to that country only which is in the vicinity of Kátmandu, the capital; but at present it is usually given to the whole territory of the Gurkhá King.

To the present day even Gurkhás when talking of "Népál" are generally, if not always, referring to Kátmandu.

In this book "Népál" will refer to the whole territory of the Gurkhá King.

The aboriginal stock of Népál is most undoubtedly Mongolian. This fact is inscribed in very plain characters in their faces, forms, and languages.

Amongst the aborigines of Népál must be counted the Magars, Gurungs, Newárs, Sunwárs, Khambus,* Yakkas,* Yakthumbas,* Murmis, and Lepchas.

All of these are undoubtedly descended from Mongolian or Thibetan stock.

The Newárs, owing to the geographical position of their valley which practically prevented them from wandering, and to the sanctity of the same, which, for centuries before Christ, drew devout Hindus and Buddhists, have more marked racial characteristics than the other aboriginal tribes. They were also more civilized, having a literature of their own, and being skilled in arts.

Physically speaking, there is a very strong resemblance between Magars, Gurungs, Sunwárs, Rais and Limbús.

Writing about aboriginal tribes of Népál, Brian Hodgson says:—

"That the Sub-Himalayan races are all closely affiliated, and are one and all of northern origin, are facts long ago indicated by me, and which seem to result from sufficient evidence

* Khambus are Rais. Yakkas are practically Rais also. Yakthumbas are Limbús. Khambus, Yakkas, and Yakthumbas form the Kiránti group.

from the comparative vocabularies* I have furnished. But to it, lingual evidence in a more ample form will, however, in due time be added, as well as the evidence deducible from the physical attributes, and from the creeds, customs, and legends of these races.

"The transit from the north into Népál was certainly made before the Thibetans had adopted from India the religion and literature of Buddhism.

"This fact is as clearly impressed upon the crude dialects and cruder religious tenets of the Sub-Himalayans, as their northern origin is upon their peculiar forms and features, provided these points be investigated with the requisite care. That physiognomy exhibits, generally and normally, the Scythic or Mongolian type of human kind, but the type is often much softened and modified and even frequently passes into a near approach to the full Caucasian dignity of head and face.

"The broken or depressed tribes which originally peopled Népál, passed the Himalayas at various periods, but all long antecedent to the immigration of the dominant tribes, and prior to the least whisper of tradition, and the lingual and physical traits of these broken tribes, as might be expected, constitute several links of connection between the Altaic tribes on the north and Dravirian on the south. The general description of the Himalayans, both of earlier and later immigration, is as follows: Head and face very broad, usually widest between the cheek bones, sometimes as wide between the angles of the jaws; forehead broad, but often narrowing upwards; chin defective; mouth large and salient, but the teeth vertical and the lips not tumid; gums, especially the upper, thickened remarkably; eyes wide apart, flush with the cheeks, and more or less obliquely set in the head; nose pyramidal, sufficiently long and elevated, save at the base, where it is depressed, so as often to let the eyes run together, coarsely formed and thick, specially towards the end, and furnished with large round nostrils; hair of head copious and straight; of the face and body deficient; stature rather low, but muscular and strong. Character phlegmatic, and slow in

* Briar Hodgson says:—

"Within the modern kingdom of Népál there are thirteen distinct and strongly marked dialects spoken, *viz.*, the Khas, Magar, Gurung, Sunwár, Kachari, Haiyun, Chepang, Kasúnda, Múrmi, Newári, Kiránti, Limbúan and Lepchan.

"With the exception of the first these are all of Trans-Himalayan stock and are closely affiliated. They are all extremely rude, owing to the people who speak them having crossed the snows before learning dawned upon Thibet."

intellect and feeling, but good-humoured, cheerful and tractable, though somewhat impatient of continuous toil.

"Drunkenness and dirtiness are more frequent than in the plains. Crime is much rarer, however, and truth more regarded and the character on the whole amiable.

"The customs and manners have nothing very remarkable, and the creed may be best described by negatives.

"The home population is intensely tribual, some races being bound together by a common appellation, as the Limbús and Rais for example. A few tribes such as the Newárs have long become stationary cultivators; and the Gurungs are still, for the most part, pastoral.

"There are no craftsmen, generally speaking, proper to these tribes; strangers and helot races, located among them for ages untold, being smiths, carpenters, curriers, potters, etc., and the women of each tribe being its domestic weavers."

---

## MILITARY TRIBES OF NÉPÁL.

The military tribes of Népál from which the fighting element is almost exclusively drawn for the army are the following:—

The Khas, Magar, Gurung, and Thákur.

There are also a few Limbús, Rais, and Sunwárs to be found in most of our Gurkhá regiments, and numbers of them are yearly enlisted into the various Military Police Battalions of Assam and Burma.

Experience gained in Sikkim, Burma, and elsewhere, would prove Limbús, Rais, and Sunwárs to be excellent soldiers, and the prejudice which existed against them would seem rightly to be dying out rapidly.

A few Nagarkotis (Newárs) are also found in most of our regiments.

Murmis (Lámás) also have been enlisted in fairly large numbers in Military Police Battalions, and seem to have acquitted themselves well in service.

With the exception of the Khas and Thákur, all the above tribes were the aborigines of the country, and to this day show an undoubted Mongolian origin.

The Khas and Thákurs also show a strain of Mongolian blood but to a lesser degree.

The most ancient records would seem to prove that Népál was originally inhabited by Mongolians. Probably from one of the great waves of Mongolian conquest, which spread through the breadth of Asia from east to west, some side wave was washed over the bleak snows of the mighty Himalayas, into the fertile plains and valleys of Népál. Finding here a cool and bracing climate and a fertile soil, this mass of Mongolians settled down and adopted the country as their own.

But again the southern boundary of Népál rested on India, from whence continual streamlets of natives were finding their way into Népál.

We have historical evidence of the existence in Népál, long prior to the advent of Sakia Simha, of Hindus from the plains of India.

We hear of the daughter of Asoka (about B. C. 250) being married in Népál to the descendant of a Chattri, who had settled there centuries before.

It can, therefore, reasonably be presumed that for centuries before and after our Christian era, a continual dribbling of natives of India was finding its way into Népál and settling there, and we therefore have these two races, *viz.*, Mongolians and natives of India, meeting and mixing ;—perhaps at one time fighting each other, at others resting peacefully side by side, but nevertheless ever meeting, and mixing their blood in legitimate marriage or otherwise.

From this was created a race which, owing to the preponderance of Mongolian blood, would ethnologically be called Mongolian, but yet has sufficient mixed blood to show a decided foreign strain too.

The northern wave, which originally peopled Népál, probably consisted of a most uncivilized ignorant race, with, perhaps, no religion at all. Those who came from the south, on the other hand, were Hindus, whose religion even then was an old-established one, and who were famous for their intelligence and civilization.

Although, perhaps, immensely in the minority, it can be easily conceived how the civilized and intelligent minority would affect the ignorant masses, and in time imbue the aborigines to a certain degree with their customs, manners, and religion.

The immigration of Hindus seems to have been most heavy in the western and south-western portions of Népál, *viz.*, about Júmla and Sallian. Hence we find the men of Doti and Western Népál generally, in language, customs, religion and appearance, far more like the natives of India than the rest of the inhabitants of Népál, whilst the further north and east we go, the stronger become the Mongolian appearance and peculiarities.

Of the early history of Népál we know little more than that, prior to the Gurkhá conquest, the country of Népál was divided, roughly speaking, from west to east, into

(1) Baisia Ráj.
(2) Chaobisia Ráj.
(3) Nepál Ráj.
(4) Rai or Kirant Ráj.
(5) Limbú Ráj.

Each of these was subdivided into a number of petty principalities and small independent States, which, though constantly warring amongst themselves, had but little or no connection with the plains of Hindustan.

The vast tract of forest, and of marshy malarious land, which skirts almost uninterruptedly the southern face of the Himalayas, from Assam in the east, almost to the Sutlej in the north-west, formed an insuperable bar to any regular intercourse between the natives of the plains and those of the hills.

Thus isolated from connection with Hindustan, the hill Rájás and their subjects became, as it were, "a peculiar people." Absorbed in their own internal affairs—at one time warring with neighbouring chiefs, at another occupied in pastoral pursuits, or in hunting expeditions in their own territories—they knew little, and cared less, about the political changes and revolutions which were occurring in Bengal.

Inhabiting a cool and bracing climate, with mixed blood of the Mongolian and the native of India, they were physically far superior to the languid and enervated residents of Bengal.

The original purity of their soil had never been sullied by the foot of the Mahomedan conqueror.

Morally, therefore, as well as physically, they looked, and they to this day still look, upon themselves as superior to any of the plains-men.

These feelings induced a proud independence and energy of character almost unknown in other parts of India.

Such of these mountaineers as had adopted Hinduism, did so only to a certain degree, and they and their descendants refused to be hampered by all the bigotry and prejudices of Brahminical law. Whilst they retained the substance they rejected much of the shadow of Hinduism, and openly disregarded many observances which were and are considered as essential by the more orthodox professors of that religion in the plains. Such conduct naturally gave great offence. The Hindus of the Himalayas began to be looked upon by the Hindus of the plains very much as the Protestant is looked upon by the Roman Catholic. As the orthodox Roman Catholic calls the Protestant a "heretic," so the orthodox Brahman of Benares calls his brother Hindu of Népál a "Páriah."

These various differences in religion, in customs, in occupations, and in language, engendered great bitterness of feeling between the races of the plains and the races of the hills.

Hence to this day we find the vigorous hill races of Népál speaking with contempt of the "Madhesia," whilst the orthodox Hindu of the plains looks upon the "Pahariáhs" (Highlanders) as more or less unconverted barbarians.

Such tribes of Népál as are enlisted into the army or military police will now be briefly discussed, commencing in the next chapter with a few remarks on the "Gurkhás" as a nation, and then dealing separately with the four tribes of which the Gurkhá nation consists.

## CHAPTER V

# GURKHÁS;

## THEIR CUSTOMS, MANNERS, CHARACTERISTICS, AND TRIBES.

As already mentioned we know that, prior to the Gurkhá conquest, Népál was divided into, broadly speaking, five Rájs, each of which was sub-divided into various little principalities. Within the Chaobisia Ráj existed a district called Gurkhá.

Gurkhá.

This district is situated in the north-east portion of the basin of the Gandak, occupying the country between the Trisulgana and the Sweti Gandak. The chief town is called Gurkhá and is about 55 miles to the west of Kátmandu.

This town, and eventually the district, is said to have obtained its name from a very famous saint called Gurkhánát, or Gurákhánat who resided in a cave, which still exists, in the hill on which the city of Gurkhá is built.

Definition of the term "Gurkhá."

The ancestors of the present race of Gurkhás derived their national name of Gurkhá from this district in which they first established themselves as an independent power. The term "Gurkhá" is not limited to any particular class or clan; it is applied to all those whose ancestors inhabited the country of Gurkhá, and who from it subsequently extended their conquests far and wide over the eastern and western hills.

The men of Doti, Júmla, and other western portions of Népál and the Kumáon hills, are Parbattias (Highlanders), but they are not Gurkhás, and never were so; whilst some Damáis and Sárkhis are recognized as "Gurkhális," notwithstanding their very low social standing, from the mere fact of their ancestors having resided in the Gurkhá district.

The inhabitants of the town and district of Gurkhá, or anyhow the fighting classes of the same, were almost entirely Khas, Magars, and Gurungs, whilst the rulers and nobility were mostly Thákurs.

The only fighting classes, therefore, that have a right to the term "Gurkháli" would be the Thákurs, Khas, Magars, and Gurungs.

These four are therefore treated in this book under the heading of Gurkhás, after which follow a few remarks on the remaining military tribes of Népál.

It is said that about 600 years before Christ, Sakya Simha (Buddha—the wise one) visited the Népál Valley, and found that the fundamental principles of his religion had already been introduced amongst the Newárs by Manjusri from China.

To Manjusri by the Buddhists and to Vishnu by the Hindus are assigned, respectively, the honour of having by a miracle converted the large mountain lake of Nága Vása into the present fertile Népál Valley, by cutting with one blow of a sword the pass by which the Bhágmati river leaves the valley of Népál. To this day this pass is called "Kot bar," Sword cut."

It is known as a fact that 300 years before Christ, Buddhism flourished in Népál, and it is still nominally the faith of the majority of Newárs (some Newárs have been Hindus from time immemorial); yet it is steadily being supplanted by Hinduism, and before another century may possibly have entirely disappeared.

The Khas are Hindus. The Magars and Gurungs are so also nominally, but their Hinduism is not very strict.

The Gurungs in their own country are really Buddhists, though they would not admit it in India.

To this day their priests in their own homes are Lámás and Giábrings, but when serving in our regiments they submit to the Brahmans and employ them for all priestly functions.

The fashionable religion is Hinduism, and it may therefore be said that Gurkhás are Hindus, and with them, therefore, Brahmans are the highest caste, from whose hands no impurity can come. The Brahmans wear the thread (Janái).

Connection of higher with lower castes.

In the case of Brahman with Khas, or Khas with lower grades, there can be no marriage.

Neither can a Magar marry a Gurung or *vice versá*, nor can a Solábját Gurung marry into the Chárját or *vice versá*.

Religious rites.

On the occasion of the birth of a child a rejoicing takes place for eleven days, and no one except near relatives can eat or drink with the father for ten days.

On the eleventh day the Brahman comes, performs certain ceremonies, after which the father is supposed to be clean, and all friends are feasted and alms are given. The same ceremony exactly takes place for a daughter as for a son, but the birth of the latter is hailed with joy, as he has to perform the "Kiriya" or funeral rites of the parents. The girl is looked upon more or less as an expense.

In our regiments eleven days' leave is always granted to a man when a child is born to him.

The Brahman (Opadia) selects a name for the child on the eleventh day. Boys up to the age of six months, and girls up to five months, are suckled from their mothers' breasts only.

On arriving at that age a grand dinner is given, and the Brahmans are feasted and propitiated.

Every friend and relation that has been invited is supposed to feed the child with grain, but this is merely a form, each man just putting a grain in the child's mouth.

The ceremony is called "Bhát Khiláná," "to feed with rice."

All the friends and relations are also supposed to give the child presents, which generally take the shape of bangles of silver or gold.

Betrothals.

Betrothals (called Mángni) take place at any age over five years.

When a marriage is agreed upon, the parents of the boy give a gold ring to the girl, as a sign of betrothal.

This is called "Sáhi Mundri."

Five or six friends of the parents of the boy, and these must belong to the same clan as the boy, and five or six friends of the parents of the girl, and these must belong to the same clan as the girl's father, assemble to witness the agreement in the presence of a Brahman.

A dinner is then given to the friends and relations of the contracting parties by the father of the girl, but the father of the boy is supposed to take with him some dahi (sour milk) and plantains as his share towards the dinner.

After a betrothal, except by breaking off the engagement which can be done by going through a certain ceremony before witnesses, but which is considered very bad form, neither party can marry any one else, unless on the death of one of them when, if the real marriage has not taken place, or been consummated, they can do so.

Marriages can take place at any time after the age of 7. It is considered good to get a girl married before she reaches the age of 13.

Marriages.

A widow cannot marry a second time, but it is not considered disgraceful for her to form part of another man's household.

A widower can marry again.

If a boy, without being engaged to her, meets a girl, falls in love, runs away and marries her, he and his bride cannot approach the girl's father until called by him. When the father-in-law relents, he will send word telling the boy that he may present himself with his wife at his home on a certain hour of a certain day. On their arrival the father-in-law will paint a spot on their foreheads with a mixture of rice and dahi (Tika {Dinnu / Garnu}), and then the boy and girl will have to make submission by bending down and saluting him. This is called "Dhok Dinnu."

"Dhok Dinnu," to make submission.

Amongst Magars it is customary for marriages to be performed by Brahmans, and the ceremony is conducted in much the same way as the ordinary Hindu marriage. There is the marriage procession Jantí, which is so timed as to reach the bride's house after midday, and which is first greeted with a shower of rice-balls, and then feasted by the parents of the bride. The actual marriage takes place at night, when the ceremony of Phera (circumambulation round the sacred fire) is performed, and afterwards the Anchal Ghátá (knotting a cloth which is stretched from the bridegroom's waist over the bride's shoulder).

The latter ceremony is said to constitute the essential marriage tie.

After marriage a divorce can be obtained by a Gurung (and often amongst Magars too) by going through a ceremony called "Sinko Dágo" or "Sinko Pángrá," but both the husband and wife must agree to this. A husband has to pay R40 for his divorce, and the wife R160. Two pieces of split bambú are tied together, placed on two mud balls, and the money is put close by. If either party takes up the bambús, breaks them, and picks up the money, the other party can go his or her way in peace and amity, and marry again legally.

*Divorce*, Sinko Dágo or Sinko Pángrá.

In Népál, Lámás, assisted by Giábrings, fulfil the priestly functions of the Gurungs, both of the Chárját and the Soláhját, but in our regiments Gurung marriage ceremonies are performed by Brahmans. They say with true philosophy, "Jaisá des vaisá bhes," which might be translated as "do in Rome as the Romans do."

In Népál, no ceremony, whether that of marriage, burial, or naming a child at birth, is performed until the officiating Lámá has determined the propitious moment by consultation of astrological tables, and by casting the horoscope. On this much stress is laid. In the marriage* of Gurungs some ceremony resembling the Anchal Ghátá is performed by the Lámás, and red-lead is sprinkled by the bridegroom over the head of the bride. This completes the actual ceremony. All friends and relations are supposed to look away from the bride whilst the red-lead is actually being sprinkled. This ceremony is called "Shindúr Hálnu," "to sprinkle red-lead."

A Magar will not allow his daughter to marry into the clan from which he may himself have taken a wife, but Gurungs have no objection to this. Neither Magars nor Gurungs, however, will take wives from the clan they may belong to themselves.

No Chárját Gurung can marry a Soláhját or *vice versâ*.

Breaches of conjugal fidelity are punished most severely by the Gurkhás in Népál.

Adultery.

An erring wife is imprisoned for life, and the dishonoured husband was expected to cut down the seducer with his kukri the first time he encountered him. Sir Jang Bahádar, however, placed restrictions on this custom, as it was found open to much abuse.

The culprit is now arrested, and after his guilt is proved, the injured husband is allowed to cut him down in public, the victim being allowed a chance of escaping by running away, for which purpose he is given a start of a few yards.

Practically, however, his chance of escaping is very small, as he is generally tripped up by some bystander.

The adulterer, however, can save his life, with the loss of caste, if he passes under the lifted leg of the husband, but this is so ignominious that death is usually preferred. The woman can save her

* *Shindúr Hálnu.*

paramour if she persits in saying that he is not the first man with whom she has gone astray.

In Népál cow-killing and murder are punished with death maiming cows and manslaughter by imprisonment for life, and other acts of violence by imprisonment and fines.

Punishments as inflicted in Népál.

Prisoners are used in Népál for all public works. They get no pay and are merely fed and clothed with prison garb. No one seems to be in charge of them when returning to prison. They apparently are expected to do so of their own accord, and, strange to say, they do.

In Népál, if a low-caste person pretends to belong to a higher one, and induces a high-caste person to partake of food or water at his house, he renders himself liable to a heavy fine or imprisonment, or confiscation of all his property, or he may even be sold into slavery.

The victim of his deception is re-admitted to his caste on payment of certain fees to the priests, and the performance of certain fasts and ceremonies (prayás chit).

Brahmans and women are never capitally punished. The severest punishment for women, *publicly*, is imprisonment for life, and for Brahmans the same with degradation from caste.

Slavery is one of the institutions of Népál. Every person of any means has several slaves (kamáras) in his household. Most of these have been born slaves in the country, but free men and women with all their families may be sold into slavery as a punishment for certain crimes, such as incest and some offences against caste.

The price of slaves ranges for females from 150 to 200 rupees, and for males from 100 to 150 rupees. They are usually well treated and seem quite contented and happy.

Should a slave have a child by her master, she can claim her freedom.

In Népál astrologers form a large class of the learned community. Some of them are priests, but in general the professions are distinct.

In Népál the time for everything, from taking a dose of physic to the declaration of war, is determined by the astrologers.

Baidis, or medical men, are very numerous in Népál. All families of any pretension have at least one permanently attached to their service.

The duties of clerks and accountants are performed by a special class of people, chiefly Newárs.

The old savage code of punishments involving mutilation, stripes, etc., was abolished by Sir Jang Bahádar on his return from England. Treason, rebellion, desertion in time of war, and other offences against the State are punished by death or imprisonment for life; bribery and peculation by Government servants, by fines, imprisonment, and dismissal from office.

Every district now has its kutcherry, where cases are tried and disposed of, but any man may appeal, if dissatisfied, to Bir Sham Sher. Justice on the whole is pretty fairly administered.

The people of Népál are poor but contented. They have few taxes to pay, and their customs and prejudices are not interfered with.

Deaths and mourning. "Dukkha Baknu" (to mourn).

In our regiments, on the death of a near relative, leave is granted for 13 days. For a father the son mourns 13 days. If an unmarried daughter dies, the father mourns 13 days, unless she was still a suckling, when he would only mourn for five days. If a married daughter dies, the father mourns her for one day only, but the father-in-law will mourn for 13 days.

Men shave their heads, lips, cheek, chins, and eyebrows for parents; also for an elder brother if both parents are dead, but not otherwise.

Men shave their heads only for sons, younger brothers, and daughters if unmarried.

On the death of a Gurung in his own country he is buried. The following ceremony takes place. The body is wrapped round with many folds of white cloth, pinned together by splinters of wood; it is then carried by friends and relations to the grave-yard. At the entrance of the cemetery it is met by the officiating Lámá, who, dressed in a long white garment, walks round the cemetery, singing a dirge, and the body is carried behind him until he stops opposite the grave. It is next lowered into the grave, and then all friends and relations are supposed to throw a handful of earth upon the body, after which the grave is filled up, and stones placed above.

In our service Magars and Gurungs on death are either buried or burned (but nearly always buried), according to the wish of the nearest relative. If they die either of cholera or of small-pox, they are invariably buried.

Every regiment, if possible, should be provided with a cemetery. The men much appreciate this.

Inheritance.

The laws of inheritance are the same in Népál as throughout Hindustan. The eldest son obtains the largest portion of the property of his deceased father, but provision is made for the younger children and widow.

In our regiments sepoys are allowed to make any one they choose their heirs.

Superstitions.

Magars and Gurungs are exceedingly superstitious. The most ordinary occurrences of every-day life are referred by them to supernatural agency, frequently to the malevolent action of some demon. These godlings have in consequence to be continually propitiated. Among the minor Hindu deities, Diorâli, Chandi, and Dévi are those specially worshipped in Gurkhá regiments. Outbreaks of any epidemic disease, such as cholera or small-pox, are invariably regarded as a malign visitation of Diorâli or Dévi. When going on a journey no one will start on an unlucky day of his own accord. After the date has been fixed, should any unforeseen occurrence prevent a man from starting, he will often walk out a mile or two on the road he intended taking, and leave a stick on the ground, as a proof of his intention having been carried out.

In March 1889 a Gurkhá woman died of cholera in the Gorakhpur recruiting depôt. Every Gurkhá officer, non-commissioned officer, and man at the depôt at once subscribed. The recruiting officers gave their share, and with the proceeds three goats, three fowls, four pigeons, and food of sorts, were purchased. Of these, one goat and the four pigeons were let loose, and the food thrown away in the name of Dévi, and the balance of animals were sacrificed to her, and then divided and eaten up. Before killing the animals, they all prayed together: "O mother Dévi, we kill these beasts in thy name; do thou in return keep away all sickness from us."

As no fresh case occurred, although there was some cholera about in the district, all the Gurkhás in the depôt were more firmly convinced than ever that this was due entirely to their having propitiated Dévi.

Every Gurkhá regiment has a shrine to Deoráli, and on the seventh day of the Dasehra this is visited by the whole battalion in state procession.

Festivals.

The following is a table of the festivals observed by Gurkhás in our service, with the leave allowed:—

| | |
|---|---|
| Basant Panchmi (in honour of Spring) . . | 1 day. |
| Shibrátri . . . . . . . . | 1 „ |
| Holi (carnival) . . . . . . . | 9 days. |
| Sawan Sakráti . . . . . . . | 1 day. |
| Riki Tarpan . . . . . . . . | 1 „ |
| Janam Asthmi (called Janmasthami) . . . | 1 „ |
| Dasehra (called Dasain) . . . . . | 10 days. |
| Diwáli (called Tiwar, the feast of lamps in honour of the goddess Bhowáni, at new moon of month of Khátik) . . . . . . . . | 4 „ |
| Mághia Sakrát (Hindu New Year) . . . | 1 day. |

The ceremonies at these festivals and their observance are with a few minor points, the same as in Hindustan.

These holidays should not in any way be curtailed or interfered with, but should be granted in full.

Dasehra.

The Dasehra is the chief festival of the Gurkhás, and they endeavour to celebrate it whether in quarters or the field.

Great preparations are made for it in procuring goats, buffaloes, etc., for the sacrifice.

Every man in the regiment subscribes a certain amount towards the expenses. The commanding officers often give a buffalo or two, and every British officer subscribes a certain amount also.

The arms of the regiment are piled, tents erected, and spectators invited to witness the dexterity of the men in severing the heads of buffaloes, the children performing the same office on goats. The period of this festival is considered an auspicious time for undertaking wars, expeditions, etc.

## PECULIARITIES REGARDING CERTAIN FESTIVALS AS OBSERVED IN NÉPÁL.

The "Diwáli" festival takes place about 20 days after the Dasehra on the 15th of Khátik. The people worship Lakshmi, the goddess of Wealth, illuminate their houses and gamble all night long. In Népál gambling in public (which is illegal at all other times) is allowed for three days and nights during the Diwáli.

Many curious tales are told regarding the heavy stakes the Népálese will put on the throw of a dice, such as staking their wives, etc.

One man is said to have cut off his left hand and put it down under a cloth as his stake. On winning, he insisted on his opponent cutting off his hand, or else restoring all the money he had previously won.

The Dasehra or Durga Puja.—This festival commemorates the victory of the goddess Durga over the monster Maheshur and takes place generally early in October and lasts for ten days.

Buffaloes, goats, etc., are sacrificed.

In Népál, however, the clay image of Durga is not made as in Bengal. On the first day of the festival the Brahmans sow barley at the spot where they worship and sprinkle it daily with sacred water.

On the tenth day they pull up the young sprouts, and present small bunches of it to their followers, in return for the presents which they receive from them.

During this festival the Gurkhás worship their colours and implements of war, and ask protection of them throughout the year, under the belief that it is to the favour of the sword they owe their prosperity.

"Janmasthami" is in memory of the birthday of Krishna, and takes place on the eighth day after the full moon of Sáwan.

The "Holi" festival is held in honour of Krishna and in Népál takes place eight days before the full moon of Phágun, and eight days after the Sheoratri festival. A wooden post or "chir," adorned with flags, is erected in front of the palace, and this is burned at night representing the burning of the body of the old year.

## FOOD, DRINKS, DRESS, ETC., ETC.

Food, and manner of cooking.

Caste rules with regard to food only apply to one description, *viz.*, "dál and rice."

*All* other food, excepting "dál and rice," *all* Gúrkhás will eat in common.

With Magars, unmarried Thákurs, and with Gurungs, it is not necessary to take off *any* clothes to cook or to eat *any* kind of food, including "dál and rice."

In Népál the Khas need only remove their caps and shoes to cook or eat their food.

Should a Brahman of the Opadhia class prepare "dál and rice," all castes can eat of it.

Magars and Gurungs will not eat the above if prepared by a Jaici Brahman.

Superior castes will not eat dál and rice with inferior ones. In our regiments men generally form little messes of their own, varying in size from two or three to a dozen.

As long as they are unmarried, Gurkhás of the same caste will eat everything together.

All Gurkhás will eat "shikar" in common, a word they use for all descriptions of meat.

No Gurkhás, except some menial classes, will eat cows, neilgai or female goats.

Gurungs eat buffaloes in their own country, though they will stoutly deny it if accused.

All kinds of game are prized by Gúrkhás, deer of all varieties, pigs, porcupines, pea-fowl, pigeons, pheasants, etc., etc., but beyond all things a Gurkhá likes fish.

Whilst bachelors, Magars and Gurungs will eat every kind of food in common, and after marriage even, the only thing they draw the line at is "dál and rice."

Food cooked in ghee, including "rice," but not "dál," is eaten by all classes in common.

Thákurs who have not adopted the thread will eat everything with Magars and Gurungs.

All classes will drink water from the same masak, which, however, should be made of goat-skin.

Brian Hodgson gives the following true and graphic account of the contrast between the way the Gurkhá eats his food, and the preliminary ceremonies which have to be observed by the orthodox Hindu :—

"These highland soldiers, who despatch their meal in half an hour, and satisfy the ceremonial law by merely washing their hands and face and taking off their turbans before cooking, laugh at the pharisaical rigour of the Sipáhis, who must bathe from head to foot, and make puja ere they can begin to dress their dinners, must eat nearly naked in the coldest weather, and cannot be in marching trim again in less than three hours.

"In war, the former readily carry several days' provisions on their backs : the latter would deem such an act intolerably degrading. The former see in foreign service nothing but the prospect of glory and spoil : the latter can discover in it nothing but pollution and peril from unclean men and terrible wizards, goblins, and evil spirits. In masses the former have all that indomitable confidence, each in all, which grows out of national integrity and success ; the latter can have no idea of this sentiment, which yet maintains the union and resolution of multitudes in peril better than all other human bonds whatsoever, and once thoroughly acquired, is by no means inseparable from service under the national standard.

"In my humble opinion they are by far the best soldiers in Asia ; and if they were made participators of our renown in arms, I conceive that their gallant spirit, emphatic contempt of madhesias (people residing in the plains), and unadulterated military habits, might be relied on for fidelity ; and that our good and regular pay and noble pension establishment would serve perfectly to counterpoise the influence of nationality, so far as that could injuriously affect us."

The above was written by Mr. Brian Hodgson in 1832, and 25 years later, namely, in 1857, he writes :—

"It is infinitely to be regretted that the opinions of Sir H. Fane, of Sir Charles Napier, and of Sir H. Lawrence, as to the high expediency of recruiting largely from this source, were not acted upon long ago."

On service the Gurkhás put aside the very small caste prejudices they have, and will cook and eat their food, if necessary, in uniform, and with all accoutrements on.

Gurkhás will eat all and every kind of vegetables and fruits. They have a great partiality for garlic and pepper, and are very fond of potatoes, cabbages, cucumbers, and squash (kadu).

Stimulants.

Gurkhás will drink any English spirits, wines, or beer.

They manufacture a kind of beer out of rice, which they call Jánr, and a spirit called Raksi, and although they will drink this freely, they far prefer good commissariat rum.

They will smoke any English or Indian tobacco, and are very fond of cheroots.

They will smoke out of any English-made pipe, even if with a horn mouth-piece, although they are likely to make a little fuss over the latter, just to save their consciences.

Arms.

The kúkri, a short, curved, broad-bladed and heavy knife, is the real national weapon of the Gurkhás, and it is worn by all from the highest to the lowest. In our regiments they are carried in a frog attached to the waist-belt.

From the beginning of the handle to the end or point of the blade they average about 20 inches in length.

Where wood is plentiful, they are very fond of practising cutting with the kúkri, and they will cut down with one blow a tree the size of an ordinary man's arm.

A really skilful cutter will cut off slice after slice from the end of a piece of green wood, each slice being not thicker than an ordinary piece of shoe leather. They call this "chinnu," "to slice off."

They are also skilful with the Golel, knocking down and killing the smallest birds with ease. All who can manage to raise the funds endeavour to possess themselves of some sort of fire-arm.

Dress.

The national dress of the Gurkhás of the poorer class, such as we enlist, is one that shows them off to the greatest advantage, and consists of the following:—

A piece of cloth (langote) worn, as natives of India do, round the loins, etc.

A thin waistcoat fitting tight and buttoned all the way up to the throat.

A long piece of cloth (patuga), which is often a pagri, and is wrapped round the waist, and by which the kukri is carried.

A pair of brown Gurkha shoes, as described further on.

A black round cap, high on one side and low on the other, and finally a kind of thin blanket or thick sheet, called Khádi, which is worn as follows :—

The two corners of the breadth are first taken. One is carried over the right shoulder and the other is brought up under the left arm, and the two corners tied together about the centre of the chest.

A third corner, the one diagonally opposite No. 1, is now taken, and brought over the left shoulder and tied in a knot with the fourth corner, which is brought up under the right arm and opposite the centre of the chest.

This dress leaves the arms quite bare from above the elbows, and the legs are naked from half-way down to the knees, thus showing off his grand limbs.

The khádi, by being tied as described above, forms a kind of large bag, which extends all the way round the back, and in this Gurkhás generally carry their goods and chattels.

The Gurkhá shoe is square-toed, fits well up over the instep, passes just under the ankle, and then round and pretty high up above the heel. It is made of rough-looking but good brown leather, and all sewing in it is done with strips of raw hide.

It is an excellent, durable shoe, is not affected by water in the same way that an ordinary native shoe of India is, and it is much less liable to come off in boggy ground.

When the sun is very hot, Gurkhás will often unwind their waist-belt and tie the same over their heads in the shape of a pagri, taking it off again in the afternoon, when it begins to cool down.

National dress of upper class and residents of cities.

The upper classes of Népál and most of the residents of Kátmandu wear the following :—

The above-mentioned national cap, or one much like it.

A kind of double-breasted frock-coat called chaobandi, fitting tight everywhere, especially over the arms, and fastened inside and outside by means of eight pieces of coloured tape, four inside and four outside. The four outside pieces of tape when tied show two on the left breast and high up, and the other two on the left side about level with the waist.

A white or coloured waist-cloth or pagri, with the invariable kúkri, a pair of pyjámas very loose down to just below the knee, and from thence fitting the leg down to the ankle, and a pair of the national shoes.

Under the coat is worn a shirt, of which three or four inches are invariably allowed to show. They never tuck their shirts inside their pyjámas.

The frock coat and pyjáma above mentioned are made of a double layer of a thin shiny cotton cloth. Between the two layers a padding of cotton wool is placed, and these secured by parallel lines of sewing, which run close to each other.

To make this still more secure, diagonal lines of sewing are also resorted to. This makes a very comfortable, and warm, but light suit.

Amusements and sports.

Gurkhás delight in all manly sports, - shooting, fishing, etc.—and are mostly keen sportsmen and possess great skill with gun and rod. They amuse themselves in their leisure hours, either in this way in the field, or in putting the shot, playing quoits or foot-ball, and they are always eager to join in any game with Europeans.

General Sir Charles Reid, K.C.B., says: "All Gurkhás are keen sportsmen, and are never so happy as when they are on a tiger's track. A man I lost at Delhi had killed twenty-two on foot; they never waste a shot; they call ammunition 'Khazána,' 'treasure.'"

They are good gardeners, but very improvident, as they never will save up seed for the next season's sowing.

They are very fond of flowers, and will often go a long distance to procure some. They often make necklaces of flowers, which they wear, and will also put flowers away in a glass of water in their barracks.

General character.

As compared with other orientals, Gurkhás are bold, enduring, faithful, frank, very independent and self-reliant; in their own country they are jealous of foreigners and self-asserting.

They despise the natives of India, and look up to and fraternize with Europeans, whom they admire for their superior knowledge, strength and courage, and whom they imitate in dress and habits.

They have the following saying: "Topiwár Kámwár, Lungiwár Khánnewár"—"The cap wearer works, the lungi-wearer eats."

They are very jealous of their women, but are domestic in their habits, and kind and affectionate husbands and parents.

As a consequence their wives are less shy and reserved, and have more freedom, and reciprocate their affection, carefully looking after uniforms and all culinary and domestic matters.

As a rule recruits on joining are very unsophisticated, very truthful, but dirty, and the first lesson that has to be taught them is that "cleanliness is next to godliness." They have then few prejudices of any description, caste or otherwise.

Gambling.

The great vice of Gurkhás is gambling, to which they are greatly addicted. Though hot-tempered and easily roused, they are in general quiet, well-behaved men, and extremely amenable to discipline. With a firm, just hand over them, punishments are rare.

Gurkhás are capable of being polished up to a degree of smartness that no native troops can approach, and which cannot be much surpassed even by British troops.

No officer can be too strict with them on parades, but they hate being "nagged at."

With a slack hand over them they very soon deteriorate and become slovenly.

Education.

In Kátmandu good schools exist in which English and Hindi are taught, but our recruits, being almost entirely drawn from the agricultural classes, are quite ignorant of reading or writing.

In our battalions schools exist for their instruction in reading, writing, and doing accounts, both in English and vernacular, and these are generally well attended. Numbers of men learn to read and write from friends in their barracks.

It may seem strange, but it is an undoubted fact, that a number of recruits are yearly obtained who profess to enlist merely for the sake of learning to read, write, and do accounts.

Traditions.

The Gurkhá, from the warlike qualities of his forefathers, and the traditions handed down to him of their military prowess as conquerors of Népál, is imbued with, and cherishes, the true military spirit.

His physique, compact and sturdy build, powerful muscular development, keen sight, acute hearing, and hereditary education as a sportsman, eminently capacitate him for the duties of a light infantry soldier on the mountain-side, while his acquaintance with forest lore makes him as a pioneer in a jungle almost unrivalled, whilst his national weapon the kúkri has in Burma and other places proved itself invaluable.

The bravery displayed by the Gurkhás in their contests with the British has already been alluded to, and their own traditions afford ample proof of the dogged tenacity with which they can encounter danger and hardship.

The return of the Népál army from Diggarcheh in the year 1790, amongst other instances, affords a distinguished proof of their daring and hardihood. The following extracts from Captain T. Smith's book are very characteristic:—

"At Bhartpur it was an interesting and amusing sight to witness the extreme good-fellowship and kindly feeling with which the Europeans and the Gurkhás mutually regarded each other. A six-foot-two grenadier of the 59th would offer a cheroot to the "little Gurkhi," as he styled him; the latter would take it from him with a grin, and when his tall and patronising comrade stooped down with a lighted cigar in his mouth, the little mountaineer never hesitated a moment in puffing away at it with the one just received, and they were consequently patted on the back and called 'prime chaps.'"

"At the assault of Bhartpur, the Gurkhás were ordered to follow in after the 59th.

"These directions were obeyed, with the exception of going in with them instead of after them; for when the British grenadiers with a deafening "hurrah" made their maddening rush at the breach, at that glorious and soul-stirring moment it was impossible to restrain them, and they dashed into the thick of it.

"In the morning after the storming of Bhartpur, when being praised for their gallantry by their British comrades, they returned the flattering partiality of the latter by the following characteristic remark: 'The English are brave as lions, they are splendid sepoys, and *very nearly* equal to us!'"

The following story is given as illustrative of their coolness and amenability to discipline:—

"A tiger had been seen within a few miles of Dehra, and Colonel Young (then Captain, and the gallant Commanding Officer of the Sirmur Battalion), accompanied by Colonel Childers of Her Majesty's 11th Dragoons, mounted an elephant and hastened to the spot. They, however, were unsuccessful in rousing him; and after a long and tedious search were returning home.

"A Gurkhá sepoy was following the elephant with his gun on his shoulder, when he suddenly dropped on one knee and presented his rifle as if in the act to fire. Having, however, roused the attention of the sportsmen, he did not pull the trigger, but kept his gun fixed in the same position. He had suddenly caught sight of the fiery eyes of the tiger, who was crouching amongst the underwood, within three paces of his gun; in this situation they steadily regarded each other. The elephant was immediately pushed up close to the kneeling Gurkhá, but neither of the sportsmen could succeed in catching a glimpse of the animal. In order, if possible, to observe the direction more accurately, Captain Young called out 'Recover arms.' The sepoy came to the 'Recover' as calmly and collectedly as if on his own parade. 'Present.' Down went the gun again; this was repeated, but still the tiger was invisible.

"Captain Young exclaimed: 'That gallant fellow shall not be left unassisted,' and in a moment dropped from the elephant and placed himself close to the sepoy. He looked along the levelled barrel, but to no purpose; the brute was not to be distinguished.

"Cocking his gun, therefore, he told the Gurkhá to fire; there was a terrific roar, a rush forward for one instant, and all was still. When the smoke had just cleared away, there lay the tiger perfectly dead. The ball had struck the centre of his forehead and entered his brain."

Doctor Oldfield in his book points out that there is not a single instance of a Népál Chief taking bribes from, or selling himself for money to, the British or any other State. This loyalty to themselves is only equalled by their loyalty to us during the fiery ordeal of the Mutiny, the records of which, as well as of Ambela, of the Cabul campaign, and many other wars and battles, amply testify the value of the services rendered us by our Gurkhá regiments since incorporation in our army in 1815.

Their fighting qualities, whether for sturdy, unflinching courage, or daring *élan*, are *nulli secundus* amongst the troops we enrol in our ranks from the varied classes of our Indian Empire and no greater compliment can be paid to their bravery than by quoting one of their sayings—

"**Káfar hunnu bhandá, manrnu rámro!**"

"It is better to die than to be a coward!"

## THÁKURS.

Of all Gurkhás, excepting the Brahman, the Thákur has the highest social standing, and of all Thákurs the Sáhi is the best. The Máharája Dhiráj (King of Népál) is a Sáhi.*

The Thákur claims royal descent, and even to this day a really pure-bred Sáhi Thákur is not charged rent for land in Népál.

Thákurs, on account of their high social standing, intelligence, cleanliness, and soldierly qualities, should invariably be taken if belonging to good clans. As soldiers they are excellent, and they can be obtained in small numbers, with quite as good physique and appearance as the best Magar or Gurung.

A Thákur who has not adopted the thread, which until marriage is with him an entirely voluntary action, has no more prejudices than the ordinary Magar or Gurung, and even after adopting the thread his caste prejudices are not so very great, nor does he ever allow them to obtrude.

The Hamál Thákur should not be enlisted by any regiment.

The best Thákur clans are the following: Sáhi, Malla, Sing, Sen, Khan, and Súmál.

The "Singála Uchái" is really a Sáhi by descent and is excellent, but all other Ucháis and the balance of Thákur clans are not up to those above mentioned, although all Thákur clans claim to be equal, with the exception of the Hamál. The Hamál is no Thákur at all, but the progeny of an Opadhia Brahman with a Thákur woman.

A Thákur king, it is said, in the course, of his conquests, came to a very high hill called Singála. This he captured from his enemies, and on the top of the same he established a garrison of Sáhi Thákurs. These in time came to be spoken of as the "Uchái Thákurs," from the fact of their living at a high elevation.

The clan Uchái will be found amongst many tribes, and is said to be derived from a similar reason.

With the exception of the Singála Uchái, all other Thákur Ucháis are the progeny of a Thákur with a Magar.

---

* Shái and Sáh are one and the same—*vide* Brian Hodgson.

## THÁKUR CLANS.

| | |
|---|---|
| Bam. | Mán. |
| Bansi. | Raika. |
| Chand. | Rakhsia. |
| Chohán (doubtful). | Rúchál. |
| Hamál. | Sáhi or Sáh. |
| Jiú. | Sen. |
| Jiva. | Sing. |
| Khan. | Súmál. |
| Malla or Mal. | Uchái. |

The Sáhi clan* is subdivided into the following:—

| | |
|---|---|
| Birkotia (from Birkot). | Ismáli. |
| Dhamar. | Kallian. |
| Galkotia (from Galkot). | Navakotia (from Navakot). |
| Gurkháli. | Surajbánsi. |

* Sáhi and Sáh are one and the same—*vide* Brian Hodgson.

## THE KHAS.

Khas.

That the Khas have existed as a nation at some period prior to A. D. 1100 cannot be doubted, as we find mention made of the "Khas nation" in the reign of Narendra Deva of Népál, who remarks on the kindness of an ascetic Bandhudatta Achárya in having taken much pains and trouble to fetch a god to the Khas country, whereby the people were relieved from distress of a drought by plentiful rain.

In ancient Hindu writings, the country between the Népál Valley and Kashmir is called Khas, and its inhabitants are called Khasiyas. Whenever mentioned in ancient records, like the Kiránts, the Khasiyas are considered as abominable and impure infidels.

We also find mention made about 1000 A. D. of a race of Hindus called the Khas, residing about Pálpá and the southern portion of Népál, whilst further north lived a barbarian race called Magars, to whose north again resided "an abominable and impure race" called Gurungs.

Probable origin.

This would seem to give the Khas a far more ancient origin than is usually accepted, as it is generally considered that they have their origin from some period subsequent to the Mahomedan invasions of India.

Now, considering that Hindus are known historically to have existed within Népálese territories for centuries before the birth of Christ, it seems to me that a mixed breed must have sprung up and have multiplied, and although, perhaps, not called Khasiyas till a later period, must nevertheless have been the same as what afterwards was so called.

It is stated in ancient history that during the reign of Stunko, the fourteenth king of the Kiránti dynasty, Asoka, the Rájá of Pátaliputra (Patna), having heard of the fame of Népál as a sacred place, came on a pilgrimage to Népál (about 230--250 B. C.).

He gave his daughter Chárumati in marriage to a "descendant" of a Chettri, named Devapála.

Here we have proof of the existence of Hindus in Népál in a very far back age.

The polished Hindus no doubt found the women of the various

hill races only too willing to welcome them to their arms, but their progeny were called Khas, perhaps, as a term of reproach, from the word "Khasnu"—"to fall."

In time, however, the number of Khas must have become so great as to form a nation, and to the nation stuck the name of Khas.

The original seat of the Khas is ordinarily said to be Gurkhá, but merely because it was thence that they issued under Prithwi Narayan on their conquering excursion into Népál. As a matter of fact, we hear of Khas in Pálpá and Botwál long before any mention is ever made of Gurkhá, and it is far more likely that the Khas were to be found all over the southern portion of Central Népál.

Previous to the advent of natives from India, in far gone ages, the country (Central Népál) was inhabited by Magars and other impure and infidel tribes. Hamilton says: "It is generally admitted that most of the chiefs who, coming from the low country, sought refuge in the Népál hills, entered into the service of the various mountain chiefs, and having gained their confidence by a superior knowledge and polish of manners, contrived to put them to death and to seize their country.

"Many of these permitted the mountain tribes to remain and practice their abominations, and have themselves relaxed in many essential points from the rules of caste, and have debased their blood by frequent intermixtures with that of the mountaineers; while such of these as chose to embrace the slender degree of purity required in these parts, have been admitted to the high dignities of the military order—Kshatriya."

It seems to me much more likely that, having converted the chiefs of various mountain tribes, they gave them high-born lineages invented for the occasion, but which in time came to be looked upon as their real origins, and gave rise to the belief that their ancestors had been pure Rájputs or Brahmans. This theory, or conquest by the sword, seems much more likely than that the mountain princes were such fools as to allow themselves to be supplanted one by one by their own employés.

Oldfield says:—

"The progress of Mahomedanism in Hindustan daily drove fresh refugees to the Népálese mountains. The '*Khas tribes*' availed themselves of the superior knowledge of the strangers to subdue the neighbouring aboriginal tribes. They were uniformly successful; and in such a career, continued for ages, they gradually merged the greater part of their own ideas, habits and language (but not physiognomy) in those of the Hindus. The Khas language became, and still is, a corrupt dialect of Hindi, retaining not many traces of primitive barbarism."

Here, again, we have fresh proof that the Khas existed as "*tribes*" at some period long anterior to the Mahomedan invasions, as we find the Khas availing themselves of the services of the Hindu refugees to conquer and subdue the neighbouring tribes.

Ektháriah.

The Ekthariahs are the descendants, more or less pure, not of the Brahmans by a Khas female, but of Rájputs and other Kshatriyas of the plains who either sought refuge in Népál from the Musalmans, or voluntarily sought military service as adventurers.

Not having the same inducements as the Brahmans had to degrade their proud race by union with Parbattiah females, they mixed much less with the Khas than the Brahmans had done.

Hence to this day they claim a vague superiority over the Khas, although in all essentials the two races have long been confounded.

Those among the Kshatriyas of the plains who were more lax in their alliances with Khas females, were permitted to give their children the patronymic title only, but not the rank of Kshatriya.

But their children, again, if they married for two generations into the Khas, became pure Khas, and at the same time re-acquired all the privileges and rank, though they no longer retained the name, of Kshatriya.

While in Népál they were Khas, not Kshatriya; but if they revisited the plains,* they bore the name and were entitled to every privilege attached to Kshatriya birth in Hindustan.

Advent of Rájputs.

It is stated by Colonel Todd that the Gurkhá dynasty was founded towards the end of the twelfth century by the third son of the Rájput Rájá Samarsi, Ruler of Chitor,† who settled in Pálpá.

---

* Since the day that Sir Jang Bahádar returned from England, a number of Khas have taken to calling themselves Chettris. This is getting more and more the fashion, and almost every man who, prior to 1850, would have been proud of being called a Khas, now returns himself as Chettri.—(Native information.)

† This would account for the numerous Chitoriah clans.

Népálese tradition.

A Népálese tradition exists which says that the Rájá of Udeipúr, probably Hari Singh, was besieged by the Mahomedans in his capital. He made a long and gallant defence, but at last food and water began to fail him, and foreseeing the horrors of famine, he destroyed all the women and children within the city, to the number of 70,000, set fire to the town, and with his garrison attacked and cut his way through the Mahomedan hosts and took refuge in the hills of Népál to the west of the Gandak river, where he was hospitably received by the aborigines.

Whatever truth there may be in the above traditions, there can be no doubt that large numbers of Rájputs and Brahmans did make their appearance in Western Népál about the twelfth century, and it can easily be understood how in time, from their superior intelligence and civilization, they obtained positions of influence and importance amongst the barbarians who inhabited the land.

Converts to Hinduism.

In time also it would appear that a number of the Magar mountaineer princes were persuaded to follow the doctrines of the Brahmans, and many of the subjects and clans of these princes were induced to follow the example set them, but a large number refused to be converted.

To the former the Brahmans granted the sacred thread, whilst they denied it to the latter, and hence have sprung up tribes called Thápás, Ghartis, Ráuás, etc., etc., some of whom wear the thread and are called Khas, whilst the others do not wear the thread and remain merely Magars.

The Brahmans, to completely reconcile their most important converts, worked out marvellous pedigrees for them, and gave them the right to claim descent from various famous origins, such as "Súrja Bansi," "born of the sun," "Chandra Bansi," "born of the moon," "Rájá Bansi," "born of a king," etc., etc.

The progeny of the women of the country by Brahmans and Rájputs were, possibly as a term of reproach, called "Khas," or the "fallen," from "Khasnu," "to fall," but the Brahmans invested this progeny with the sacred thread also, and thereby gave them a higher social standing than the Magars and Gurungs. But this is most clearly and graphically described by Brian Hodgson.

After describing how the Mahomedan conquest and bigotry continued to drive multitudes of Brahmans from the plains of Hindustan to the proximate hills which now form the western territories of Népál, Brian Hodgson says :—

"The Brahmans found the natives illiterate, and without faith, but fierce and proud. They saw that the barbarians had vacant minds, ready to receive their doctrines, but spirits not apt to stoop to degradation, and they acted accordingly. To the earliest and most distinguished of their converts they communicated, in defiance of the creed they taught, the lofty rank and honours of the Kshatriya order.

A new race arises.

"But the Brahmans had sensual passions to gratify as well as ambition. They found the native females—even of the most distinguished—nothing loth, but still of a temper, like that of the males, prompt to resent indignities.

"These females would indeed welcome the polished Brahmans to their embraces, but their offspring must not be stigmatized as the infamous progeny of a Brahman and a Mléchha. To this progeny also, then, the Brahmans, in still greater defiance of their creed, communicated the rank of the second order of Hinduism; and from these two roots (converts and illegitimate progeny), mainly, spring the now numerous, predominant, and extensively ramified tribe of Khas, originally the name of a small clan of creedless barbarians, now the proud title of Kshatriya, or military order of the kingdom of Nepál. The offspring of the original Khas females and of Brahmans, with the honours and rank of the second order of Hinduism, got the patronymic titles of the first order, and hence the key to the anomalous nomenclature of so many stirpes of the military tribes of Népál, is to be sought in the nomenclature of the sacred order."

It may be added, as remarkably illustrative of the lofty spirit of the Parbattias (Highlanders), that, in spite of the yearly increasing sway of Hinduism in Népál, and the various attempts of the Brahmans in high office to procure the abolition of a custom so radically opposed to the creed both parties now profess, the Khas still insist that the fruit of commerce (marriage is out of the question) between their females and males of the sacred order shall be ranked as Kshatriya, wear the thread, and assume the patronymic title.

It will thus be seen that the Khas are derived from three sources :—

1. Progeny of Brahman and Chatris with women of the hill tribes.
2. Converted barbarians.
3. Ekthariahs.

The famous Prime Minister Bhim Sen was the descendant of a Magar Thápá, as was also General Amar Sing.

A new language arises.

Now, as has been shown, from the advent of these thousands of foreigners and their numerous progeny sprang up a new race, called Khas, and with this new race also came a new language, a kind of Hindi *patois*, which was called the language of the Khas, or Khas-Kúra, which is nowadays the *lingua franca* of Népál.

"The only language of southern origin spoken in Népál is the Khas-Kúra brought there by colonies from below, and now so generally diffused that, in the provinces west of the Kali River, it has nearly eradicated the vernacular tongues, and though less prevalent in the provinces east of that river, it has even with them, as far as the Trisulganga, divided the empire of speech almost equally with the local mother-tongues."

Brian Hodgson wrote this about fifty years ago, since which the Khas language has made immense strides, and is now understood more or less all over Népál from the Káli to the Michi.

Brian Hodgson says :—

"Khas-Kúra is terse, simple, sufficiently copious in words, and very characteristic of the unlettered but energetic race of soldiers and statesmen who made it what it is.

"At present it is almost wholly in its structure, and in eight-tenths of its vocables, substantially Hindi. Yet several of its radical words still indicate an ancient barbarous stock, and I have no doubt that the people, who more especially speak it (the Khas), were originally what Menu calls them, *viz.*, barbarous mountaineers of a race essentially the same with the several other races of Népálese Highlanders.

"The Gurkhális speak Khas-Kúra, and to their ascendency is its prevalence, in later times, to be mainly ascribed.

"The emigrations from the south, which caused the birth of the Khas language, set chiefly in the provinces west of the Trisulganga.

"There to this day Brahmanical Hinduism principally flourishes, its great supporters being the Khas, and next to them the Magars and Gurungs.

"These southern immigrants were so numerous as to be able to give the impress of their own speech and religion to the rude and scattered Highlanders."

The Khas are the predominant race of Népál. They are generally slighter, more active, and more intelligent, than either the Magar or Gurung.

They are Hindus, wear the thread, and are more liable to Brahmanical prejudices than the Magar or Gurung. They, however, make little of the ceremonial law of the Hindus in regard to food and sexual relations. Their active habits and vigorous characters could not brook the restraint of ritual law. Their few prejudices are rather useful than otherwise, inasmuch as they favour sobriety and cleanliness.

They are temperate, hardy and brave, and make good soldiers. They intermarry in their own castes, and have a high social standing in Népál.

In the Népálese army almost all the officers above the rank of Lieutenant are Khas, and so are by far the greater proportion of officers below the rank of Captain.

They are intensely proud of their traditions, and look down upon Magars and Gurungs.

In their own country any Khas who runs away in a battle becomes an outcast, and his very wife is unable to eat with him. They are very national in their feelings.

In the Népálese "Rifle Brigade," which consists of the picked men of all classes, are to be found numbers of Khas of 5′ 8″ and over, with magnificent physique.

Colonel Bahádar Gambar Sing, who at present commands the "Rifles," served as a private under Sir Jang Bahádar at Lucknow during the Mutiny. He there greatly distinguished himself by single-handed capturing three guns and killing seven mutineers. He received an acknowledgment from the British Government for his bravery, and the Prince of Wales presented him in 1875 with a claymore, with an inscription thereon. In this fight Colonel Gambar Sing had no other weapon than his kúkri, and he received twenty-three wounds, some of which were very dangerous, and to this day his face is scarred with huge sword-cuts. He also lost some fingers, and one of his hands was nearly cut off. Sir Jang Bahádar had a special medal struck for him, which the gallant old gentleman wears on all great parades.

Under the native army reorganization scheme of 1893, the 9th Bengal Infantry has been converted into a Regiment of Khas Gurkhás. They should be a splendid body of men, who will undoubtedly give a great account of themselves whenever called upon to do so.

Khattris.

About Khattris, Dr. L. Hamilton says:—

"The descendants of Brahmans by women of the lower tribes, although admitted to be Khas (or impure), are called Kshattris or Khattris, which terms are considered as perfectly synonymous."

It would seem, however, that some proper Khattris, called "Deokotas," from Bareilly, did settle in the country, and intermarried with the Khas Khattris. All the Khattris wear the thread, and are considered as belonging to the military tribes.

Since the return of Sir Jang Bahádar from England, a number of Gurkhá Khas have taken to calling themselves Chettris. There is no such man in the whole of Népál as a Gurkhá Chettri.

Khas there are and Khattris there are also, but Chettris there are none, and it is merely a title borrowed latterly from India.

Brian Hodgson also mentions a tribe called Ekthariahs, the descendants of more or less pure Rájputs and other Kshatriyas of the plains. They claimed a vague superiority to the Khas, but the great tide of events around them has now thoroughly confounded the two races in all essentials, and therefore they will not be shown as a separate tribe, but be included with Khas. Brian Hodgson says:—

"The Khas were, long previously to the age of Prithwi Narayan, extensively spread over the whole of the Cháubisia, and they are now to be found in every part of the existing kingdom of Népál, as well as in Kumáon, which was part of Népál until 1816. The Khas are more devoted to the house of Gurkhá as well as more liable to Brahmanical prejudices, than the Magars or Gurungs; and on both accounts are perhaps somewhat less desirable as soldiers for our service than the latter tribes.* I say somewhat, because it

* This was written in 1832,—namely, only sixteen years after our war with Népál,—and it is on that account that Brian Hodgson says the Khas are somewhat less desirable as soldiers for our service—not for want of bravery or soldierly qualities.

is a mere question of degree; the Khas having certainly no religious prejudices, nor probably any national partialities which would prevent their making excellent and faithful servants-in-arms; and they possess pre-eminently that masculine energy of character and love of enterprise which distinguish so advantageously all the military races of Népál."

Matwala Khas.

To the north and to the west of Sallián, numbers of Matwala Khas are to be found. They are rarely if ever found to the east of the Gandak river. There can be no doubt that this race found its origin somewhere about Sallián, or perhaps still further west.

The Matwala Khas is generally the progeny of a Khas of Western Népál with a Magar woman of Western Népál.

If the woman happens to belong to the Ráná clan of the Magar tribe, the progeny is then called a Bhát Ráná.

The Matwala Khas does not wear the thread. He eats and drinks and in every way assimilates himself with the Magars and Gurungs. He invariably claims to be a Magar.

Amongst the Matwala Khas are to be found those who call themselves Bohora, Roká, Chohán, Jhánkri, etc.

These are easy to identify, but it is more difficult to find out a Matwala who calls himself a Thápá. His strong Magar appearance, his not wearing the thread, and his eating and drinking frooly with the real Magars, all tend to prove him to be what he almost invariably claims to be, *viz.*, a real Magar. The writer has found men in the ranks who for years had served as, and been considered, Magars, but who really were Matwala Khas. Some very excellent recruits are obtained amongst the Matwala Khas, although the greater proportion are coarse-bred and undesirable.

1. ADHIKÁRI.

| | | |
|---|---|---|
| Alina. | Khadsena. | Musiah. |
| Bajgai. | Khaptari. | Pokriál. |
| Bhatta. | Khirkiseni. | Powrel. |
| Bhaltala. | Khirsing. | Thákuri. |
| Dangal. | Khushiab. | Thámi. |
| Dhami. | Man. | Thararái. |

2. BÁNIYA.

Sinjapati.

### 3. BASNIET.

Khairákoti.
Khaptari.
Kholya.
Khulál.
Lámchania.
Porel.
Puwár.
Rakmi.
Sripáli.

### 4. BANDARI.

Bamba.
Bhajgai.
Gianwáli.
Kálá.
Kálákotia.
Lámá.
Raghúbangsi.
Rikhmel.
Sinjáli.
Sinjápati.

### 5. BISHT.

Bagduwal.
Bayal.
Dabál.
Kálá.
Kálikotia.
Khansila.
Khaptari.
Puwár.
Oli.
Sinjúli.
Somal.

### 6. BOHORA.

Dewakota.
Jureli.
Máharáji.
Khaptari.

### 7. BURHA.

### 8. BURHATHOKI.

Baraj.
Chandra.
Deobar.
Mohat.
Nare.
Khaptari.
Puwár.

### 9. GHARTI.

Bagalia.
Barwál.
Godar.
Kálákotia.
Khandka.
Khulál.
Lámchania.
Machiwál.
Machel.
Malájí.
Powrel.
Sripáli.
Suyal.

### 10. KARKI.

Himál.
Kálá.
Khulál.
Lámá.
Mula.
Mundala or Murula { Lepholi. Piutháui
Rukmel.
Rumi.
Sripali.
Sutár.

## 11. KHANDKA.

Bagália.
Basniet.
Gimiria.
Kálakotia.
Karka.
Khaptari.
Khulál.
Lakangi.
Lámchania.
Máháráji.
Pálpáli.
Partiál.
Powrel.
Púwár.
Ráj.
Sarbe.
Sewáli (or Siowli).
Sobe.
Sujál.

## 12. KHATTRIS.

Achárja.
Adikbári.
Alphatopi.
Amgai.
Arjal.
Arjel.
Armel.
Arulie.
Bagália.
Bajgai.
Balia.
Bámankoti.
Banstala.
Barál.
Barwal. }
Basyal. }
Bastakoti.
Batiál.
Bemsal.
Bhakati.
Bhandári.
Bhát Ojha.
Bhat Rai.
Bhattari.
Bhikral.
Bhiriál.
Bhusál.
Bhustarimal.
Bhurtel.
Bikral.
Bohra.
Budal.
Chalataui.
Chalse.
Chanial.
Chapagái,
Chapain.
Chanvalagai.
Chokan.
Chuain.
Chundáni.
Chunjali.
Chonial.
Dahal.
Dal.
Dalál.
Dámi.
Dangáli.
Dangi.
Danjal.
Deokota.
Dhakál.
Dhamál.
Dhilál.
Dhingáná.
Dhongiál.
Dhungana.
Ditál.
Gairia.
Ganjál.
Gartaula.
Gewáli.
Ghimiria.
Gilal.
Gothámi.
Hamiagai.
Jakri.
Jamakotel.
Kadária.
Kaksel
Kala.
Kálákhathi.
Kanál.
Kandel.
Kanhál.
Kaphle.
Karal.
Karka.
Karki.
Karwal.
Katiora.
Khana.
Khandál.
Khaptari.
Kharal.
Khatiwáta.
Khijal.
Khilatáni.
Khulál.
Kirkiseni.
Koerálá.
Koniel.
Konwár.
Kosil.
Kukriál.
Kumai.
Label.
Lámchania.
Lamsál.
Langail.
Loyál.
Luentel.
Lubáli.
Mahatra.
Máji.
Makraula.
Maraseni.
Mari Bhus.

Megain.
Mohara.
Mohat.
Mondibhusa.
Naipal.
Neupáni.
Newgaura.
Oli.
Osti.
Oupreti.
Pachain.
Paingni.
Pánde.
Panth.
Parajaikamla.
Parajuli.
Parsai.
Parseni.
Partak.
Pekurel.
Phania.
Phuljel.
Pinsinga.
Pokrel.
Porel.
Porseni.
Porjál.
Pungiál.
Puwár.
Ráwal.
Regmi.
Remi.
Rigál.
Rijál.
Rimdl.
Rupkheti.
Sabane.
Saktial.
Sangrola.
Sápkotia.
Satania.
Sáte.
Satingai.
Saun.
Seora.
Sikhdicl.
Sikhimlal.
Sijal.
Silaula.
Silwal.
Sureri or Sureri.
Takmel.
Tandan.
Tewari.
Thápá.
Thapthaila.
Timsena.
Tumrakal.
Wagle.
Zodri.

## 13. KONWAR.

Arjál.
Arthi.
Bagale.
Basnayet.
Jogi.
Kándka.
Khulál.
Porel.
Rana.

## 14. MANJHI.

Rai.

## 15. MAHAT.

Kálákotia.
Sinjapatti.

## 16. RÁNÁ.

Atharapanthi.
Bárápanthi.
Bhát.
Deokota.
Dhuhana.
Máski.
Pandel.
Puwár.
Simauli.

## 17. RÁWAT.

Basnayet.
Khaptari.

## 18. ROKA.

Dud.
Lamchania.
Sijial.

### 19. THÁPÁ.

| | | |
|---|---|---|
| Bagale. | Khaptari. | Pulámi. |
| Bagiál. | Khulál. | Puwár. |
| Deoga. | Konwár. | Sauiál. |
| Gagliya. | Lámchania. | Singhdáli. |
| Ghimiria. | Máhárájí. | Sinjáli. |
| Gudár. | Parajuli. | Suyál. |
| Kálákotia. | Pujar. | Thakuriál. |

The following, although they mostly appear as clans amongst the tribes shown above, are said also to be tribes. I doubt the existence of all of them as tribes, but as some may be so, I enter them all. Probably they are progeny of Brahmans or Matwala Khas of Western Népál :—

| | | |
|---|---|---|
| Ankhle. | Godar. | Rokahá. |
| Bagale. | Kathait. | Remál. |
| Balkote. | Marseni. | Sahani. |
| Barwál. | Oli. | Sinjáli. |
| Bhattarai. | Pánre. | |
| Dangi. | Rami. | |

## GURUNGS.

Magars and Gurungs are by common consent recognised as the *beau ideal* of what a Gurkhá soldier should be.

As these tribes have submitted to the ceremonial law of purity, and to Brahmanical supremacy, they have been adopted as Hindus, but they have been denied the sacred thread, and take rank as a doubtful order below the Kshatriya.

They are practically only Hindus because it is the fashion; they have gone with the times, and consequently their Hinduism is not very strict, and they are decidedly the least prejudiced in caste matters of all classes of Népál who seek our service. They participated in all the military successes of the house of Gurkhá and although they have less sympathy with the Government, they are still very loyal to it.

The Gurungs lent themselves less early, and less heartily, to Brahmanical influences, and they have retained to a greater extent than the Magars their national peculiarities and language. In stature the Gurungs are generally larger and more powerful than the Magars and Khas.

The Magars and Gurungs have already been referred to as being of the Tartar race; they in Népál follow agricultural pursuits; they are square-built, sturdy men, with fine, muscular, and large chest and limb development, low in stature, and with little or no hair on face or body, and with fair complexions. They are a merry-hearted race, eat animal food, and in Népál drink a kind of beer made from rice called *janr* and a kind of spirit called *raksi.* In our battalions they will drink any English wine, spirits, or beer. They are intensely fond of soldiering. They are very hardy and extremely simple-minded. They are kind-hearted and generous, and as recruits absolutely truthful. They are very proud and sensitive, and they deeply feel abuse or undeserved censure. They are very obstinate, very independent, very vain, and in their plain clothes inclined to be dirty. They are intensely loyal to each other and their officers in time of trouble or danger.

Brian Hodgson says about Magars and Gurungs:—

"From lending themselves less early and heartily to Brahmanical influences than the Khas, they have retained, in vivid freshness, their original languages, physiognomy, and, in a less degree, habits. Their two languages differ materially, though both belonging to the unpronominalised type of the Turanian tongues.

"The Gurungs are less generally and more recently redeemed from Lámáism and primitive impurity than the Magars.

"But though both the Gurungs and Magars still retain their own vernacular tongues, Tartar faces, and careless manners, yet, what with military service for several generations under the predominant Khas, and what with the commerce of Khas males with their females, they have acquired the Khas language, though not to the oblivion of their own, and the Khas habits and sentiments, but with sundry reservations in favour with pristine liberty.

"As, however, they have, with such grace as they could muster, submitted themselves to the ceremonial laws of purity, and to Brahman supremacy, they have been adopted as Hindus, but they have been denied the thread, and constitute a doubtful order below it."

The participation of the Magars and Gurungs in the political success of the now dominant Khas, has spread them as peaceful settlers, in no scanty numbers, easterly and westerly from the Káli to the Michi. The *locale* of the Magars and Gurungs, however, not more than 130 years back, or before the conquest by the house of Gurkhá, was to the west of the Népál Valley.

The Gurungs resided in a line of country running parallel to that occupied by the Magars, and to the north of it, and extending to the snows in that direction.

The manners of the Magars and Gurungs are, in most respects very similar, and both these tribes were much addicted to arms.

Of the ancient history of the Gurungs we scarcely know anything.

Gurung Chieftain.

It would appear that a chief, who was Rájá of Káski, settled in Ghándrúng, where the Gurungs were most predominant. These people were strongly attached to his descendants, by whom they were not disturbed in their religious opinions or customs, and in their own homes they practically still continue to follow the doctrines of Sakia as explained to them by Lámás of their own tribe.

No Gurungs have as yet ever been admitted to the dignity of Khas, but with their constant intercourse with the Khas, who are

Hindus, their original faith is getting weaker and in time will disappear.

It may here be pointed out that none of the high-sounding titles which are to be found amongst the Magars, and which were evidently brought in by the Brahmans from Hindustan, are to be found amongst the Gurungs.

Amongst the thousands of Gurkhás the writer has seen, he has never met a Surja Bansi Gurung, and he doubts the existence of any.

Two great divisions. The Gurung tribe consists of two great divisions :—

| 1. The Chárját. | 2. The Soláhját. |
|---|---|

The Chárját, as its name implies, is composed of four castes, *viz.* :—

| 1. Ghallea. | 3. Lámá. |
|---|---|
| 2. Ghotáni (or Ghundáni). | 4. Lámchania. |

Each of these four castes comprises a number of clans, and some of these are again subdivided into families.

The Chárját Gurung might be called the Gurung aristocracy.

Every Gurung recruit knows perfectly well whether he belongs to the Chárját or to the Soláhját, but numbers of the latter will try to claim the former. A little trouble will almost invariably bring out the truth.

The Chárját Gurung is very much looked up to by the Soláhját.

A Soláhjat Gurung cannot marry a Chárját, nor can he ever by any means become a Chárját.

Questioning a Chárját Gurung would be much as follows :—

"What is your name?" . . . "Jasbir Gurung."
"What Gurung are you?" . . . "Chárját."
"Which of the Chárját?" . . . "Lámchania."
"Which Lámchania clan?" . . . "Plohnian."
"What Plohnian?" . . . . "Atbai."

Of the Chárját Gurungs the Ghallea is by far the most difficult to obtain.

The Plohnian and Chenwári clans of the Lámchania are both subdivided into families; the best Plohnian family is the Atbai, and the best of the Chenwári is the Chárghari.

It will be noticed that nearly all Ghotáni clans end with "ron."

Some excellent recruits are also obtained from the Soláhját.

In olden days the Ghalleas ruled the country about Lámzúng and had their own king, a Ghallea.

Their kingdom nominally exists to this day.

Traditions. The following tradition regarding the birth of the Chárját exists:—

A Thákur King asked the King of Lámzúng for his daughter's hand in marriage.

The Ghallea King accepted the proposal favourably, and sent a young and beautiful maiden as his daughter to the Thákúr King, who duly married her, and by her begot several children.

Some years afterwards it transpired that this young maiden was no king's daughter, but merely one of her slave-attendants; whereupon the Thákúr King was very angry, and sent a message threatening war, unless the Ghallea King sent him his real daughter.

The King of Lámzúng thereupon complied, and this time sent his real daughter, whom the Thákúr King married, and by whom he begot three sons. (From these three sons are descended the Ghotáni, Lámá, and Lámchania clans.)

It was then ruled that these three sons and their descendants should rank equal to the Ghallea clan, and that they should be called the Chárját Gurungs, whilst the descendants of the children of the slave-mother should be called Soláhjáts and should for ever be servants to the Chárját.

From this it would appear that the Ghallea Gurung is the oldest and the purest of all Gurung clans. They certainly are splendid men of the purest Gurkhá type.

The Gurungs have for centuries kept up their history, which is called in Khas Kúra "Gurung ko Bangsáoli."

When the famous case of Colonel Lachman Gurung took place, Sir Jang Bahádur, being anxious to elucidate, if possible, the difference between Chárját and Soláhját Gurungs, had the history of the Gurungs brought to him, and having read the same, declared that the Soláhját Gurung must remain satisfied with his present position, and be for ever the servant of the Chárját.

The Soláhját Gurung will always make obeisance to the Chárját, and when travelling in their own country, the Soláhját will generally carry the Chárját's load.

It is said that Colonel Lachman Gurung offered his daughter's weight in gold to any Chárjat who would marry her. A poor man of the Ghotáni clan, being sorely tempted by the bribe, offered himself as a husband, but was at once outcasted and reduced to a Soláhját, and so the marriage never came off.

Tradition regarding the "Tutia" clan.

Many centuries ago, it is said, a landslip occurred which buried a whole village, and destroyed all the inhabitants, except one small boy, who was found by a Lámchania Gurung amongst the *débris*.

He took the boy home and adopted him, but as he did not know who the father of the boy was, a difficulty arose in time as to what clan this boy should belong to.

The Lámás, on being consulted, ruled that the child and all his descendants should be called Tutia Lámchanias (Tutia means broken, rugged), because he had been found on broken, rugged ground.

Tradition regarding "Plohnian" clan.

A boy that had been deserted was found by a Lámchania Gurung amongst some reeds. It was settled that this boy and all his descendants should be called Plohnian Lámchanias (Plohn means reeds), because he had been found amongst reeds.

There are two regiments of Gurungs in the Népálese army—the Káli Bahádar and the Káli Persád. The former is absolutely a Gurung regiment, and most of the men are Chárját Gurungs.

They are a magnificent body of men, consisting of all the picked Gurungs of Népál. They must average over 5′ 6″ in height, with splendid physique.

The Gurungs of Eastern Népál are, in my opinion, with a few exceptions, very much inferior to those of Central Népál, for physique, appearance, and in all respects.

Through intermarriage with other races of Eastern Népál, or through other causes, they have deteriorated in physique, and in most cases have lost all idea as to what clan, and even as to what tribe, they belong.

I give no list, and take absolutely no notice, of such clans and tribes as were given to me by Gurung recruits of Eastern Népál, as I find they are almost invariably unrecognizable corruptions of real Gurung names, or else titles borrowed from other races of Eastern Népál.

The Gurungs (and Magars also) of Eastern Népál, with a very few exceptions, are practically not Gurungs or Magars at all.

Although, perhaps, the actual descendants of the conquerors of Eastern Népál, what with intermarriage, and what with residing in the minority, amongst an immense majority of foreigners, they have lost all individuality, and I might almost say that they take in Eastern Népál much the same place that Eurasians do in India.

In my opinion, a good Limbú, Rai, or Sunwár, is a more desirable lad to enlist than the average Magar or Gurung of EASTERN NÉPÁL.

See also remarks at page 100 under heading of Magars.

## GURUNGS OF CHÁRJÁT.*

### GHALLEA CLANS (*Chárját*).

Gerlen.
Gyapsing.
Kialdung.
Khági.
Lámchania.
Parja.
Pyling.
Rájbangsi.
Rilli.
Rilten.
Sámri.†
Samunder.
Sinjáli.
Surajbansi.

### GHOTÁNI CLANS (*Chárját*), also called GHUNDÁNI.

Adunron.
Chomron.
Gholron.
Harpu.
Kaliron.
Kamjai.
Kelonron.
Kilat.
Kongron.
Kudlaron.
Lámkunia.
Logon.
Mazuron.
Migiron.
Mlogron.
Morlon.
Nagiron.
Naikron.
Pachron.
Pochkiron.
Rijoron.
Singoron.
Tagren or Tagron.
Tari.
Tenro or Tengron.
Thákúron.
Walron.

### LÁMÁ CLANS (*Chárját*).

Chelen.
Chenwári.
Fáche.
Hurdunga.
Karki.
Kelung.
Khimu.
Kib.
Kurungi.
Lohon.
Megi.
Muktan.

* The Gerlen, Rilten and Sámri clans are the best of the Ghalleas. The Samunders, Kialdung, Khági and Parja clans I have also met. I have never met a single case of a Sinjáli, Rajbansi, or Surajbansi Gurung of any kind, nor after the most careful enquiry do I believe in their existence. Sinjáli, Rajbansi, and Surajbansi are distinctly Rájput names, and are continually occurring amongst Magars, but never amongst Gurungs.

† The Sámri Ghallea is supposed not to eat goat's flesh.

Nakchia.
Pachron.
Pengi.
Pipro.
Pungi.
Pyung.
Tengi.
Tidun or Titun.
Timji.
Tonder.
Urdung.
Yoj.

## LÁMCHANIA CLANS (*Chárját*).

Adi.
Chen.
Chenwári.
Chingi.
Chipling.
Chomron.
Dungli.
Kahreh.
Kaliron.
Kroko.
Kurbu.
Lem.
Lengra.
Lunam.
Marenu.
Naikron.
Nasa.
Nasuron.
Nizain.
Pachen.
Pajji Lem.
Pángi.
Plitti.
Plohnian.
Prob.
Puráni.
Silangi.
Sinjoron.
Támme.
Tasuron.
Thankia.
Toson.
Tutea.
Twidian.

## GURUNGS OF THE SOLÁHJÁT.

Allea.
Baindi.
Bhaju.
Bhuj or Bhujia.
Bokati.
Chágli or Chákli.
Chárlang.
Chime.
Chohomonu.
Chornu.
Chumaru.
Darlámi.
Diál.
Dingiál.
Duriál.
Gelang.
Ghabbu.
Ghorenj.
Gonor.
Gulangia.
Giabring { Ku.
Sil.
Siuri.
Tu.
Hinj.
Hurdung.
Jelting.
Jhimál.
Jimiel.
Jumreli.
Kepchen.
Khaptari.
Khatrain.
Khulál.
Kiapchain.
Kinju.
Kokia.
Kongi Lámá.
Kubchen.
Kúmai.
Kromjai.
Labor.
Langwaja.
Leghen.
Lenghi.
Lohon.
Lyung.
Main.
Mapchain.
Mareu.
Masrangi.
Migi.
Mobjai or Mahbrijai.
Mor or Mor main.
Murum.
Nánra.
Nánsing.
Pajju or Pachun.
Palanja.
Pália.
Pálná.
Parjun.
Phiwáli, Piwáli, or Phinyáli.
Plen.
Plopo.
Pomai.
Ponju.
Pudusa.
Pulámi.
Remni.
Rilah.
Rimál.
Sarbujá.
Tahiu.

| | | |
|---|---|---|
| Tamain. | Thár. | Tormain. |
| Tamme. | Tingi Lámá. | Tute. |
| Telej. | Tol. | Uze. |
| Tendur. | Tolangi. | Yoje. |
| Tenlája. | Torjain. | Yujáli. |

NOTE.—Several Gurung clans, both of the Chárját and Solàhját, are called by a certain name in Khas-kúra, and by a different in Gurung-kúra, thus :—

| | | | | | |
|---|---|---|---|---|---|
| Dingiál | is | Khas-kúra | for | Kepchen | in Gurung-kúra. |
| Darlámi | ,, | ,, | | Plen | ,, |
| Chenwári | ,, | ,, | | Pacharon | ,, |
| Pajji Lem | ,, | ,, | | Kroko Lem | ,, |

Allea is Khas-kúra for a clan whose Gurung-kúra name I have forgotten.

Several clans, therefore, are no doubt repeated twice, once in Khas-kúra and once in Gurung-kúra ; but, for facility of reference, I think it best to leave them thus alphabetically arranged.

Members of the Giabring clan are often used for priestly or religious ceremonies. Giabrings are supposed not to eat fowls. Personally I have seen them enjoying "murghis" on many occasions.

## MAGARS.

Of very ancient Magar history we know nothing, and the first time that they came into prominence as a great power is about A. D. 1100, when we hear that Mukúnda Sena, the Magar King of Pálpá and Botwál, invaded and conquered the Népál Valley, and committed terrible atrocities during the reign of Hari Déva, King of Népál.

First mention of Magars.

The principal seat of the Magars was most of the central and lower parts of the mountains between the Jingruk (Rapti of Gorakhpur) and Marsiangdi rivers.

That they resided about Pálpá from times immemorial is well known.

Doctor F. Hamilton in his book published in 1819 says that the Magars, who resided to the west of the Gandak river, seem to have received the Rájpút princes with much cordiality.

Until the arrival of the Rájputs and Brahmans, the hill tribes seem all to have eaten every kind of animal food, including the cow.

Each tribe appears originally to have had a priesthood and duties peculiar to itself, and to have worshipped chiefly ghosts.

The Magars have for many centuries more or less admitted the supremacy of the doctrines of the Brahmans, and consequently they have adopted many Rájput customs, ceremonies, and names. The Gurungs also, but to a very much lesser degree, have borrowed from the Rájputs, but this does not give either of these two tribes any claim to any other descent than Mongolian.

Owing to the geographical position of the tract of country inhabited by the Magars, they were the first to receive immigrants from the plains of India, and thus conversions were more numerous amongst the Magars than any of the other hill tribes living further north or east.

Effects of Hindu influence on Magars.

The Magar women have consequently had more connection with the Brahmans and Rájputs, and probably the greater proportion of original Khas were the progeny of Brahmans and Rájputs of India with Magar women.

Hence we find amongst Magars many high-born titles such as Surajvansi, Chandravansi, etc., etc., which undoubtedly never existed amongst the Magars themselves, but were introduced from India.

Some of the Magars having been converted assumed the sacred thread, whilst others did not; hence we find Ghartis, Ránás, and and Thápás, who appear as tribes belonging both to the Magars and to the Khas.

Hamilton says in 1819:—

"The Ghartis are of two kinds, Khas and Bhujiál. The former are admitted to the military dignity, but the latter wallow in all the abominations of the impure Gurungs, and do not speak the Khas language.

"The Ránás (Hamilton might also have added the Thápás and Burhathokis, etc.) are divided into two kinds, the Khas and the Magar. The latter are a branch of the Magar tribe and totally neglect the rules of purity. It is not even all the Rájputs that have adopted the rules of purity, and whilst some branches of the same families were pure, others rejected the advice of the sacred orders, and ate and drank whatever their appetites craved.

"The family of Gurkhá, which now (1802) governs Népál, although it pretends to come from Chitor, is in reality of the Magar tribe, and, at any rate, these people are now firmly attached to its interests, by having largely shared in the sweets of conquest; and by far the greatest part of the regular troops of that family is composed of this nation.

"When the colony from Chitor first took possession of Pálpá it belonged to a Magar chief, and the people were of that tribe.

"I shall not take it upon myself to say whether the Pálpá family, said to be descended from Chitor, really were so, or were impure mountaineers, who had this pedigree invented to flatter them when they turned from their impure ways and were induced to follow the Brahmans."

The chiefs of Rising, Ghiring and Gajarkot were related to the Pálpá family by birth, and yet they are described by Hamilton as "wallowing in all the ancient abominations of the mountaineers," from which it seems very probable that the rulers of Pálpá and all other Chaubisia chiefs were really Magars, and that perhaps in after time, to hide their ignoble birth, they invented stories of being descended from Rájputs whom they made to appear as having ousted the Magar chief and seized the government of the country.

Since the conquest of Népál, Magars are to be found anywhere from the Sardáh in the west to the Michi on the east, but their proper habitat is west of the Népál Valley, and there undoubtedly the best and purest Magars are found to this day in large numbers.

The following tradition given by Pandit Sarat Chandra Dass proves the existence of Magars in Eastern Népál at no great distance west of Kinchanjanga :—

"The legend which I heard of the Kangpachan people (west of Kanchan Gonga), and of the Magars the ruins of whose forts and town we saw in the Kangpachan valley, is very interesting. People say the account is correct and true.

"The upper valley of the Kangpachan river, through the grace and blessing of the Royal Kanchan Gonga, was peopled by men of Thibetan extraction, called the Sherpa, whose original home was in the mountains of Sher Khambu, or Eastern Kiránta.

"The lower valley, a few miles below the Kangpachan village, on account of the comparatively sluggish course of the river, contained many spacious banks fit to be the habitation of hill-men. The Magar tribe of Népál occupied these tracts. Their chief, who had become very powerful, extended his sway over the people of Kangpachan, and exacted a heavy tax from them.

"His deputies always oppressed the people to squeeze out money from them, so that at last they were driven through desperation to take revenge upon their enemies.

"The Magar chief accordingly was murdered with all his followers upon their visiting the Kangpachan village on a certain occasion.

"The wife of the Magar chief thereupon planned the best means of wreaking vengeance on the Kangpachan murderers.

"She therefore ordered grand funeral observances for the honour and benefit of the departed soul. The funeral was appointed to take place six miles up the river, midway between the two great villages of the Kangpachan valley, so that all the villagers might assemble there.

"After the Queen's followers had finished drinking, poisoned wine was given plentifully to the Kangpachan villagers, who, suspecting nothing, drank freely and all died. In this way nearly one thousand men and women died.

"The infants in arms were taken away by the Queen's followers.

The place where this foul deed was committed is now called Tong-Shong-phug, or "the place which witnessed a thousand murders."

"In consequence of this a Thibetan army invaded the several Jongs belonging to the Queen, when she shut herself up in one of her castles.

"She had made no preparations to fight the enemy, but her soldiers defended the place for three months.

"The Thibetans then tried to compel the Magars to surrender by depriving them of water. At last the Queen, aware of this intention, threw all the water she had in store towards the Thibetan camp. The Thibetans, thinking that she had abundance of water inside the castle, raised the siege, and went to a distance to watch the movements of the Magars. She immediately collected her men and pursued the enemy, when a skirmish took place, in which she fell fighting nobly. The Thibetans expelled all the Magars from the country, *viz.*, Kangpachan and Tambar valley, and left their property to the Kangpachan people."

The Magars are divided into six distinct tribes and no more, although the following all claim to be Magars, and try in every way to establish themselves as such :—

Bohra (really a Matwala Khas of Western Népál).
Roka ( ditto ditto ditto ).
Chohán ( ditto ditto ditto ).
Jhánkri ( ditto ditto ditto ).
Konwár (progeny of mendicant).
Uchái ( ditto Thákúr).

In days of old a certain number of Magars were driven out of their own country, and settled in Western Népál amongst strangers. From the progeny of these sprang up many clans of mixed breeds, who now claim to be pure-bred Magars, but are not recognized as such.

In addition to the few mentioned above, are some others who also claim to be Magars, such as Rawats, Dishwas, etc., but as they have no real relationship to Magars, it is considered unnecessary to enter a list of them here.

The real and only Magars are divided into the following six tribes, which are here entered alphabetically :—

1. Allea.
* 2. Búrhathoki.
3. Gharti.
4. Pún.
5. Rána.
6. Thápá.

These tribes mostly intermarry with each other, have much

* Real Magars of Burha tribe also exist, but I have treated them as if they were Búrhathoki, as I can find no difference between them.

the same customs and habits, and are in every way equal as regards social standing, with perhaps a slight preference in favour of the Ráná.

The original home of the Magars was to the west of the Gandak river (Káli-war*), and, roughly speaking, consisted of that portion of Népál which lies between and round about Gúlmi, Argha, Kháchi, Pálpá and Bhirkot.

This bit of country was divided into twelve districts (Báráh Mangránth†), and the residents of the same in time came to be spoken of as the Magars of the Báráh Mangránth.

Brian Hodgson and Captain T. Smith both give the following as the Báráh Mangránth: Satúng, Pyúng, Bhirkot, Dhor, Garhúng, Rising, Ghiring, Gúlmi, Argha, Kháchi, Musikot, and Isma.

By the term "Báráh Mangránth Magars"‡ no particular set of tribes was meant. The term had a purely local meaning, and referred to all such Magars, of whatever tribe they might be, whose ancestors had resided for generations within the Báráh Mangránth.

Each of these twelve districts had its own ruler, but it would appear that the most powerful kings were those of Gúlmi, Argha, Kháchi, and that the remaining princes were more or less tributary to these three.

Since the rise of the house of Gurkhá, towards the close of the eighteenth century, the country has been redivided, and the twelve districts no longer exist as such, and the term "Báráh Mangránth Magar" has no signification now, and is therefore falling into disuse. Not one recruit out of five hundred knows what the term means.

---

* Dr. Hamilton in his book published in 1819 says :—

"Before the arrival of the Rájputs, it is said that the Magar nation consisted of twelve Thams, the whole members of each being supposed to have a common extraction in the male line. Each Tham was governed by a chief, considered as the head of a common family."

† The Sardáh on the west, and the Gandak in the centre of Népál, are both spoken of as the Káli.

‡ This information I obtained by personal and careful enquiry both at Gorakhpur and in Népál itself. I also consulted many native officers and men, and the Prime Minister of Népál was good enough to cause enquiries to be made on this point from the most learned men in Népál. Brian Hodgson also says : "The original seat of the Magars is the Báráh Mangránth," and he then proceeds to give the names of the twelve districts which collectively were called Báráh Mangránth.

As mentioned before, the original home of the Magars was to the west of the Gandak river, but it would seem that some clans had for ages occupied certain portions of Népál on the east bank.

The city of Gurkhá was originally the residence of the Chitoriáh Ránás. It is said that the city was built by them, and to this day numbers of Chitoriáh Ránás are found there.

The Magars having participated in the military conquests of the house of Gurkhá, spread themselves far and wide all over Népál, and numbers are now to be found to the east of the Gandak river.

Alleas.

The Alleas in appearance seem a very pure-bred race. As a rule they are very fair, well-made men. The tribe must, however, be rather a small one, as the percentage of Alleas enlisted yearly is very small. They are most desirable men to get.

Búrhathokis.

*Búrhathokis are also apparently very limited in number. Some excellent specimens of Gurkhás are, however, every year obtained from this tribe. They are very desirable men to get.

Ghartis.

The Ghartis are pretty numerous, but care should be taken in enlisting from this tribe, as they seem to be far more mixed than any of the other five pure Magar tribes. By careful selection, however, excellent Ghartis can be obtained.

The Bhújiál Gharti lives in the valleys and high mountains to the north of Gúlmi, above the Púns, but immediately below the Karántis.

Their tract of country runs along both sides of the Bhúji Khola (river), from which they probably derive their name.

The Bhújial Gharti is generally a shepherd. He lives principally on the milk of sheep, and is almost invariably a man of very good physique and heavy limbs. He is remarkably dirty when first enlisted.

Amongst the Gharti clans are two that should not be confounded, although from their similarity in pronunciation one is

* I have occasionally met recruits who called themselves "Búrha." They are so few, however, that I have incorporated them with "Burhathokis."

very apt to do so. The Paháre or Pahária is a good Magar. The Páre or Pária (from *pár*, outside) should never be enlisted. He is, as his name indicates, an outcast or a descendant of an outcast.

Púns.

The Pún* tribe seems a small one, as but a small percentage of them is obtained annually. They are generally men of heavy limbs and excellent physique. They much resemble Gurungs. They live about Gúlmi principally, although of course they are found in other places also. They are most desirable men.

Ránás.

Of all Magars there is no better man than a Ráná of good clan. In former days any Thápá who had lost three generations of ancestors in battle became a Ráná, but with the prefix of his Thápá clan. Thus a Reshmi Thápá would become a Reshmi Ráná.

An instance of this is to be found in the 5th Gurkhás, where a havildar, Lachman Thápá, and a naick, Shamsher Ráná, are descendants from two Thápá brothers; but three generations of descendants from one of these brothers having been killed in battle, Shamsher Ráná's ancestors assumed the title of Ráná; Lachman Thápá's ancestors not having been killed in battle for three generations, he remains a Thápá.

From this custom many Ráná clans are said to have sprung up, and this would lead one to believe that the Ráná tribe was looked up to amongst Magars.

The original Ráná clans were few, amongst them being the following: Chitoriá, Máski, Rúchál, Húnchún, Thára, Láye, Thárali, Súrjabansi or Súrjavansi, Hiski, and Masrángi.

Thápás.

The Thápá tribe is by far the greatest of all, and amongst them, yearly, hundreds of excellent recruits are obtained. Care should, however, be exercised in the selection of Thápás, as a very large number of men adopt the title of Thápá, although they have no right to the same.

The Sáru and Gáhá clans of the Thápá are each subdivided into five or more families, and in each case the Kálá family is the best.

* I cannot help thinking the Púns are in some way allied to the Gurungs.

The Púrána Gorakh Regiment in Népál consists entirely of Magars, and is a splendid body of men. All the finest Magars of Népál, excepting those in the Rifle regiments, are put into this regiment. They must be nearly if not quite as big as the Káli Bahádar.

The Magars of Eastern Népál are, in my opinion, with a few exceptions, very much inferior to those of Central Népál, in physique, appearance, and in all respects.

The remarks which I have made on Gurungs of Eastern Népál at pages 99 and 100, under heading of Gurungs, apply equally forcibly to the Magars of Eastern Népál, and for the same reason therefore I give no list and take absolutely no notice of such corrupted names of Magar clans and tribes, as have been given to me by Magars of Eastern Népál.

Central Népál is the real, original, and actual home of the Magars and Gurungs, and it is there that all the information must be sought for, and the lists, which I give after years of careful enquiry, are, I believe, fairly complete and correct, and I see no reason why I should add the contorted corruptions of names which both Magar and Gurung recruits of Eastern Népál give as their clans and tribes, whenever they know any.

Taking it for granted that the Magars and Gurungs of Eastern Népál are the descendants of Magars and Gurungs of Central Népál, they should be of the same clans and tribes as their ancestors, and therefore if my lists of Magars and Gurungs of Central Népál are true and complete, as I believe them to be, any new name which comes from Eastern Népál is probably an untrue one, which no real Magar or Gurung would claim.

### ALLEA CLANS.

Arghúli or Arghounle.
Biji.
Chángi.
Chármi.
Chidi.
Dhoreli.
Dukcháki or Durcháki.
Dura.
Gar.

Gonda.
Gyangmi.
Hiski.
Hunchun.
Kalámi.
Kháli.
Khaptari.
Kharri.
Khichman.
Khulál.

Kilung.
Khulangi.
Kiapcháki.
Lahakpa.
Lámchania.
Lamjál.
Limiál.
Lungchia.
Magiam.
Máski.

Meng.
Pachain.
Panmgi.
Panthi.
Phiwáli Piwáli or Phiuyáli.
Pulámi.
Pungi.
Rakhal.
Ramiál.
Rimal.
Roho.
Sarangi.
Sarbat.
Sarthung.
Silthung.
Sinjápati.
Sirpáli.
Sithung.
Surjavansi or Surjabansi.
Suyál.
Tarokche or Torokcháki.
Thakcháki.
Yángmi.

BÚRHATHOKI CLANS.

Baijáli.
Balkoti.
Barkwánri.
Darlámi.
Deobal.
Gamál.
Karmani.
Lámchania.
Paháre.
Ramjáli.
Ramkháui.
Ranju.
Sialbang.
Sinjapati.
Siris.
Ulangia.

GHARTI CLANS.

Arghuli or Arghounli.
Atráse.
Baima.
Bainjáli.
Bhánta.
Bhujiál.
Bulámi.
Chanchal or Chantial.
Dagámi.
Darlámi.
Galámi.
Gamál.
Garbuja.
Gial.
Hunjáli.
Kagja.
Kahucha.
Kálá.
Kálákotia.
Kengia.
Konsa.
Lámchania.
Masrangi.
Nishál.
Pahare or Paháría.
Páre or Pária.
Paza or Paiza.
Phágámi.
Phukan.
Purja.
Ramjáli.
Rangu.
Rankhani.
Rawál.
Rijál.
Salámi.
Sámia.
Sáru.
Sawangi.
Senia.
Sinjáli.
Sinjapati.
Sirasik.
Sunári.
Sutpaháre.
Taláji.
Thein.
Theri.
Tirgia.
Ulángia.
Wália.

PÚN CLANS.

Baijáli.
Balámi.
Bapál.
Barangi.
Dagain.
Dagámi.
Darlámi.
Dud.
Gore.

NOTE.—The Siris clans of the Ránás and Thápás are the descendants of children who were brought up from babyhood on the milk of goats, their mothers having died in child-birth.

No Ráná or Thápá of the Siris clans will eat goat's flesh.

The Roho clan of Allea are said not to eat the fish called Roho.

Hunjáli.
Jagonlia.
Kámi.
Naya.
Pahàre.
Pajansi.
Phungáli.
Poingia.
Rákaskoti.
Ramjáli.
Ramkam.
Rángu.
Ratuwá.
Rúhan.
Sabangi.
Sain.
Samia.
Sarbuja.
Sinjáli.
Sinjápati.
Sothi.
Sutpahare.
Tajáli.
Takália.
Támia.
Tendi.
Tháni.
Tirkhia.
Ulángia.

## RÁNA CLANS.

Allea.
Archami.
Arghuli or Arghoule.
Aslámi.
Bangling.
Barál or Balál.
Barkwánri.
Báráthoki.
Bhusál.
Byangnási.
Charmi.
Chitoriah.
Chumi.
Darlámi.
Dengáli.
Dud or Dut.
Durungcheng.
Gáchá.
Gághá.
Gáhá.
Gandharma.
Garancha.
Gelang.
Gomul.
Gyándris.
Gyangmi.
Hiski.
Hunchun.
Jargha.
Jhiari.
Jiandi.
Kamchákí.
Kandkha.
Kanoje.
Kiapcháki.
Khiuyáli.
Lámchania.
Laye.
Lungeli.
Mákim.
Máski.
Masrangi.
Merassi.
Namjáli.
Pachain.
Pachrai.
Palli.
Panti.
Parta.
Phiwáli-Piwáli or Phiuyáli.
Pulámi.
Pusál or Bushál.
Rángu.
Reshmi.
Rilámi.
Ruchál.
Sarángi.
Sartungi.
Sáru.
Sinjáli.
Siris.*
Suiel.
Sunári.
Surjavansi or Surjabansi.
Thára or Tháda.
Uchai.
Yahayo.

## THÁPÁ CLANS.

Allea.
Arghuli.
Aslámi.
Báchia or Báchio.
Báchún.
Bagális { Átghari. Darlámi. Palungi. Sátighari. }
Baigália.
Bailick.
Bakabal.
Balál or Barál.
Balámi.
Bankabarál.
Baola.
Báràghari.
Bareya.

* Will not eat goat's flesh.—E. V.

Barkwanri.
Begnáshi.
Bhomrel.
Biangmi.
Birkhatta.
Bopál.
Buráthoki.
Chahari.
Chantial.
Charti.
Chidi.
Chitoriah.
Chohán.
Chumi.
Dálá or Dália.
Damarpal.
Darga.
Darlámi:
- Bagália.
- Kálá.
- Palungi.
- Puráni.
- Sing.

Denga or Dhenga.
Dengabuja.
Dengál.
Dhanpáli.
Dishwa or Disuwa.
Durel.
Fal or Phal.
Gághá.
Gáhá:
- Bádoha.
- Barda.
- Chidi.
- Gora.
- Kálá.
- Kan.
- Malangi.

Gáhab.
Ganchake.
Gandharma.
Garanja.
Garja.
Gejal.
Gelung.
Giángmi.
Giangdi or Giami.
Gianris.
Gidiel or Gindil.
Gurmachang.
Gyal.
Hiski.
Hitan.
Hunchun.
Ismála.
Jargah.
Jehare or Jhiádi.
Jhánkri or Jhángdi.
Jhenri.
Kaikálá.
Kámchá.
Kámu.
Kángmu.
Kánlu or Kánluk.
Kanojia.
Kanrdlu.
Kásu.
Kejung.
Keli.
Khánga.
Khaptari.
Konwar.
Koral.
Kulál.
Lámchania.
Lamtari.
Lanchia.
Langakoti.
Langkang.
Láye.
Lingjing.
Lungeli.
Mákim.
Mamring.
Mandir.
Marpa.
Maruncha.
Máski.
Masrangi.
Medun.
Mobchan.
Mogmi.
Námjlái.
Niar.
Nidun.
Nimiál.
Pachbáya.
Pajangi.
Palli.
Pátá.
Pengmi.
Phal.
Phiwáli-Piwáli or Phiuyál.
Phunjlái.
Pitakoti.
Pochun.
Powan.
Puánri.
Pulámi.
Rai.
Rájvansi or Rájbansi.
Rákaskoti.
Rakshia.
Ramjali.
Ramkhani.
Regámi.
Rehári.
Reshmi:
- Bagále.
- Dangále.
- Gore.
- Kálá.
- Thárá.

Rijai.
Rilámi.
Roka.
Rokim.
Ruchal.
Sain.
Sámi.
Salámi.
Sanmáni.
Saplengi.
Sarangi.
Sarbuja.
Sartungi.
Sáru:
- Gorá.
- Janrup.
- Japarluk.
- Jhenri.
- Kálá.
- Malengia.
- Paneti.

Sátighari.
Sinjáli.
Sinjápati.

| | | |
|---|---|---|
| Sirnia. | Suniál. | Thagnami. |
| Siris. | Supári. | Thamu. |
| Somare. | Surajvansi or Surjabansi. | Thárá or Thádá. |
| Sonwánri. | Surpák. | Tharun. |
| Sothi. | Susaling. | Thurain. |
| Sahnakhári. | Swial. | Tumsing. |
| Sumái or Some. | Tarbung. | Uchai. |
| Sunári. | | Untáki or Wantáki. |
| | | Yángdi. |

NOTE.—Bagále means "many." This clan is said to be derived originally from a large family of brothers.

# CHAPTER VI.

## LINE-BOYS.

THE progeny of Gurkhá soldiers, who are born and brought up in the regiment, are called line-boys, and these might be divided into two distinct classes :—

1. The progeny of purely Gurkhá parents.
2. The progeny of a Gurkhá soldier with a hill-woman.

From the first class, if carefully selected, some excellent soldiers can be obtained.

The second class should be avoided. The pure-bred line-boy is just as intelligent as the half-bred, and if boys are required for the band, or men as clerks, etc., it would be better to select them from out of the first class. Only a small percentage of line-boys, even of the first class, should be enlisted.

The claims of line-boys to be provided for in the service are undoubtedly very great, as Government has always, and very wisely too, encouraged Gurkhá colonies, and their fathers and grandfathers, having in many cases been all their lives in British employ, they have no other home than their regimental lines.

In their first generation their physique does not deteriorate much, and they almost invariably grow up to be extremely intelligent men and full of military ardour. Their military education begins with their perceptive powers, as they commence playing at soldiers as soon as they can toddle about. The worst point against line-boys is that unfortunately they often prove to be men of very loose habits.

Sir Charles Reid, K.C.B., mentions that out of seven men who obtained the Order of Merit for the battles of Aliwal and Sobráor, five were line-boys; and out of twenty-five Order of Merit men for the siege of Delhi, twelve were line-boys.

## OTHER CLASSES OF CENTRAL NÉPÁL.

Kamárá. The Kamárá is a slave. Most of the higher officials in Népál retain Kamárás as attendants.

The offspring of a Magar, Gurung, or Khas with a Kamárá would be a Kamárá.

Khwás. Khwás is the offspring of a slave-mother with a Thákur. The children of this union become Khwás, and their posterity retains the name. Khwás is also the name given to the illegitimate children of the King or Royal Family.

Konwár. A Konwár who claims to be a Magar is the offspring of the connection between a mendicant and any woman. He is generally an ill-bred-looking man, and should not be enlisted. The Khas Konwár is all right.

Dhotiáls. The Dhotiáls live in the extreme west of Népál, and south of Júmla. They are not Gurkhás at all, and should never be enlisted.

Bánda. Any man can become a Bánda, which practically means a bondsman. For instance, A will go to B and say, "Give me sixty rupees cash and I will be your bánda for two years." On receipt of money he becomes a bánda and is bound to work for the two years for nothing beyond his food, but at the expiration of his two years, if he has contracted no fresh debt, he becomes free again.

"Jaici." The offspring of an Opadhia Brahman with a Brahman's widow is called "Jaici."

"Khattri." That of a Jaici, and certain Brahmans with a Khas, is called Khattri. The Khattri wears the thread, but is below the Khas.

The offspring of a Khas with a Magarni or Gurungni is a titular Khas, but his very father should not eat with him, nor any pure Khas.

"Hamál." The progeny of an Opadhia Brahman with a Thákur woman, or a Thákur with Brahman woman of Opadhia class, gives a Hamál.

That of a Thákur with a Magarni gives an Ucháí Thákur.

Tháru. The Terái is inhabited by certain tribes of low-caste Hindus called Thárus, who manage to live here throughout the year, and who brave with impunity the deadly malaria and the savage beasts with which these districts are infested.

These people follow the calling of agriculturists, of potters, and, where the neighbourhood of rivers allows it, of ferrymen or fishermen.

They live from hand to mouth, they sow a little rice and grain, but scarcely enough for their own consumption, and they get occasional but uncertain supplies of animal food from the carcasses of cattle which die, as well as by catching fish and hunting the wild pigs and deer which abound in the forest.

Though they probably belong to the same original stock as the natives of the adjacent plains of India, yet their continued residence for many successive generations in the most unhealthy and malarious districts, as well as their scanty food and their system of only marrying amongst themselves, has caused the breed to deteriorate most painfully; and whoever their early ancestors may have been, the inhabitants of the Terái are, at the present day, a puny, badly developed, and miserable-looking race. Living almost in a state of nature, they never seem to suffer from any exposure to the weather, and to be entirely exempt from all danger of jungle fever; and though they look half-starved, and as if they were deficient in muscle and bone, yet they are capable of undergoing very considerable exertion and fatigue. This is shown by their supplying not only the class of dâk runners, but also mahuts and others who, during the hot and rainy months, are employed in the dangerous and difficult business of catching wild elephants. They seem to combine the activity of an animal with the cunning and craftiness so characteristic of the human savage.

## MENIAL CLASSES.

The following is a list of some of the menial classes of Népál.

No man belonging to any of these should be enlisted as a soldier.

If it is found necessary to enlist any of them on account of their professional acquirements, they should be given separate quarters, and as far as possible be kept entirely away from all military duties.

Their being allowed to take their share as soldiers at guard-mounting, etc., etc., cannot raise, in the eyes of a real Gurkhá, the glory of being a soldier :—

| | |
|---|---|
| Agri . . . . . . | . Miners. |
| Bhánr . . . . . | . Musician.—But prostitute their women. |
| Chamákhalá . . . . | . Scavenger. |
| Chunára . . . . . | . Carpenters. |
| *Damái . . . . . | . Tailor, Musician. |
| Drái . . . . . . | . Seller of pottery. |
| Gáin . . . . . . | . Bard. |
| Kamárá . . . . . | . Slave. |
| *Kámi or Lohár . . . . | . Ironsmith. |
| *Kasái (Newár) . . . . | . Butcher. |
| Kumhál . . . . . | . Potter. |
| Mánji . . . . . | . Boatman. |
| Pipa . . . . . | . Klasi. |
| Pore . . . . . | . Sweeper. |
| Sárkhi . . . . . | . Worker in leather. |

## SARKHI CLANS.

*Workers in leather, a menial class.*

| | |
|---|---|
| Basiel. | Hitung. |
| Bhomrel. | Madkoti. |
| Bilekoti. | Mangránti.† |
| Chitoriah. | Ramtél. |
| Dankoti. | Rimál. |
| Gaire. | Sirketi. |
| Hamália. | Sirmal. |

* These three classes, if enlisted from Central Népál, are immeasureably finer men in every way than those of Eastern Népál.

†This clan is derived from the fact of the ancestors of the same having resided within the Báráh Mangránth.

# CHAPTER VII.

## NEWÁRS.

WHEN Nanya Déva was marching with Newár troops to the conquest of Népál (about A. D. 1323-24) it is said that *en route* they were in danger of perishing from hunger, when their goddess Kangkali appeared to one of their chiefs in a dream, and told him that in the morning she would grant them a supply of provisions, and that she gave them permission ever afterwards to use the kind of food which she was about to send. Accordingly, in the morning a large herd of buffaloes appeared, and were killed by the people, who have ever since indulged in that kind of food.

Reputed origin of Newár.

The Newárs themselves totally deny their origin from Simraun, and allege that they are the original inhabitants of the Népál Valley. Their houses have a great resemblance to those of the Bhutias, while in many points their customs resemble those of the other tribes of Mongolian descent.

Reputed origin denied by Newárs.

The Népál Valley is undoubtedly the real home of the Newárs.

Of the Newár language Brian Hodgson says :—

"The language of Népál proper, or the Newári, has much in common with that of Thibet. It is, however, a poorer dialect than that of Lhássa and Digarche, and it has consequently been obliged to borrow more extensively from Sanskrit, whilst the early adoption of Sanskrit, as the sole language of literature, has facilitated this infusion."

This would seem to conclusively prove the Newárs to be of Thibetan extraction originally, whatever admixtures of blood may have been introduced in after-times.

In 1793 Kirkpatrick wrote :—

"The Newárs are of a middle size, with broad shoulders and chest, very stout limbs, round and rather flat faces, small eyes, low and somewhat spreading noses."

Hamilton says :—

"If the morals of the Newár women had been more strict, I believe that the resemblance between Chinese and Thibetans and

Newárs would have been complete; but since the conquest the approach to Hindu countenance is rapidly on the increase, women in most cases giving a decided preference to rank, especially if connected with arms or religion.

"Until the conquest there was probably little intermixture, except in the descendants of the governing family."*

When the writer of this work was in Kátmandu in 1888, and during his frequent shooting trips with Máharája Bir Sham Sher, 1889-90 and 1891, he had many opportunities of observing Newárs, and he is of opinion that they show more of Hindu blood in their features than either the Magars or Gurungs. Not that they struck him as being darker-skinned, but that their faces seemed longer, their eyes larger, and the bridges of their noses more strongly marked than in the Magars or Gurungs.

The present race of the Newárs is a mixed one, derived from Indian and Thibetian stocks, and their religion naturally presents a corresponding mixture of the Indian and Thibetian creeds. The predominance of the Thibetian over the Indian stock in the composition of their blood is as evident in the religion of the Newárs as it is in their language, their characters, and their physical appearance.

The pure Bhuddhism, which they originally inherited from their Thibetian ancestors, is still the basis of their natural faith, but it has been very much modified by the adoption or retention of many Hindu doctrines and practices derived from the natives of Hindustan, with whom those Thibetian ancestors intermarried.

There is every reason to believe that the earliest or aboriginal inhabitants of the valley of Nepal, and of the country lying between it and the Himalaya snows, were of Chinese or Thibetian origin.

The Newárs are not a warlike or military race, but there can be no doubt that they occasionally produce good soldiers.

The best Newár caste is the Sirisht, and one, Súbádár Kishnbir Nagarkoti, of the 5th Gurkhá Rifles, belonging to this caste, won the Order of Merit three times for gallantry displayed during the Kábul war, and was given a gold clasp when recommended a

---

* Considering that Hindus existed in Nepal Valley for centuries before the Christian era, the intermixture of blood had permanently been going on from earliest ges and not only from after conquest.

fourth time for conspicuous gallantry displayed at the time of Major Battye's death, in the Black Mountains, in 1888.

Súbádár (then Jemádár) Birbal Nagarkoti of the 43rd Gurkhá Rifles greatly distinguished himself in 1891, during the Manipur troubles. He received the Order of Merit for bravery displayed, as well as for coolness and soldierly qualities.

The Newárs also fought very bravely and in a most determined way against the Gurkhá conquerors—a fact proved by their twice defeating Prithwi Narayan, as before mentioned.

They have letters and literature, and are well skilled in the useful and fine arts, having followed the Chinese and also Indian models; their agriculture is unrivalled in Népál, and their towns, temples, and images of the gods are beautiful, and unsurpassed in material and workmanship.

They are a steady, industrious people, and skilled in handicraft, commerce, and the culture of the earth.

The Jaicis are their priesthood and should never, on any account, be enlisted in our regiments.

All trade and manufactures of the country may be said to be in the hands of the Newárs and a few foreigners. Some families of Kashmiris have been settled in Kátmandu for generations.

All mechanics of the country are Newárs, except a few workmen from the plains of India employed by Government in the public workshops and arsenals.

The chief manufactures of the country are few, consisting chiefly of cotton and coarse woollen cloth, a peculiar kind of paper (made from the inner bark of several species of Daphne), bells, brass, and iron pots, ornaments of silver and gold, and coarse earthen ware.

The great bulk of the population is employed in agriculture, and almost every family holds a small piece of land. Most land yields two crops every year, and some even three; the work of cultivation is done almost entirely by hand, though of late years the plough is being more extensively used.

Every Newár girl, while a child, is married to a "Bel" fruit, which after the ceremony is thrown in some sacred river. When she arrives at puberty, a husband is selected for her. The marriage tie, however, amongst Newárs, is by no means so binding as amongst Gurkhás.

Widows are allowed to re-marry; in fact, a Newárni is never a widow, as the "Bel" fruit to which she was first married is presumed to be always in existence.

Adultery is but lightly punished among the Newárs; the woman is divorced, and her partner in guilt has to make good the money expended by the husband in the marriage, or failing this he is imprisoned.

The repayment of bride price by the guilty man to the injured husband is a practice also found amongst Limbús and Rias.

The Newárs burn their dead.

## BRIEF ACCOUNT OF BUDDHISM AND SAKYA SIMHA.

The following is a brief account of Buddhism and its apostle Sakya Simha, and is a condensed extract from Oldfield's book :—

The origin and first progress of the religion of Buddha is obscure and confused, in consequence of the many mythological legends which the superstition of its supporters has mixed up with its early history. Not only have they attributed to its founder, Sakya Simha, a supernatural origin, and invested him with supernatural powers, but they have incorporated with their creed the fabulous chronology of the Hindus, in order to exaggerate the antiquity of what is in reality a comparatively modern faith.

There can, however, be but little doubt that Buddhism had its origin in the valley of the Ganges, whence it spread over the whole continent of India about the middle of the sixth century B. C., and it is equally certain that it commenced, not as a new and independent system of religion, but as an offshoot or schism from the more ancient faith of the Hindus.

The gross idolatry encouraged by the Brahmans, and more particularly the cruel characters of their ritual, which enjoined the constant slaughtering of animals, and the occasional sacrifice of even human victims, caused great disgust to many of the Vaishnavas (followers of Vishnu), as well as to many other Hindus who gradually seceded from the ancient faith.

As, according to the mythology of the Hindus, all of Vishnu's previous incarnations had been destined to accomplish certain definite purposes to the benefit of mankind, it was a natural course for the early followers of Buddha to represent that their deity had become incarnate for a ninth time, in the form of Buddha, with the object of reclaiming Hindus from all bloody sacrifices, and purifying their religion of the numerous errors and abuses with which it was corrupted.

They therefore set up Buddha as an incarnation or "avatar" of Vishnu.

As their numbers increased, and emboldened by their success, they openly denounced the errors of Hinduism, threw off the allegiance of the Brahmans, and denied the sacred character and spiritual authority of the Vedas.

As the basis of the new creed they adopted from the Hindus the belief in one Supreme Being, but they denied his providence and active interference, either in the creation or government of the universe.

They believed in the eternity of matter, and identified the powers of nature with the Supreme Being.

Although they incorporated with their system many if not most of the Hindu deities, yet they ranked them not as gods, but as mere superior servants of the Supreme Being, and regarded them as subordinate even to their own deified saints. They borrowed from the Hindus, with but little change, the doctrine of the reputed transmigrations of the soul, and of its ultimate absorption into the Supreme Being;— the difference being that the Hindus looked forward to absorption into Brahma, and the new religionists looked forward to absorption into Buddha.

They agreed with the Hindus in looking on the present world merely as a sphere of probation for man.

The most important point of difference between the Brahmans and the Buddhists consisted in the latter denying the divine authority of the Vedas and Puranas, which were the most sacred scriptures of the Hindus.

They rejected entirely the system of caste, and with it they threw off all social or spiritual superiority of the Brahmans and other privileged classes. They abolished also the hereditary priesthood, maintaining that priests were not essential; as, in the eyes of God, all human beings were equal, and that all were alike able, unassisted, to work out their own salvation, and to obtain ultimate absorption into the Supreme Being. For the assistance of their weaker brethren, however, priests were permitted, and their holy character recognized; but they were selected from any class of the community, and were only required to be distinguished for the purity of their morals, their learning, and for the greater asceticism of their lives.

To avoid the shedding of blood (so common among the Hindus, and especially among the worshippers of Shiva and Durga), every kind of sacrifice was prohibited as being repugnant to the mild and benevolent character of the Supreme Being, who was represented as looking with abhorrence on the effusion of blood, and as requiring from his worshippers an excessive respect for every form of animal life.

In the year 623 B. C., Savartha Siddha was born. He was the son of Rájá Sadudhana, who was a Kshatriya by caste, and a king of the Solar race, and who reigned over the powerful kingdom of Magadha (modern Behar).

Savartha Siddha was reared with the greatest care. When he was sixteen years old he was married to the Princess Yasodhara, having obtained her hand as a reward for his prowess and skill in martial accomplishments in a public contest.

For several years after his marriage the young Prince devoted himself exclusively to the pleasures and gaieties of the world, after which he gradually became impressed with the conviction that the pursuit of religion was the only one worthy of following.

Savartha Siddha was 28 years of age at the time of his conversion, and having dropped his former name, he adopted that of Sakya Simha,* by which he was ever afterwards known, and devoted himself entirely to asceticism.

He studied the most abstruse doctrines of religion until the age of 35, when he started for Benares, where he openly preached the new doctrines of philosophy and religion.

Sakya's royal lineage, his piety and learning, his talents, zeal and moral courage, enabled him to reconcile the conflicting jealousies of the various rival sects, and to lay the solid and lasting foundations of a new religion, based upon a simple, a pure, and a widely accepted creed.

As head of the various heretical sects, Sakya soon succeeded in uniting them all into one powerful party, who looked up to him as their spiritual father, and who, even during his lifetime, invested him with the title, as they believed he possessed the attributes, of a divine being.

They called him "Buddha," the "Wise one," and the new religion was called by his followers after his name.

This religion may be described as a system of deism, in which the supreme deity is represented by the powers of nature; in

* Sakya Simha is avowedly a Kshatriya; and if his six predecessors had really any historical existence, the books which affirm it, affirm too that all the six were of Brahmanical or Kshatriya lineage.

which a fundamental doctrine is the transmigration of the soul, which necessarily involves a belief in the sanctity of every form of life; which assumes the original equality, social as well as spiritual, of all classes of men, and is therefore opposed to the system of caste; and which enjoins on its followers a life of virtue and self-denial in this world as the only means of securing an immortality of peace and rest in the world to come.

Sakya was wonderfully successful as a missionary; thousands crowded to his preaching and many neighbouring monarchs embraced his religious opinions.

Having travelled through the greater part of north-western India, he made a pilgrimage to Népál, accompanied by one thousand three hundred and fifty Bhikshas (or mendicant ascetics) and having with him the Rájá of Benares and an immense crowd of all sorts and conditions.

In Népál Sakya found the doctrines, of which he was the apostle, had already taken a firm root.

They had been introduced into the country by a distinguished teacher from Thibet, named Manjusri,* who had led the first colony from China into Népál, and had built on a hill within the confines of the valley, a temple to the eternal self-existent spirit Swayambhu.

This hill is still known as the hill of Swayambhu or Sambhunath.

Sakya recorded with pious pride the great doings of Manjusri, he told how tradition assigned to him the honour of having by a miracle converted the large mountain lake of Nagávasa into the rich and habitable valley of Népál.

When Sakya returned to Hindustan, most of the followers who had accompanied him from thence, settled in Népál, and became gradually blended, by intermarriage, with the original inhabitants of the country. It was probably at this time, and in this way, that the system of caste, which had been rejected by the Buddhist of the plains, was introduced in a modified form among the Buddhists of Népál.

Sakya is known by various other names, of which Gotáma, Sakya Muni, and Mahamuni are those most commonly used.

---

* Sri and Manju, *viz.*, the "Sri," "wise one" of "Manju" or "Manchuria."

There is quite enough that is authentic in the history of Sakya to show that he was a very eminent and extraordinary character.

His piety was sincere, his learning great, his zeal untiring, and his talents were only exercised in the cause of virtue and religion. He founded hospitals for the sick and infirm, he established monasteries and convents for those who were desirous of leading a pure and holy life. Although he encountered the bitter and unscrupulous opposition of the Brahmanical priesthood, yet he never was betrayed into any retaliatory acts of cruelty and violence.

# CHAPTER VIII.

## KIRÁNTIS.

### SHORT RÉSUMÉ ON THEIR HISTORY, TRADITIONS, MANNERS, CUSTOMS, AND DIVISIONS OF TRIBES.

KIRÁNTIS INCLUDE :

1. LIMBÚS—YAKTHUMBAS.
2. RÁIS— { KHAMBUS. YAKKAS.

Definition of term "Kiránta."

The term "Kiránta" requires some explanation.

By right it should apply to the Khambus only (Ráis).

The Yakkas claim to be a separate nation and so do the Yakthumbas (Limbús).

But as Khambus, Yakkas and Yakthumbas can and have intermarried for many generations, the three nations, although at one time quite separate, have, for all practical purposes, been fused into one and the same nationality.

Hence we find their manners, customs, religious ceremonies and appearance almost the same.

To the Khambus, Yakkas, and Yakthumbas, therefore, might for all practical purposes be applied the term Kirántas.

In this book by Kiránta will be understood the three nationalities of Khambus, Yakkas, and Yakthumbas.

Although the Khambus, Yakkas, and Yakthumbas have almost the same manners, customs, religious ceremonies and physical appearance, yet each nation has retained its own language in a great degree.

Marriage and progeny.

It should be noted that the Kiránt group can intermarry by the Biah ceremony, and that the progeny invariably becomes of the nationality of its father, never of its mother.

Adoption into nationality.

Another point is of interest, *viz.*, the adoption of a member of any one of the three nations which compose the Kiránt group, into either of the other two.

For instance, say a Sángpang Khambu expresses his desire to become a member of the Limbú nation of the Maniyámbo tribe.

After certain ceremonies, such as paying certain sums, exchanging rupees three times with a Maniyámbo man, giving and receiving scârves, etc., he will be admitted into the Limbú nation and as a member of the Maniyámbo tribe, ***but he must retain the name of his Khambu tribe***, and thus he and all his descendants will become Sángpang Maniyámbo—the name of his Khambu "*tribe*," sinking into the name of a *clan* of the Maniyámbo tribe.

The Yakkas and Khambus have mixed together more freely than either of them have with the Limbús.

Term Subah and Rái.

The term-Subah* or Suffah is generally adopted by Limbús, whilst Rái is a name often claimed by Yakkas and Khambus.

But both the terms Subah and Rái are of modern origin, and signify practically the same thing, *viz.*, chief.

When the Khambus first, and the Limbús afterwards, were conquered by the Gurkhás, the Gurkhá king, probably anxious to conciliate his vanquished enemies, conferred upon the most influential men amongst them, commissions sealed with the red seal, conferring upon them powers to rule certain districts.

With these commissions to the Khambus were given the title of Rái, and to the Limbús the title of Subah, each title meaning practically the same.

These titles were given, to begin with, to the most, influential of each nation, and the title remained hereditary; but nowadays most Limbús call themselves Subahs, whilst Khambus and Yakkas call themselves Ráis.

Khambu and Yakka recruits, when first brought in for enlistment and asked what class they belong to, will reply "Jimdár," and when further pressed will answer "Rái."

The Kiránta group therefore consists of the following:—

Practically the same now.
1. Khambus, also called Jimdars, Ráis.
2. Yakkas, also called Jimdars, Ráis.

(These two will be treated in this book as Ráis only.)

* In Central Népál "Subah" is the title applied to certain civil authorities, who practically represent our Deputy Commissioners in India.

3. Yakthambas, also called Limbús, Chang, Tsong, Subah, and Das Limbús.

Claim descent from Benares.

They all three have a tradition that they originally came from Benares (Kási).

Although often mentioned in the oldest of Hindu writings, no history of the Kiránts is obtainable on which any dependence can be placed.

Like the Magars and Gurungs, the Kiránts show a decided Mongolian origin, but there is also some foreign strain in them.

The following tradition taken from Sarat Chandra Dass seems to clearly indicate an immigration from Thibet into the northern mountains of Népál and their sunny valleys:—

" The village of Yangma in ancient time was not inhabited. Once upon a time a cowherd of Tashi-rabka (in Thibet) lost one of his yaks, which grazing in towards the Kangla Chen pass, entered the Yangma valley. Here the cowherd, having followed the tracks, found his hairy property lying on a rock with a full stomach. In the morning he again missed his yak, and proceeding further down in the interior met it at a place called Shophug, grazing in a rich pasture land.

" Here, being charmed with the luxuriance of the pasture as compared with his bleak and barren country, he sowed a few grams of barley, which he had obtained from a certain priest as a blessing.

" On his return to his village in Thibet he gave a good account of this place to his fellow 'dokpas' (cowherds), but nobody would believe him, nor would any one undertake to visit his discovery on account of its position beyond the snows.

" The cowherd, however, with his wife went to Yangma valley to tend his flock. To their surprise they found the barley well grown. On his return he showed the barley ears to his friends, who were now induced to emigrate to the new land to grow corn.

" Thus was the village of Yangma first inhabited. It is indeed a purely Thibetan settlement, as the houses testify."

Roughly speaking, the Limbús inhabit the easternmost portion of Népál, and the Khambus and Yakkas the country between the Limbús and the valley of Népál.

Habitat of Limbús and Ráis.

They are mostly cultivators or shepherds; their physique is good, and in appearance they are much like an ordinary Magar or Gurung, although perhaps

Occupation.

not quite so thickly built. They are said to be very brave men but of a headstrong and quarrelsome nature, and taken all round are not considered as good soldiers as the Magars or Gurungs.

There is one regiment composed entirely of Limbús in the Népálese Army; it is called the Bhairanáth, but on account of the quarrelsome nature of the men is always quartered at some distance from other regiments.

The First Burma Rifles, which was raised about 1889, consists chiefly of Limbús and Ráis, and has on every occasion won approval.

It seems to me highly probable that once we have a regiment consisting entirely or almost entirely of Kirántas, that it will be found they are nearly as easy to manage as the ordinary Gurkhá regiment.

Limbús and Ráis, when found in our Gurkhá regiments, have so far always been immensely in the minority, and being looked upon with disgust by the Khas and Thákurs on account of their very late (if not actually still existing) beef-eating propensity, the y have probably been subjected to insults.

Now Magars, and even Gurungs (in public), are also obliged to show indignation at this custom, and hence it can easily be understood how the Limbús and Ráis would be bullied, thereby causing ill-feeling and its consequent trouble, which may possibly account for the bad name given them as to their quarrelsomeness.

No doubt the Limbús and Ráis are of a more exciteable nature than the Magars and Gurungs, but I cannot help thinking that the explanations given as to their peculiar position in our old Gurkhá regiments may have had much to do in earning them the character they are credited with.

Hamilton says:—

"East from Népál proper, the mountainous territory was occupied by Kiránts, who in remote times seem to have made extensive conquests in the plains now constituting the district of Dinapur.

"Father Guiseppe in 1769 recognised the Kiránt country as being an independent State. Now, although this would not appear to be strictly exact, as the Kiránts had long been subject to Rájput princes, yet the Kiránts formed the principal strength of these Rájput chiefs, and their hereditary chief held the second office in the State, and the Rájputs, who were united with them, did not presume to act as masters, to invade their lands, or to violate their customs. These Kiránts are frequently mentioned in Hindu legend as occupying the country between Népál and Madras (Bhotan)."

The Kiránts seem always to have been a warlike and enterprising people, but very rude, although not so illiterate as many of their neighbours. The Lámás made great progress in persuading them to adopt their doctrines, but many adhered to their old customs.

The Rájputs on obtaining power induced many to abandon part of their impure practices, but in general this compliance was only shown when they were at court. The abstinence from beef which the Gurkhális enforced was exceedingly disagreeable to the Kiránts.

It is stated that the Gurkhális threatened and eventually carried out war against the Kiránts, because they would not give up their beef-eating propensities.

Hindu action in Eastern Népál.

It would appear that the Rájputs and Brahmans acted in Eastern Népál very much as they did on the western side of the Népál Valley, and we eventually find the chiefs of Eastern Népál claiming descent from Chitor.

Makwanpur originally formed part of the estate of the Ruler of Pálpá. There is no doubt that Makúnda Sen possessed very extensive dominions, but on his death he divided his kingdom amongst his four sons. To the youngest, Lohanga by name, Makwanpur was given. A mountain chief, by name Bajúhang Rai, joined Lohanga with all his Kiránt troops, and they conquered all the petty principalities lying to the east of Makwanpur independent until then, and took possession of Bissipur.

Bajúhang was killed during these wars, and his son relinquishing the title of Hang, in its stead took that of Chautaria, and all his successors assumed Hindi names.

Lohanga now possessed a very extensive territory reaching from Mahananda in the east to Adiya on the west, and from Thibet to Julagar, near Purneah.

One of Lohanga's successors was called Subha Sen, and had two sons, who on their father's death divided the kingdom. In 1774 the Gurkhás overran the country.

Sarat Chundra Dass says :—

"The country between the Arun and Tambar is called 'Limbúan' by the Népáli natives, and the aboriginal people, who have resided there from time immemorial, are designated by the name of Limbú, though they call themselves by the name of Yakthumba. In the same manner the tribes inhabiting Kiránta, or the regions between the Dúdkosi and the Arun, are called Kiránta,* which name is as old as that of the great Hindu deity Mahádeva. The Kiránt of the north, now called Khambu, and the Limbú of the south are allied tribes, intermarrying among themselves.

"They were known to the ancients by the name Kiránta, on account of their living by hunting and carrying on trade with the natives of the plains in musk, yaktails, shell-lac, cardamum, etc., from the earliest Hindu periods.

"Hence Arrian heard of the Kirhœdi of Népál and Bhot.

"The Kiránta includes Rongshar, Sharkhambú, Madhya Kirantá, Limbúan, and Pánthar.

"Rongshar is a country of defiles through which the Dúdkosi flows. It lies between the great mountain range running from north to south, of which the culminating point is Lapchhyikang (called Mount Everest in English maps), and that lofty range which commences east of Nanam (or Nilam) to terminate at the junction of the Sún and Dúdkosi rivers.

"Sharkhambú lies to the west of the Arun and south of the Pherák district of Thibet.

"Madhya lies between the Arun and Tambar rivers, the most remarkable places in it being Tsanpúr, Walung, and Shingsa.

"Limbúana includes the eastern defiles, forming the valleys of the Tambar and Tangpachan rivers.

"Pánthar, or Páthar in Hindi (probably the region of rocks), includes the eastern and western flanks of the lofty range which runs north to south full one degree between 28th and 27th north latitude, having for its culminating points Gesang-La in the north, the Kanchanjanga group in the middle, and Samdúkphi of the Darjeeling frontier to the south.

* Ancient Newár mythology mentions that the "Kirántis," who originally dwelt to the eastward, came and conquered Népál and ruled there, and that after them came the gods.

"The Thibetians and the Bhutias of Népál and Sikkim call the Limbús by the name of Tsang, which is probably given to them on account of their having emigrated to Limbúana from Tsang, in Thibet.

"The Limbús are said to be derived from three sources :—

(1) Emigrants from Tsang in Thibet.

(2) Emigrants from Káshi (Benares) in Mádhya Desh (*viz.*, from the plains).

(3) From those sprung from underneath a huge rock in the village of Phedáb situated to the north-east of Tsanpur.

"Originally, therefore, the Limbús were divided into three great tribes, according to their original homes—Tsang, Káshi, and Phedáb,—which three tribes in later times were split up into numerous clans.

"The first branch from Tsang spread themselves over Tambar Khola, Phalung, Maiwa Khola, Mewa, and Yangrop, being designated by the Thibetans as Tsang Monpa, or the Limbús inhabiting the defiles.

"Those who came from Káshi occupied Chaubisa, Kaikhola, and Chaothar.

"Those who came from Phedap were called Bhaiphuta, and were widely distributed in the valleys of Wallung, Tambar, Mewa, Máiyá, Chaothar, Páthar, and Chaubisa.

"The Bhaiphuta Limbús were the most powerful and numerous. Their chief, Bhaiphuta Hang, ruled over Eastern Népál.

"All the Limbú tribes, as well as the Kirántas, paid him tribute and military assistance in a manner resembling the feudal system of Europe.

"The family of the Bhaiphuta Hang ruled for many years; after its decline the Káshi tribe became powerful, and its chief massacred all the members of the Hang royal family.

"In this act of bloodshed the Tsang Limbús helped the Madhesia (Káshi) Limbús.

"After the fall of Bhaiphuta Hang's dynasty there was anarchy all over Eastern Népál, there being no supreme ruler to keep all the clans of the Limbús and Kirántas in peace and unity.

"In this way they continued for several years, when at length there sprang from among the Srisobha tribe a powerful man called Marang, who succeeded in reconciling the different tribes to each other.

"The Srisobha tribe claims to be of Thibetan origin.

"Marang was elected king by common consent of the people to rule over all the aboriginal tribes of Eastern Népál, for in those days the southern part, including the great valley of the Sún Kosi, was ruled by a Newár chief.

"After a prosperous reign of many years, Marang died, and among his successors in the chieftainship founded by him, Mokani Rájá became distinguished.

"After Mokani's death the Limbú tribes again fell into anarchy, there being none able to persuade all the tribes to live peacefully together, which state of things lasted for more than a century. At last, probably in the ninth century, appeared the famous Srijanga, the deified hero of the Limbús. Srijanga taught the Limbús the art of writing by inventing a kind of character.

"Tradition says that Marang Rájá was the first man who introduced writing among them, which, however, owing to the long-prevailing anarchy, fell into disuse till revived by Srijanga."

Gurkhá division of Eastern Népál.

At the present time it would appear that Eastern Népál is divided into twelve districts. I give a list of the same as obtained by me, with names of such races as are said to preponderate in each :—

| | | |
|---|---|---|
| *Bhojpur . | Inhabited mostly by . | Ráis. |
| *Dhankota | ,, ,, . | Limbús and Ráis. |
| *Ilam | ,, ,, . | Ráis and Limbús. |
| *Okaldunga | ,, ,, . | Ráis. |
| Aisalkarkha | ,, ,, . | Limbús and Ráis. |
| Charikot | ,, ,, . | Ráis. |
| Dingla | ,, ,, . | Sunwárs, Gurungs, Ráis, Limbús. |
| Dulkel | ,, ,, . | Newárs. |
| Chainpúr | ,, ,, . | Ráis and Limbús. Magars. |
| Melung | ,, ,, . | Magars, Gurungs, Limbús. |
| Ramechap | ,, ,, . | Sunwárs. |
| Rangeli | ,, ,, . | Thárus. |

Each of these districts has either a General, a Colonel, or a Captain in charge of the same.

Dhankota is the most important of all, and next comes Ilám.

A good deal of uncertainty seems to exist about the names and number of districts.

Those marked * I believe are correct, but the remainder may be real districts or merely big villages.

That there are more than four districts,† however, I believe to be the case, and to obtain a full and correct list must be a matter of time.

Marriage ceremony amongst Kirántis.

Some families among the Limbú people consult astrologers, others do not. When marriage is contemplated, the parties, very commonly without the knowledge of their parents, meet together in some place of common resort, or in some market, should there exist any, in order to sing witty songs, in which test alone the male is required to excel his fair rival. If the candidate is beaten in the contest by the maiden whose hand he covets, he at once runs away from the scene, being ashamed of his defeat; but if, on the other hand, he wins, he seizes her hands and leads her triumphantly to his home without further ceremony, a female companion generally accompanying her.

If the candidate had previously won the maiden's attachment by any means whatsoever (the place to meet being some fountain or rill where the maiden goes to fetch water), and thereby had opportunities of discovering her efficiency in the art of singing, he pays a bribe of a couple of rupees, or its equivalent in kind, to the maiden's companion to declare him the winner in the singing competition.

Generally marriage is contracted by courtship among the parties, when the above-described means are not resorted to, before their parents are informed of their intentions. This takes place when the candidate obtains free access to the house of the maiden's father, which is easily effected by presenting the nearest relation living in the house with a pig's carcase. This kind of present is called "phudang" in the Limbú language. When the marriage ceremony takes place, the bridegroom, if rich enough, kills

† Such recruits as I have enlisted so far, belonging to the Bhojpur district, when asked what their district is, have almost invariably said Chár number, meaning number four. I am informed that each district once upon a time bore its number as well as its name, but Bhojpur is the only one whose number I have actually heard given by recruits. Okaldunga, I am told, is called Tín number.

a buffalo, or else a pig, which is presented to the bride's parent with a silver coin fixed in its forehead (ticca).

Amongst the lower people the parents of the bride seldom know anything about the marriage till the return of the girl from her victor's house. At the time of the marriage the friends and relations of the parties assemble, each bringing a present of a basketful of rice and a bottle of murwa or arack (Jáar).

Then the parties meet in a spacious courtyard attended by their friends and neighbours. The bridegroom beats a drum to the music of which the bride dances, outsiders also taking part in the dance.

This over, a priest, called Phedangba, or Bijua, conducts certain religious ceremonies, beginning with the mantra "according to the commands handed down from ancient times, and the doings of the patriarchs, we bind our son and daughter in marriage to-day," when the Bijua repeats the mantra, the bridegroom places his palm in that of the bride, they at the same time holding a cock and a hen respectively, which is then made over to the Bijua. At the end of the service the throats of the fowls are cut and the streaming blood is received on a plantain leaf, from which omens are drawn. In another leaf some vermilion paint is placed. The bridegroom then dipping his middle finger in the paint passes it by the forehead of the officiating priest to touch the bridge and tip of the bride's nose. The bridegroom then says,—" Henceforth from this day, maiden, thou art my wife," and shouting repeatedly, "Maiden, thou art my wife," puts a vermilion mark on her brow. The slain fowl is thrown away, so that whoever picks it up gets it. The following morning the priest invokes some friendly spirit, who thus advises the married couple: "You two should henceforth live as husband and wife as long as you live on this earth," to which the parties suitably reply, "We will do as you command."

Unless this period of a lifetime is mentioned, the marriage is not considered auspicious, and to make it auspicious certain other ceremonies are prescribed, which open up new sources of gain to the priest.

Those who bring bottles of murwa as presents are admitted as guests to the marriage, when first of all murwa and roasted meat (generally pork) are served, after which a dish of rice is presented to every one of the party. At the termination of the marriage ceremony the bride, released from her captor's hands for the first time, returns to her parents. Two or three days after her return comes the parmi (intermediator or umpire) to settle differences with the bride's parents, who now for the first time are supposed to learn the matter about her and the bridegroom. He brings, as a rule, three things—one bottle of arack, the entire carcase of a pig, and a silver coin—as presents to the bride's parents. Just as he goes to make the presents to the bride's parents, they are bound to fly into a passion and threaten to beat him, whereupon he entreats them not to beat him, and tries to pacify them by producing another rupee from his pocket. The bride's parents then interrogate him in an angry tone, saying, "Why did you steal away our daughter," and so on. When their anger subsides, he pays the price of the bride, which, according to his means and resources, varies from Rs. 10 or less to Rs. 120 or more. When the money is not forthcoming, its equivalent in kind is given, but in all cases a pig must accompany the price. When the bride's parents are satisfied, the demand of presents for the soffas (subahs) and village aldermen is made. (These men are the twelve elders of the village.) Usually a sum of Rs. 12 or its equivalent in kind is given, which the subahs and other officials of the village appropriate to themselves. The payment is called "turayimlag" in the Limbú language, meaning satisfaction for appeasing the anger of the bride's parents for stealing their daughter.

This amount, although due to the bride's parents, is nowadays appropriated by the village officials.

Like the Thibetans, the Limbús present white cotton scarves to all who are interested in the marriage.

At the time of delivering the bride to the "parmi" the parents must say, "Oh, our daugher is lost! She is not to be found; somebody must go and find her."

So when a couple more of silver coins are produced as remuneration, but not before, one of the relations discovers the lost bride, who generally conceals herself in the State room of her parent's house, and delivers her up to "the parmi." Nowadays this searcher does not generally make his appearance on marriage occasions, but the bride discovers herself when the money is paid.

## LIMBÚS.

### TRANSLATION OF LIMBÚ VANCÁVALI (*viz*, HISTORY).

God is called Mojingna Khiwagna. He made the world and all the creatures in it.

Limbús were first known by the name of Yakthumba, and they are descended from ten* brothers whose names are as follows:—

1. Thosoying Kanglaying Hang.
2. Thindang Sawaro Hang.
3. Thosading Hambleba Sawaro Hang.
4. Thoding Tangsak Sawaro Hang.
5. Yóphoding Sawaro Hang.
6. Moguplungma Khambeh Sawaro Hang.
7. Moguplungma Langsoding Sawaro Hang.
8. Yokphoding Sawaro Hang.
9. Yokphodingighang Laingbo Hang.
10. Totoly Tomeangbo Hang.

With these ten brothers also came three spiritual advisers Bijuas):—

1. †Phejeri Phedangma.
2. Sambahang Eblyhang Samba.
3. Samundum Yepmundum.

These above-mentioned brothers and priests did not know how to read or to write, but they knew some *tácha* (prayers) and *modhun* (traditions).

These were handed down by word of mouth and by these were they ruled.

These ten brothers and three priests were all residents of Kási (Benares), and they agreed to make themselves homes in the mountains of Népál.

Five of the brothers marched straight from Benares to Népál, but the other five went to Thibet, and from Thibet through Lásádinga, until they met their five brothers in the mountains of Népál.

The first five brothers and their descendants are called Kásigothra, and the second five brothers and their descendants are

* The Limbús often state also (see Risley) that they were originally divided into thirteen tribes. This would be accounted for by the ten brothers and three priests.

† Phejeri Phedangma is the most important of the three.

called Lásagothra, because they respectively journeyed from Benares to Thibet, and from Lásadinga to Népál.

But all ten brothers should rightly be called Kásigothra, for they all came from Benares.

Now, these ten brothers settled in a place called Ambepojoma Kamketlangma Sumhalangma.

The kings of the country where the ten brothers lived were called—

| | |
|---|---|
| (1) Honden Hang. | (5) Khesiwa Hang. |
| (2) Yekted Hang. | (6) Ekangso Hang. |
| (3) Chasbi Hang. | (7) Khadi Hang. |
| (4) Larasopangbo Hang. | (8) Ime Hang.* |

The ten brothers had many children, and their descendants multiplied very quickly, till they became a nation and were called Limbús.

The Limbús were, however, subject to the kings of the country and they were very much oppressed. The kings ruled them with such a hard rule, and oppressed them so greatly, that eventually the Limbús having joined together in the place called Ambepojoma Kamketlangma Sumhalangma, consulted together, and determined to fight the kings of the country, and drive them out of the country.

So every Limbú swore upon the holy place (Ambepojoma, etc.), that he would conquer in the fight or die, and every man swore that he would not return from the war until the kings had been driven from the country, and that he would die sooner than run away in battle.

So there was a great war between the Limbús and the kings, and the former won many victories and drove out the kings from the land, and the Limbús seized the country as their own and fixed its boundaries on the north by Thibet; on the south up to the Mades (plains); on the west up to the Arun Khola; and to the east up to the Michi Khola.

Then the Limbús assembled again together and consulted, and they determined to elect unto themselves ten chiefs (Hangs), one from each tribe, and so the following ten chiefs were elected, and

*Ime is another name for Lépchá and evidently the 8th king was King of the Lépchás.

each chief built himself a fort and called it by a name, and each chief marked the boundaries of his country and called it by some name :—

1. Samlupley Samba Hang called his country Tambar Khola, and his fort Tambar Yiokma.

2. Tampeso Perúng Hang called his country Thérathar, and his fort Thala Hiokma.

3. Thoktokso Angbo Hang called his country Áthrai, and his fort Poma Jong.

4. Sengsenggum Phedáp Hang called his country Phedáp, and his fort Poklabang Yiokma.

5. Tindolung Koya Hang called his country Yangroke, and his fort Hastapur.

6. Sesiane Sering Hang called his country Mewakhola, and his fort Meringdem.

7. Yenangso Pápo Hang called his country Pánchthar, and his fort Yasok Pheden Yiokma.

8. Taklung Kajum Hang called his country Chethar, and his fort Chamling Chimling Yiokma.

9. Soiyok Ládo Hang called his country Cháobisia, and his fort Sánggori Yiokma.

10. Ime Hang called his country Chárkhola, and his fort Angdang Ilam Yiokma.

The above are the names of the first ten Limbú chieftains, together with the names of the ten principalities as first marked out, and their respective forts (capitals).

After this division of the country the Limbús remained rulers of their country until the Gurkhás waged war against them.

For twelve years did the Das Limbús fight with the Gurkhás, after which they were defeated The Gurkhás then killed all the Limbús whom they could catch, whether men, women, or children; and the Limbús had to hide in the mountains because of the cruelty and oppression of the Gurkhás.

[NOTE.—It should here be noted that the second name of the majority of these ten chieftains is the name of some known Limbú tribe: thus Sámba, Angbo, Phedáp, Sering, Pápo, and Kajum.

The first name of each chief is probably his real name, the second that of the tribe he belonged to, and Hang might be translated as Baron.

2. The districts ruled over by these chiefs are all named either after the rivers which runs through the same: for example, Tambar Khola, Mewa Khola, etc.; or by the number of tribes that constituted the rulers of the country for example Chethar, Chaobisia, Therathar, etc.

3. I have been assured by many Limbús that the ten forts with their original names exist to this present day, but many have now given their names to cities: thus, Hastapur, Ilám, etc.]

After some time the Gurkhá king, thinking of all the heavy troubles that were upon the Limbús, called them together, and on their promising to look upon him as their king, he granted unto the chief men amongst the Limbús, Támápúttras,* Lálmohars,† and Sobangjis† (*viz.*, sealed and stamped warrants) with certain powers for the ruling each chief of a certain district.

Each holder of Támápúttra, Lálmohar, and Sobangji was granted full power according to his warrant, to try all cases in his district, and to rule in every way as he deemed fit, with the exception only of cases of *khúni* (murder), cow-killing, and with regard to taxes or money matters.

Every case of murder, cow-killing, and all matters connected with taxes has to be referred to and settled by the King of the Gurkhás.

The Limbús after this ceased from making war with the Gurkhás and became their friends, and acknowledged the King of the Gurkhás as their king.

They have now begun to learn to read and write in the Gurkhá character and language, and many have taken service in Gurkhá regiments.

Here ends the vernacular history of which I was able to obtain a copy.

Although very wearisome reading, I consider it of value on account of the light it throws on the original districts of the Limbú nation.

The following is a translation which I made of a vernacular document kindly lent to me by Mr. Paul, and contains some of the last wise sayings of Srijangga, the deified hero of the Limbús.

I have attempted to produce the same in readable English whilst keeping as near as possible to the wording of the vernacular document.

* Támápúttra is a commission engraved on a copper-plate.
It is said the Thibetans owned a "támápúttra" for the temple of Sambunath in Népál.

† A Lálmohár is a commission sealed with a red seal.
Sobangji is a rank and corresponds practically and on a small scale to a Deputy Commissioner.

## WISE SAYINGS OF SRIJANGA.

He that plays continually on the banks of a large river will some day be drowned.

He that plays too much upon a rock may fall down some time.

He that continually climbs trees will fall down some day.

Pigs secured by wooden clogs will become tame.

Fowls shut up in a basket will get tame.

Goats secured by wooden clogs will get tame.

Dogs tied up with iron chains will get tame.

Elephants secured by twisted cotton ropes will get very tame.

If yokes are put on bulls they will become very tame.

If salt is given to cows they will become quiet and manageable.

Wives should be treated with kind words, and they should treat their husbands as dearly as guests.

Mothers should suckle their own children.

Servants should be kindly treated.

He that steals another man's wife should be killed.

A man should consider another's wife as his own mother.

A woman should consider another's husband as her own father.

A wife's duty is to rise early in the morning, clean the house, and prepare the food.

After preparing the food she should carefully wash all utensils.

If a visitor calls she should first offer water to wash his hands, and treat him with every respect.

As soon as she has risen in the morning, a wife should bow down before her husband and place his feet upon her head.

Wives should obey the commands of their fathers-in-law and mothers-in-law.

Do no murder.

Do not steal.

Do that faithfully which your religion teaches you, and read your sacred books.

If the water is clear, fish will gather there.

If the tree is good and large, all birds and squirrels will live here.

Do not hate and abuse the poor, because he may become rich some day.

Boast not of your riches.

Do not covet thy neighbour's goods.

Be satisfied with what is your own.

Do not envy others.

Be not anxious to defend thy neighbour's honour.

Husband and wife, love each other, or ruin will come upon you.

Such wives as obey not their husbands' commands and insist upon acting according to their own wishes, will bring ruin to their own home, and after death will be born again in the shape of itchy bitches.

Those who steal iron implements will be born again as beasts.

Those who steal household plates will be born again as blind or lame persons.

Those who steal cotton will be born again as lepers.

## LIMBÚS AND THEIR DIVISIONS.

*Example:*

| | |
|---|---|
| Name | Purandhoj. |
| Nationality | Limbu, or subah. |
| Tribe (*Swang*) | Kajum. |
| Clan (*thar*) | Chongbang. |
| Original home or *kipát* | Chethar. |

Origin.

The Limbús in their own history claim to be descended from ten brothers, who left Benares to make them, selves a home in Népál; five of these brothers went direct to Népál, whilst the other five went *viá* Thibet.

Limbús say that they were first of all divided into thirteen tribes, but that three of these were lost, so that from ten tribes were created the present nation of Limbús.

Risley, in his "Tribes and Castes of Bengal," divides the Limbús into the following ten tribes :—

| | |
|---|---|
| 1. Pánthar | Classed as Kási gothra, supposed to have immigrated into Népál from Benares. |
| 2. Chothar | |
| 3. Ahtharai | |
| 4. Yangorup | |
| 5. Chaibisá | |
| 6. Miákhola | Classed as Lhása gothra, supposed to have come from Lhása. |
| 7. Charkhola | |
| 8. Maikhola | |
| 9. Phedáb (Bhaiphuta) | |
| 10. Tambar khola | |

Risley then continues and gives the clans, which belong to each of these ten tribes.

After the most careful and searching enquiries I have come to the conclusion that the ten tribes given by Risley are in eight cases not the names of tribes but of districts.

Districts, composing Limbú land.

I divide the Limbú country into the following ten districts :—

| | |
|---|---|
| Pánchthar | (The residence of five tribes.) |
| Chethar | (The residence of six tribes.) |
| Athrai | (The residence of eight tribes ?) |
| Yangrok or Yangrup | (Name of a place.) |
| Chaubisia | (The residence of twenty-four.) |
| Mewa-khola | (Name of river.) |
| Chárkhola | (Four rivers.) |

| | |
|---|---|
| Máiwakhola . . | (Name of river.) |
| Phedáp . . . | (Name of famous rock and cave.) |
| Tambarkhola . . | (Name of river.) |

Of these the first five districts, it is said, were originally peopled by members of the Kásigotra, whilst the last five were inhabited by the Lhásagotra.

These districts most certainly held a preponderance each of certain tribes.

For instance, to this day even all Limbús of the Phágo tribe claim Máiwakhola as their residence, and very few, if any, Phágos will be found in any other district, except Máiwakhola.

However few the number of Limbú tribes may have been originally, at the present time there are a large number. Some of these tribes are divided into a large number of clans, some into two or three only, whilst others, although recognized as true tribes, have no subdivision.

Thus Phágo, Tegim, Kewa, etc., etc., are tribes with numbers of clans, whilst Ijam, Chemjong, Kurungbang, have but two or three clans, and Lingkim, Moden, Nogo, Sámi, etc., etc., although tribes (*swang*), have no clans of their own.

Of the ten districts which I have given, two appear also as the names of tribes, *viz.*, Áthrai and Phedáp.

Phedáp is the name of a famous rock and cavern visited and described by Sarat Chandra Das, and the original residents of this cave, it is said, assumed to themselves the name of the rock, or gave the rock and thence the district the name of their tribe. Phedáp was the country of the Bhaiphutas. See history given under Kiránt chapter, page 130.

Tribes of Limbús.

All Limbús, whatever may be their tribe or their district, nevertheless claim common descent.

Every single recruit I have met as yet will invariably, if asked, give his "swang," also his clan if there be any, and his district.

Questioning a Limbú will be much as follows :—

| | |
|---|---|
| * What are you? . . | Subah (or Limbú). |
| What Limbú? . . | Phágo. |
| What Phágo? . . | Nálibo. |
| What is your district (kipat)? . . | Máiwakhola. |

* If asked by a Limbu in Limbú kura, he will generally reply Yakthumba.

As pointed out very truly by Risley, an immense number of clans have sprung up amongst the Limbús (and this applies to the whole of the Kiránt group), through some peculiarity of the founder of the same.

Thus, within the Chaubisia district, there existed once upon a time a man of the Yongya Hang tribe who had two sons. One of these was very fond of wearing the red rhododendron flower (topetlágu), whilst the other showed much partiality to a fruit called yambhota, and from these peculiarities arose the Topetlágu and Yambhota clans of the Yongya Hang, the nicknames having stuck to the posterity of each.

Again, the existence of many tribes has been caused by a nickname, either given on account of some peculiarity or from local reason, which nickname has superseded the original tribal name.

Thus the Chemjong tribe derives its name from the fact that its founder was a resident of Chem, who settled in some foreign part.

| | |
|---|---|
| Tegim . . . | The wicker-worker. |
| Menyangbo . . . | The unsuccessful one. |
| Libang . . . | The archer. |

It can easily be conceived what a number of tribes and clans can be produced from such a peculiar custom, and how complicated matters must get in time.

Religion of Limbús.

Owing to the great progress the Lámás made amongst the Kiránts, and their consequent adoption of Buddhism, there is no such thing as caste amongst the Limbús (the same applies to Ráis).

The result is that all Limbús are, socially speaking, equals.

Menials exist, no doubt, in Limbú land : for instance, Sárkhis, Damais, etc., are found, but these menials are foreigners. They are not, and never can be, Limbús.

A Limbú may take up the profession of Damai (tailor), (he would probably refuse to do any such thing), but it would not make him a Damai, nor would it sink him socially in the eyes of other Limbús. Being a Limbú, and there being no such thing as caste amongst his nation, he may adopt any trade he likes, and yet remain the equal of any other Limbú.

Limbús recognize Ráis as being their equals and will eat and drink with them, and intermarry by the *biah*-ceremony.

Yet a Limbú, although recognizing no social superiority in any member of his own nation, will refuse to eat or drink or have any dealings with foreign menials, such as Sárkhis, Damais, etc.

It must be noted, however, that since the conquest of Eastern Népál by the Gurkhás, the Hindu religion, with its caste customs, is beginning to make itself felt.

Cows, for instance, can no longer be slaughtered, nor having been killed can their flesh be eaten.

The Limbús and Ráis are still in a state of transition, if I may use such an expression. A little over a hundred years ago, if they had any religion, it leaned towards Buddhism, but even their Buddhism was of the most lax description. Under the Gurkhá rule, the observances of the Hindu religion in a more or less lax form are introduced; these are neither rejected nor adopted, but tolerated and allowed to exist side by side with their shadowy Buddhistical and pagan notions.

The religion of the Limbús and Ráis, if it can be so called, is a mixture of what seems most convenient and gives the least trouble to its devotees of Buddhism, Hinduism, and their original pagan, or ghost worship.

When celebrating a birth, marriage, or other religious ceremony, a Lámá is called in, but if no Lámá is available a Brahman will do, and if neither can be got, then any religious mendicant or none at all will do equally well.

In selecting his priest for the occasion, the Limbú will be mostly, if not entirely, influenced by the religion which is prevalent locally.

If the surrounding people are Hindus, he will call for a Brahman; if Bhuddhist, he will want a Lámá or Phedangbo.

A Phedangbo is also called in at births to foretell the destiny of the infant, and to invoke the blessing of the gods. The office frequently descends from father to son, but any one may become a Phedangho who has a turn for propitiating the gods, and for this reason the occupation shows no sign of hardening into caste.

Comparing the religion of the Limbús with the ancient religion of Thibet, Risley says :—

"We may perhaps hazard the conjecture that the original religion of the Limbús is closely akin to the Pan or ancient religion of

Thibet. In both we find the forces of nature and the spirits* of departed men exalted into objects of worship. In both systems temples and images are unknown, while propitiatory offerings occupy a prominent place.

"To complete the parallel, neither recognize a definite priestly order, while both encourage resort to medicine men, to ward off the malign influences which surround the human race."

Sarat Chandra Das says :—

"There are five classes of priests among the Limbú people to perform their religious and secular ceremonies. They are called Phedangbo, Bijuwa, Dami, Baidang, and Srijanga.

"The Phedangbo enjoy the privilege of conducting the religious ceremonies and of dealing in omens and fortune-telling.

"The Bijuwa are trained to the Shamanic or mystic worship, of which fantastic dances are the chief characteristic.

"The Dámi practise witchcraft exclusively and are said to be able to eject evil spirits through the mouth.

"The Baidang are physicians who cure diseases.

"The word Baidang is undoubtedly derived from the Sanskrit Baidya."

The Srijanga, which is the most important of the five, have the exclusive privilege of interpreting the religious books and of studying religious observances and rites.

A Srijanga can combine in himself the qualifications of the other four orders.

Marriage customs.

A Limbú may marry any girl he likes who does not actually belong to the *same clan* of his *own tribe*, For instance, a man belonging to the Chongbang clan of the Phágo tribe may marry any Limbú girl as long as she does not belong to the Chongbang clan of the Phágo tribe.

* Srijanga and Theba were two powerful chiefs or kings of the Limbús who were afterwards deified.

Risley states Theba or Thebbeh was the son of Srijanga, who fought against Prithwi Narayan.

Other authorities give Srijanga a very much older date of existence, referring him to the ninth century. I cannot find any evidence of Srijanga having fought the Gurkhás: the only General who apparently defeated the Gurkhás was Satrajit, a Lepcha, but he was himself eventually subdued. He obtained his name from the fact of having won seventeen victories, so it is said. I incline to the belief that Srijanga existed many centuries ago as a powerful chief, and at a time long anterior to the Gurkhá invasion. Mr. Paul, at Darjeeling, inclines to the belief that Srijanga existed at about the same time as Vikramaditia.

He may marry a girl belonging to any other clan of the Phágo tribe, but not with the Chongbang of the Phágo tribe.

But, again, he may marry any girl belonging to the Chongbang clan of any other tribe than Phágo.

Thus a Phágo Chongbang may marry a girl of the Húúpá Chongbang, or a Kajum Chongbang, or any other Chongbang except Phágo Chongbang.

With Limbús, therefore, and all Kiránts, a man may (with certain exceptions) marry any girl of the Limbú nation, as long as she does not belong to the same *clan and tribe* as he does.

One of the exceptions referred to above is that a Limbú mus not marry into the clan of his mother.

A Limbú, as mentioned before, can, if he chooses, become a Rái.

He can marry a Rái girl by the *biah* ceremony.

A description of Limbú marriage ceremony is given under chapter on Kiránts. (See page 138.)

Limbú customs.

When a Limbú falls ill a "Yeba" is called, who sacrifices some animal and prays to all gods and goddesses for assistance.

When any one seduced another man's wife, according to ancient custom, the seducer was killed by being cut down with a kúkri, but now a days the injured husband sometimes allows the wife to go, receiving money, cattle, or furniture as compensation.

A murderer in former days was killed, but nowadays he is sometimes merely fined.

The following is a translation of a vernacular document which I obtained from Mr. Paul, late Deputy Commissioner of Darjeeling :—

Funeral ceremony.

"When a Limbú dies his body is sometimes kept for one whole night before being buried, and sometimes it is buried at once.

"The body is properly laid out at full length, and then carried to the spot chosen as a grave.

"The officiating priest, 'Phedangma,' then receives one rupee with which he is supposed to purchase the piece of ground to be used as a grave from the gods and goddesses of that place. After the body has been buried, some of the 'Phedangma' keep the money, whilst others throw it away crying, 'This is the money with which we purchased this land.' The grave is dug deep and long. The body is laid in at full length with the toes pointing towards the sky, and with the hands upon the breast, and with the fingers of one hand clasped by the fingers of the other. Leaves are then scattered over the body.

"The rich bury their dead, first enclosing the body in a coffin, in which is placed grain of every kind.

"Earth is then piled over the body and on the top of the earth a monument of stones is erected.

"If the body is buried near a road, the top of the grave will be made so as to be a convenient resting-place for travellers, and a tree will be planted to give shade and coolness to them.

"After the actual burial is over the priest and all guests and friends will go to the house of the deceased, where a feast is provided for them. The family and relations of the dead will mourn for four days if the deceased was a man, and for three days if a woman, and are forbidden during that period to eat any meat, salt, dhal, oil or chilli.

"After the mourning is over a pig is killed, and a Phedangma and all the friends and relations having been called, a feast will be indulged in by them, and the Phedangma and the guest will say to the mourners: 'You are now allowed to partake of meat, salt, dhal, oil and chilli, and all other things from to-day.'

"The Phedangma will then again cry out loudly to the dead man's spirit: 'Go now where your forefathers and foremothers have gone before.'"

Risley in his "Tribes and Castes of Bengal" describes matters regarding Limbús so very much better than I ever could, that I will now proceed to give extracts from him, on all such points as he discusses, and on which I agree with him:—

"Limbús are a large tribe, probably of Mongolian descent, ranking* next to the Khambus, and above the Yakka among the three upper divisions of the Kiránti group.

"The name Limbú or Dass Limbú from the ten sub-tribes (really thirteen) into which they are supposed to be divided is used only by outsiders.

* From all I can gather it would seem that Khambus, Yakkas, and Limbús all profess to be socially equal one to the other. I have never heard any member of any one of these three claim that his nation ranked above or below either of the other two nations.

"The Limbús according to Doctor Campbell form a large portion of the inhabitants in the mountainous country lying between the Dudkosi and the Kanki rivers in Népál, and are found in smaller numbers eastwards to the Mechi river, which forms the boundary of Népál and Sikkim. In still fewer numbers they exist within the Sikkim territory, as far east as the Tista river, beyond which they rarely settle. In Bhutan * they are unknown except as strangers. Hodgson locates them between the Arun-kosi and the Mechi, the Singilela ridge being the boundary on the east.†

"The Limbús themselves claim to have held from time immemorial the Tambarkhola valley on the upper waters of the Tambar Kosi river. They have also a tradition that five out of the thirteen sub-tribes came from Lhása, whilst five others came from Kási (Benares). The former group is called Lhásagotra, and the latter Kásigotra; but the term 'gotra' has in this case no bearing in marriage.

"All that can safely be said is that the Limbús are the oldest recorded population of the country between the Tambar Kosi and the Mechi, and their flat features, slightly oblique eyes, yellow complexion, and beardlessness may perhaps afford grounds for believing them to be descendants of early Thibetan settlers in Népál.

"They appear to have mixed little with the Hindus but much with the Lepchas, who, of late years, have migrated in large numbers from Sikkim to the west.

"Dr. Campbell compares the two tribes in the following words: 'The Limbú is a very little taller in stature than the Lepcha, somewhat less fleshy, and more wiry in the limbs, as fair in complexion, and as completely beardless. He is scarcely ever as ruddy as the Lepchas sometimes are, his eyes are; if anything, smaller, and placed more to the front than the Lepcha, and his nose, although somewhat smaller, is rather higher in the bridge than that of the Lepcha. He wears his hair long, but does not plait it into a tail; has no fancy for head necklaces, wears a

* Owing to opening out of tea gardens in the Duars a certain number of Limbús are settling down in the Bhutan hills.

† See also, in chapter on Kirántis, Pandit Sarat Chandra Dass's opinion regarding location of Limbús.

kúkri instead of the bán, and wide trousers and a jacket or chapkan in preference to the robe and long jacket of the Lepchas.'

"At the time of the Gurkhá conquest of Népál, the country east of the Arunkhola was held by petty Limbú chiefs, on *quasi*-feudal terms, from the Hindu Rájás of Bijapur and Makwanpur, at whose courts representative Limbús discharged the duties of Chauntra or Prime Minister.

"Taking refuge in the hill forts with which each of the chiefships was provided, the Limbús offered a gallant resistance to the invading Gurkhás, and the latter underwent many repulses before their supremacy was fully established.

"Although used to bearing arms, and deeming themselves a military race, they do not rank among the regular fighting tribes of Népál.

"Their principal occupations at the present day are agriculture, grazing and petty trades.

"Some authorities believe them, with the rest of the Kirántis, to be inferior in soldierly qualities to the Khás, Magar and Gurung tribes, from whom our best recruits are drawn; but this opinion seems to be giving way to a more favourable estimate of their military capacity, and their behaviour in the Sikkim campaign of 1888 is understood to have borne out the latter view.

Internal structure.

"The internal structure of the Limbús is extremely complicated. The names of the septs are extremely curious. By far the greater number of them refer to some personal adventure or peculiarity of the original founder of the sept. Intermarriage between cousins is barred for three generations or, as some say, for seven. In practice, however, while the rule forbidding marriage within the 'thar' (clan) is most strictly observed, there seems to be much uncertainty about prohibited degrees. A further complication is introduced by the restrictions in intermarriage arising from 'mith' (Limbú Saiba) friendships, or in fictitious brotherhood among most of the hill races.

"Two men contract friendship by a special ritual at which a Brahman, or, when the parties are Buddhist, a Lámá, officiates and reads 'mantras' or mystic formulæ, while the two friends thrice exchange rupees, handkerchiefs, or scarves, and daub each other between the eyebrows with the paste made of rice and curds which is used in the marriage ceremony.*

"The effect of the union is that the friends are reckoned as brothers, and intermarriage between the two families is prohibited for several generations. Any breach of the rule is punished in Népál, I am informed, with severe punishments, such as death or slavery.†

"The children of a Limbú man, by a Bhutia, Lepcha, Magar, Gurung, Sunwár, or Murmi woman, are admitted without question into the Limbú community.‡

Religion.

"The phlegmatic and utilitarian habit of mind, which a German ethnologist has noticed as characteristic of the Mongolian races, comes out conspicuously in the *nonchalant* attitude of the Limbús towards religion. Where their surroundings are Hindu, they describe themselves as Saivas, and profess to worship, though with sparing and infrequent observance, Mahadeva and his consort Gauri,—the deities most favoured by the lax Hinduism of Népál.

"In a Buddhist neighbourhood the yoke of conformity is still more easy to bear: the Limbú has only to mutter the pious formulæ: 'Om mani padme om,' and to pay respect and moderate tribute to the Lámás, in order to be accepted as an average Buddhist. Beneath this veneer of conformity of whatever faith happens to have gained local acceptation, the vague shapes of their original Pantheon have survived in the form of household or forest gods, much in the same way as Dionysius and other of the Greek gods may be traced in the names and attributes of the saints who preside over the vintage, the harvest, and the rural festivals of various kinds, in remote parts of Greece at the present day. Under such disguises, which serve to mark departures from

* The same ceremony is used when admitting any outsider as a member of the Limbú nation,—the man admitted always first choosing some man, of such tribe and clan as he wishes to belong to, as his brother.

† Nowadays the punishment is a heavy fine, and banishment out of Népálese territory; in very aggravated cases slavery, but never death.

‡ The children of a Limbú woman by a man of other class, such as Bhutia, Lepcha, etc., are not Limbús, but of the class their father belongs to.

the popular creeds, the Limbús worship a host of spiritual beings, whose attributes are ill-defined, and whose very names are not easy to ascertain. Yumá Kápobá, and Thebá, rank as household gods, and are propitiated once in every five years, or whenever disease or loss of property threatens the family, by the slaughter outside the house, of buffaloes, pigs, or fowls. The votaries eat the sacrifice, and thus, as they express it, 'dedicate the life-breath to the gods, the flesh to ourselves.' No special days are set apart for the ceremony; but it canno be performed on Sunday, as that day is sacred to Himáriyá. Those who wholly neglected the duty are supposed to suffer in person or property, and the common hill disease of goitre is believe to be one of the special modes by which the gods manifest their displeasure.

"Temples and idolsare alike unknown, nor, so far as I can ascertain, does the imagination of the Limbús trouble itself to clothe its vague spiritual conceptions with any bodily form.

"Himáriyá, the god of the forest, is propitiated on Sundays by offerings of sheep, goats, fowls, pigeons, and Indian-corn. A stone under a tree by the roadside is smeared with vermilion and bound with thread, and this place of sacrifice is marked by consecrated rags tied to a bambú pole.

"In addition to these more or less beneficent, or at least neutral divinities, the Limbús are compassed about by a multitude of nameless evil spirits, 'who require peculiar management in warding off their caprices.' To appease and propitiate these is the special function of the Bijuas, a class of wandering mendicants peculiar to Sikkim and the eastern parts of Népál. Bijuas are wholly illiterate, and travel about the country muttering prayers and incantations, dancing, singing, prescribing for the sick, and casting out devils. They wear a purple robe and broad-brimmed hat, and are regarded with great awe by the people, into whom they have instilled the convenient belief that their curses and blessings will surely be fulfilled, and that ill-luck will attend any one who allows a Bijua to leave his door dissatisfied.

"While the Bijuas act as exorcists and devil-worshippers for all the Himalayan races, the equally illiterate Phendangma is the tribal priest of the Limbús for the higher grades of spirits, and officiates at sacrifices, marriages, and funerals.

"Both cremation* and burial are in vogue amongst the Limbús (also amongst the other Kirántis), the latter being the more common and probably the older practice.

Disposal of the dead.

"The corpse is placed lying on its back with the head to the east. The grave is lined with stones, and a cairn, consisting of four tiers for a man and three for a woman, erected on the top. The Phedangma attends at the funeral and delivers a brief address to the departed spirit on the general lot of mankind and the doom of birth and death, concluding with the command to go whither his fathers have gone and not to come back to trouble the living with dreams. Neither food nor clothes are placed in the grave, but sometimes a brass plate with a rupee (or if a poor man with a copper coin) is laid under the head of the corpse. For nine days after the funeral the sons of the deceased live on plain rice without any salt, and for a month or two the relatives must avoid wearing flowers in their hair or merry-makings.

"The special and characteristic sign of mourning is a piece of white rag tied round the head. There is no periodical ceremony for the propitiation of ancestors.

"At a man's death his sons, natural or adopted, divide his property; but an adopted son or a natural son by a wife informally married (*kacchi shádi*) takes only one-half of a legitimate son's share. The division of the property is usually made by the tribal council (*thum-thum*) who set apart an extra share for the eldest son. The youngest son† is allowed to choose his share first.

Inheritance.

* Limbús also often throw their dead into the nearest river. This is probably an innovation brought in by Hindu religion.

Being in some cases a most convenient way of disposing of their dead, it has naturally been accepted by the Limbús, who have ever shown a willingness to adopt any measure in any religion which saves trouble.

† From what I can learn this is not quite right. The eldest son on death of father practically stands in the position of father to his brothers, and is recognized as such. His share having been allotted to him by the "thum-thum" (and it is always the largest) he then turns to his youngest brother and allows him to select any one of the shares which have been previously made out by the tribal council. This custom probably exists as a check to ensure an impartial division of the property.

Sisters and daughters have no right to any share; they may be given something, but almost invariably receive nothing.

"Failing sons, the eldest surviving brother is the next heir.

Food.

"In the matter of food they have very few prejudices. They eat pork and the flesh of all clean-feeding animals and drink wine. In fact, the only restrictions in their diet appear to be those imposed on certain thars' by the obligation not to eat the 'totem'* or 'beast-eponym' of the group.

"The Kirántis will eat with Magars, Gurungs, Sunwárs, Khás Thákurs, Brahmans, Newárs, and, with very slight exceptions, with the Murmis and Bhutias."

The Magars, Gurungs, Sunwárs, and unmarried Thákúrs will eat and drink with Kirántis.

Kirántis profess not to eat beef now, it being, they say, forbidden. In their own country, when free from observation, they probably go back gladly to what they have ever considered excellent food.

It is well known that they not only ate beef in the days before the Gurkhá conquest, but that it was their favourite meat, and their refusing to give up their beef-eating propensities was in part a reason of the Gurkhá invasion. Kirántis prefer in our service drinking water out of a goatskin massak.

The following, although, perhaps very incomplete, and in places inaccurate, is a list of Limbú "swangs" (tribes) with their clans.

Opposite each "swang" is entered in brackets the "*original* home" of the same.

The "original home," or "proper habitat," is called in Khas kura "Kipat" and in Limbú kura "Láji."

Some tribes have never moved fromtheir own homes—"Phágos," for instance.

Others are to be found in several districts; thus the "Kedemma" tribe will be found in Mewakhola, Yangrok and Pánchthar, and the Songbangphe and Tumbangphe tribes will be found in Chethár, Pánchthar, and Cháobisia, as well as in their original homes.

* *Vide* "Kewa" tribe, to whom the flesh of all winged animals is forbidden. The same custom exists amongst the Gurungs and Magars—*vide* Samri Ghallcas, Giabrings, Roho, Alleas, Siris, etc.

At page (165) is entered a list of "Limbú Swangs" that either have no clans or whose clans have not yet been identified.

It will be noticed that several of the names entered in this list appear as clans amongst other "swangs," and this is probably due to marriage customs, as explained previously.

For the sake of easy reference, I give, to begin with, an index or list of the ten Limbú districts, and opposite each district I have entered the tribes whose original homes were there. Many tribes will of course be found in more than one district, but I have endeavoured to show each tribe's original home or "kipat."

# INDEX

*Showing original homes of Limbú tribes.*

| Names of original homes (kipats). | Swangs or Tribes. | Names of original homes (or kipats). | Swangs or Tribes. |
|---|---|---|---|
| (1)—Athrai | Athrai.<br>Iwa. | (7)—Pánchthar | Chemjong.<br>Leoti.<br>Pápo.<br>Nembang.<br>Pheyak.<br>Serima.<br>Tegim. |
| (2)—Cháobisia | Lingden.<br>Songyokpa. | (8)—Phedáp | Húúppá.<br>Kurungbang.<br>Phedápea.<br>Singjangjo.<br>Songbamphe.<br>Tumbamphe. |
| (3)—Charkhola | Immehang. | (9)Támbarkhola | Máhbo.<br>Máhbohang.<br>Mangyung.<br>Pheuduwa. |
| (4)—Chether | Kajum.<br>Kewa.<br>Sangwa.<br>Tokleng.<br>Tilling. | (10)—Yangrok or Yangrup. | Bakkim.<br>Ijam.<br>Kebang.<br>Meniyangbo.<br>Sambarhang.<br>Thebe.<br>Yongya.<br>Yongyahang.<br>Yungwa. |
| (5)—Máiwakhola | Phágo. | | |
| (6)—Mewakhola | Kedemma.<br>Libang.<br>Nálibo.<br>Sámba.<br>Sering.<br>Tukyuma.<br>Tunglung. | | |

## *Limbú Tribes and Clans.*

ATHRÁI—(Athrái).

Ángbahang. Bakkim. Idinggo. Inglámphen. Kondongwa. Phonpho. Pomo. Sendang. Thallang. Tinglabo. Yoksoba. Yoksoma.

BAKKIM—(Yangrok).

Bakkim. Loksomba. Máden. Yangwágo.

CHEMJONG—(Pánchthar).

Chikcho. Ládo. Máhbo.

HÚÚPA—(Phedáp).

Chongbang. Hangserung. Isubo. Lokphangwa. Máden. Pehim. Phouthak. Wabungia.

IJAM—(Yangrok).

Kongliba. Penjetamlingba.

IMEHANG—(Descended from Lepchas)—(Chárkhola and Sikkim.)

Chilikchan. Lingdam. Loktong. Loksong.

IWA—(Athrái).

Inglangphe. Phalechuwa. Waji.

KAJUM—(Chethar).

Chikcho. Chongbang. Imusong. Kádi. Kurungbahang. Kurungphong. Lahorou. Lekuwá. Léwáhang. Párgharri. Sángwa. Togleng. Tukchang. Tungchang.

KEBANG—(Yangrok).

Iringba. Keiba. Sambayu. Silingbo. Tanjamba.

KEDEMMA—(Mewakola).

Nugedemma. Sansoyang.

KEWA*—(Chethar).

| | | |
|---|---|---|
| Anglabang. | Mangáp. | Tumhah. |
| Kajum. | Mangwayak. | |
| Kebuk. | Samdangwa. | |
| Lingden. | Sing Máden. | |
| Lung Máden. | Thoksuba. | |
| Máden. | Tigalla. | |

KURUNGBANG—(Phedáp).

| | |
|---|---|
| Song.† | Tum.† |

LEOTI—(Pánchthar).

| | |
|---|---|
| Pákpasomba. | Tikapatti. |

LIBANG—(Mewakhola).

| | | |
|---|---|---|
| Lunkimba. | Panghoma. | Pemba. |
| Naidemba. | | |

LINGDEN—(Chaobisia).

| | | |
|---|---|---|
| Pambokpa. | Pothaugchere. | Sengwangyang. |
| Pánkemyang. | | |
| Pánphomá. | | |

MAHBO—(Tambarkhola).

| | | |
|---|---|---|
| Chemjong. | Lekhogwa. | Máhbo. |
| Lejenji. | | Yamoke. |
| Lumdhoyu. | | |

MAHBOHANG—(Tambarkhola).

| | | |
|---|---|---|
| Kambang. | Máhbohang. | Sukarengba. |
| Láhbung. | Moringlahang. | |

MANGYUNG—(Tambarkola).

| | | |
|---|---|---|
| | Mangyung. | Tabebung. |

MENIYANGBO—(Yangarok).

| | | |
|---|---|---|
| Lercharbo. | | Wetúpmá. |
| Sangpanggye. | | |

NALIBO—(Mewakhola).

| | | |
|---|---|---|
| Chongbang. | Máden. | Tungbamphe. |

* Kewas are supposed not to eat the flesh of any animal that has wings.

† "Song" means "new" and "Tum" "elder brother,"

NEMBANG—(Pánchthar).

Angdemba.
Ingwába.
Kudánamba.
Kugetnamba.
Lohringden.
Mápejong.
Námlakpá.
Pegwa.
Phejonba.
Pichchowa.
Sárdaphe.
Tungbanphe.
Yangdemba.
Yangsoba.

PÁPO—(Pánchthar).

Angdemba.
Ingwába.
Kugetnamba.
Láoti.
Mánglap.
Mebok.
Pákserma.
Pápo.
Pápsong.
Phegwáden.
Serima.
Song.*
Takwaden.
Tum.
Tumbrok.
Umdeme.
Wegu.

PHÁGO—(Máiwakhola).

Aláppa.
Aláppawanemba.
Chongbang.
Ehpheng.
Gnoyongba.
Hinah.
Máhsuwa.
Mangden.
Nálibo.
Nayongba.
Okrábo.
Pábem or Pabemba.
Fáugma.
Pundhak.
Sápla.
Singyemba.
Yokkippa.
Taklung.
Tegotofra.
Tengubumthúpra.
Tembeh.
Thándemba.
Thopra.
Wahek.
Wanemba.

PHEDÁPEA—(Phedáp).

Angbung.
Húúppá.
Húúppá Chongbang.
Húúppá Sering.
Isúbo.
Kawepung.
Kongwa.
Kurungbang.
Lungphuma.
Máden.
Morába.
Musuhang.
Ninglekn.
Pahtangna.
Pombo.
Ponthak.
Poniyanggu.
Sene.
Singak.
Sodemba.
Sodung.
Songbangphe.
Songbo.
Suknáwab.
Tambeden.
Tenyung.
Theguba.
Tungbangphe.

PHENDUWA—(Tambarkhola).

Ajibungia.
Máden.
Támbe.
Tungbangphe.
Usuk.
Yengdem.

* "Song" means new.

PHEYÁK.—(Pánchthar).

| | |
|---|---|
| Pák.* | Tum.† |

SÁMBÁ—(Mewakhola).

| | | |
|---|---|---|
| Chongbang. | Mayongba. | Penchangwa. |
| Lungkimba. | Mingemba. | Toadopa. |
| Máden. | Mudensong. | |

SÁMBÁHANG—(Yangrok).

| | |
|---|---|
| Panthap. | Sangsangbo. |

SANGWA—(Chethar).

| | | |
|---|---|---|
| Báragahrri. | Pák.* | Tum.† |

SERIMA—(Pánchthar.)

| | |
|---|---|
| Pák.* | Tum.† |

SERING—(Mewakhola).

| | | |
|---|---|---|
| Chongbang. | Longwa. | Nálibo. |
| Kedem. | Modengba. | Sameakamba. |
| Kedemba. | Modengsomba. | Singdaba. |

SINGJÁNGGO—(Phodáp).

| | | |
|---|---|---|
| Angbung. | Phudungbang. | Teyúng. |
| Kongwa. | Sukwába. | Toklengkya. |
| Pheyák. | Tegoba. | Unglingba. |
| | Yohimbang. | |

SONGBAMPHE—(Phedáp).

| | | |
|---|---|---|
| Longwa. | Pángenhang. | Sangwareba. |
| Musuhang. | Pángenhang Manjia. | Suknawába. |
| | Warakpa. | |

SONGYOKPA—(Chaobisia.)

| | | |
|---|---|---|
| Lingden. | Thokpeba. | Thumyangba. |
| Lokpeba. | Thoksuba. | Tumsong.† |
| Páksong.‡ | Thumba. | Wáyang Kajum. |

* "Pák" means younger brother.
† "Túm" means elder brother.
‡ "Song" means new.

TEGIM—(Pánchthar).

Angbo.
Angthumba.
Chabeghu.
Hanserumba.
Kerungma.
Libang.
Longwágo.
Lua.
Máhbo.
Mákim.
Maksingbung.
Magmu.
Mánsingbung.
Mangyungbo.
Máúba.
Mehok.
Miyongma.
Nangen.
Páhghu.
Pettehba.
Pheyák.
Sakwademba.
Sakwaden.
Samdemba.
Sángba.
Saring.
Setling.
Thoglema.
Toklehang.
Wanem.
Yekten.
Yengdemba.
Yoksuba.

THEBE—(Yangrok).

Ingwárom.
Mangthumbo.
Sing.
Thúpúkúm.

TOKLENG—(Chethar).

Angla.
Kebok.
Má.
Máden.
Tumbangphe.
Sialungma.

TILING—(Chethar).

Chongbang.
Kebok.
Máden.
Sing Máden.

TUKYÚMA—(Mewakhola).

Chongbang.
Máden.

TUMBANGPHE—(Phedáp).

Kawepung.
Kochponge.
Kurungbang.
Ningleku.
Ningleku Manjia.
Patáhá.
Phonjela.
Pongiango.
Potangna.
Potro.
Sakwáden.
Sinehang.
Singgokhang.
Songmeba.*
Songrungbang.*
Támden.
Tokleng.

TUNGLUNG—(Mewakhola).

Chongbang.
Máden.

YONGYA—(Yangrok).

Muden.
Yakka.

YONGYAHANG—(Yangrok).

Laksomba.
Topetlágu.
Yambhota.
Yokpangden.
Yongatomba.

YUNGWA—(Yangrok).

Durombo.
Koyábang.
Sámsomba.
Sáptá.
Támorangba.

* "Song" means new.

*Other Limbú Swángs (tribes) that either have no* thars *(clans) or whose* thars *have not been identified.*

| Original home. | Name of Swáng. | Original home. | Name of Swáng. |
|---|---|---|---|
| Pánchthar. | Alappo. | | Mebhak. |
| Athrai. | Angbahang. | Mewakhola. | Moden. |
| Pánchthar. | Angbo. | Tambarkhola. | Nembeke. |
| Tambarkhola. | Angchangbo. | Yangrok. | Nogo. |
| Pánchthar. | Angdemba. | Do. | Nogohang. |
| Chethar. | Anglába. | ? | Ochombo. |
| ? | Baphu. | Tambarkhola. | Pálungwa. |
| Yangrok. | Begha. | Yangrok. | Pegha. |
| Do. | Bohra. | Pánchthar. | Photro. |
| Athrai. | Chengdang. | Yangrok. | Pokim. |
| Phedap. | Chikkubung. | Tambarkhola. | Purumbo. |
| ? | Chongwá phoma. | Do. | Sabenhimba. |
| Mewakhola. | Hangam or Hangkam. | Do. | Sakwáden. |
| Yangrok. | Hembiah. | Yangrok. | Saling. |
| ? | Hizipa. | Tambarkhola. | Sámbahang. |
| Yangrok. | Idingo. | ? | Sámi. |
| Pánchthar. | Ingkim. | Tambarkhola. | Samperwa. |
| ? | Ingpung. | Do. | Sarbangtum. |
| Tambarkhola. | Ingwá. | Chaobisia. | Saiyokpa. |
| Yangrok. | Ingwába. | Tambarkhola. | Sawenhimba. |
| Pánchthar. | Ingwádokpa. | ? | Senbo. |
| ? | Kádi. | Chárkhola. | Setwa. |
| Yangrok. | Kambáhang. | Yangrok. | Sigu. |
| ? | Kambang. | Do. | Singwa. |
| Pánchthar. | Kámthak. | ? | Songmiba. |
| Chethar. | Kebuk. | Tambarkhola. | Songsangoo. |
| Tambarkhola. | Kimding. | Yangrok. | Suguwa. |
| Mewakhola. | Kogling. | Do. | Sukwahang. |
| Tambarkhola. | Lechenche. | Do. | Támling. |
| Do. | Lekogwa. | ? | Tampára. |
| Yangrok. | Lingden. | Mewakhola. | Thallang. |
| Tambarkhola. | Lingkim. | ? | Thengyong. |
| Phedap. | Lingleku. | ? | Tonggomba. |
| Chárkhola. | Loksom. | Panchthar. | Wabába. |
| ? | Longimba. | Mewakhola. | Warak. |
| Mewakhola. | Longwa. | Yangrok. | Wurji. |
| ? | Lungbongwa. | Do. | Yokwába. |
| ? | Lungso. | | |
| Pánchthar. | Makkim. | | |
| Do. | Mangmu. | | |

NOTE.—"Kipat" in Khaskhúra or "Laj" in Limbukhúra means "original home" or "country."

## RÁIS:
### WHICH INCLUDES KHAMBUS AND YAKKAS.

SWANG *means* "TRIBE."
PÁCHHA „ "CLAN."

*EXAMPLE:*

| | |
|---|---|
| Name . . . . | Randhoj. |
| Nationality . . . | Rái. |
| Tribe or swang . . | Chámling. |
| Clan or páchha . . | Lapioncha. |

Excepting occasional mention of Kirántis (Ráis) in the most ancient of Hindu writings, nothing is known of their early history. In the history of Népál it is stated that the Ráis conquered Népál Valley and ruled over it for ages, and that after the Ráis came the gods. It is probable that the Ráis conquered the Thibetan tribe (now called Murmis) which orginally held the Népál Valley.

So much has been said about Ráis under the chapter headed Kirántis, and so many of the remarks on Limbús apply equally to the Ráis, that there seems to me little necessity to add any more.

Limbús and Ráis speak of each other and seem to consider one another equal in all respects. They state that their custom and habits are in all ways identical.

An intelligent man who has studied as far as he could the history, etc., of the Ráis,told me that the real truth is that, owing to neither Limbús nor Ráis having any writings of their own all history, etc., of any remote period can only be found out with great difficulty. Everything has been handed down by word of mouth, and hence all traditions, old history, customs, etc., have become much mixed, exaggerated or forgotten.

Parubhang, quoted by Mr. Risley as a household deity, I am told, is only so regarded by certain men. A havildar of Mogoung Battalion told me that Parubhang was no household deity of his, and that he would never so much as sacrifice a *murghy* to him.

When asked why not, he replied: "Parubhang was originally only a man like myself. He is now dead and what can he do for me? Fools and ignorant men may believe in his ghost ('bhút'), but I do not, or where are all the ghosts of all the dead?"

The religion of the Limbús and Ráis is being immensely affected by the reigning dynasty of the Gurkhás.

Prior to the Rái and Limbú wars with Népál, it is said that Limbús and Ráis killed and ate all and every kind of animals, including cows. It would appear that the reigning King of Népál sent word to the Ráis first and Limbús afterwards that they must cease killing cows, as it hurt their religious prejudices to see animals, considered by them holy, being killed and eaten.

On refusal to comply, war was declared, which, after gallant resistance ended in favour of the Gurkhás.

Since that time the killing of cows has been strictly forbidden and they have come to be regarded almost as holy.

The Limbús and Ráis both now recognise Vishnu (Bishnu) as god. Mahadeo and Debi are also worshipped. In olden days Bijuás were their priesthood. Bijuás are either Limbús or Ráis who of their own accord have adopted the profession, and any Limbú or Rái can become one.

As a matter of fact, Ráis, just like Limbús, are perfectly indifferent about religion. In Hindu company they will, as long as it causes no great trouble, adopt Hindu principles, but in Buddhist company they will return to lax Buddhism.

In appearance I do not believe any one could tell the difference between a Limbú and a Rái.

Their physique and appearance are of the same kind, and until asked no one could tell whether any particular lad was a Limbú or a Rái.

A list of such tribes and clans as I have been able to find out is given further on, but this is no doubt very imperfect and will require alterations.

Experience alone can give a more detailed and correct classification, but this will be a matter of time.

As I am told by both Limbús and by Ráis that their customs and manners are very much the same, and as day by day they are becoming more and more assimilated, it would be merely a repetition of my remarks on Limbús to enter into details regarding Rái customs and manners.

It appears to me that it is a mere matter of time for the Limbú and Rái nations to become thoroughly confounded in all essentials.

Regarding " Ráis " Risley says : " Khambu, Jimdár, Rái, one of the fighting tribes of Népál, forming with the Limbú and Yakka the Kiránti group, who have their original home in the 'Kiránt des' or mountainous country lying between the Dud-kosi and Karki rivers. Like several other Népálese tribes, the Khambus (or Ráis) cherish a tradition that they came to Népál from Kási or Benares.

" A mythical ancestor, Parubhang, is still worshipped as a household deity. Khambus marry their daughters as adults, and tolerate sexual license before marriage on the understanding, rarely set at defiance, that a man shall honourably marry a girl who is pregnant by him. Men usually marry between ages of 15 and 20, and girls between 12 and 15, but marriage is often deferred in the case of the former to 25, and of the latter to 20. The preliminary negociations are entered upon by the bridegroom's family, who send an emissary with two chugas or bamboo vessels of murwa beer and a piece of ham to the bride's house to ask for her hand.

" If her parents agree, the bridegroom follows on an auspicious day about a fortnight later and pays the standard bride-price of R80. The wedding takes place at night. Its essential and binding portion is the payment of one rupee by the bridegroom as 'Saimbudi' or 'earnest money' to the bride's father, the smearing of vermilion on the bride's forehead and putting a scarf round her neck.

" The bride's price may be paid in instalments if the bridegroom's family cannot afford to pay in a lump.

" A widow is allowed to marry again, but her value is held to have declined by use, and only half the usual bride-price is paid for her if she is young, and only one-quarter if she has passed her first youth.

" Divorce is permitted for adultery ; the seducer must pay to the husband the full amount that the woman originally cost, and he can then marry her. In actual practice the marriage bond is very readily broken among the Khambus, and among many other of the Népálese tribes.

"Women are faithful to the men they live with, while they live with them, and secret adultery is believed to be rare, but they think very little of running away with any man of their own or a cognate tribe who takes their fancy, and the state of things which prevails approaches closely to the ideal régime of temporary unions advocated by would-be marriage reformers in Europe.

"By religion the Khambus are Hindus, but they have no Brahmans, and men of their own tribe, called Homé, corresponding closely to the Bijuás employed by the Thibetans, serve as priests. Their special god is the ancestral deity Parúbhang, who is worshipped in the months of March and November with the sacrifice of a pig and offerings of incense and murwa beer. Him they regard as a *Ghardevatá* or household deity, and he is held in greater honour than the unmistakeably Hindu divinity Devi, to whom buffaloes, goats, fowls, and pigeons are occasionally sacrificed. Another of their minor gods, Sidha, is honoured with offerings of dhub grass and milk. His origin is uncertain, but it seems to me possible that the name may be a survival of the stage of Buddhism through which the Khambus like many other Népálese castes have probably passed.

Religion.

"The practice of the Khambus in respect to the disposing of the dead varies greatly, and appears to depend mainly on the discretion of the Homé called in to supervise the operation. Both burial and cremation are resorted to on occasions, and the mourners sometimes content themselves with simply throwing the body into the nearest river. A Sráddh ceremony of a somewhat simple character is performed once for the benefit of the deceased in the next world, and to prevent him from coming back to trouble the living.

Funerals.

"Land owning and cultivation are believed by the Khambus to be their original and characteristic occupation, but a certain number of them adopt military service and enter Gurkhá regiments under the title of Rái. A Khambu, if asked to what caste he belongs, will usually reply 'Jimdar' (a corruption of zémindar) or Raijimdar. A few Khambus have also taken to weaving. Their social status, so far as Népál is concerned, is best marked by the statement that they belong to the Kiránti group, and are recognized as equal with the Limbús and Yakkas. In the matter of food

Occupation.

they are less particular than the Hindu of the plains, for they eat pork and domestic fowls and indulge freely in strong drinks."

What Mr. Risley has stated above applies equally to the Yakkas as well as the Khambus (Ráis).

Yakkas have become so thoroughly mixed up with Khambus hat it would be most difficult, if not quite impossible, to separate them.

They are therefore treated under one and the same heading of Ráis.

One thing more should be mentioned, *viz.*, that the divisions of the Rái nation are not so clearly marked as those of the Limbús.

To get a full and really correct list of Rái tribes and clans would, I believe, be impossible, as numbers of fresh clans are continually being added. Any peculiarity of manner, speech, thabit, is apt to give a nickname which becomes a clan. The fact of living in any particular district, or marriage into any particular clan, often causes the creation of fresh clans.

AMBOLA.

| | |
|---|---|
| Ambole. | Sám. |

AMCHOKE.

| | | | |
|---|---|---|---|
| Búnche. | Hangkem. | Mangphang. | Tanglukwa. |

ATṔAHARE.

BAINGIYE.

| | | |
|---|---|---|
| Báingiye. | Nechále. | Rumdáli. |

BANTÁWA.

| | | |
|---|---|---|
| Ámchoke. | Dilungpa. | Nehang. |
| Bárálung. | Dungmáli. | Newang. |
| Bilpáli. | Hankim. | Pungchebang. |
| Bokhim. | Harimána. | Ráhadung. |
| Bungchen. | Katonjeli. | Rájálim. |
| Bungchio. | Káúng. | Rájátang. |
| Butangpyer. | Kemyung. | Sámsong. |
| Chinamkhole. | Kimdim. | Sangpang. |
| Desámun. | Kowa. | Suthunga. |
| Dibet. | Nácha. | Tanglukwa. |
| Dilpáli. | Náchring. | |

## CHAMLING.

Bádácha.
Báráthare.
Bijahi.
Birájaoba.
Boyoncha.
Buchinámcha.
Bumácha.
Bumakámcha.
Butepáchha.
Chalipáchha.
Chamdacha.
Chámling.
Chamlingcha.
Cháripáchha.
Chibringgie.
Darbalicha.
Dibungcha.
Dikulikpa.
Dilpáchha.
Dorkalicha.
Dungpachha.
Gwápácha.
Haideungcha.
Halesecha.
Homáicha.
Harasuncha.
Homewácha.
Hongdar.
Kerasingcha.
Keresoha.
Kerupungcha.
Kolapáchha.
Kraich.
Lapioncha.
Likuácha.
Lipocha.
Lungbocha.
Maidangcha.
Malcha.
Melekungcha.
Mehrácha.
Mennucha.
Molocha.
Mompolancha.
Mukumorácha.
Nabuchácha.
Námrangnácha.
Ninámucha.
Nirpáli.
Nomanácha.
Palangmocha.
Pitrangcha.
Pulomocha.
Pumbocha.
Puntepáchha.
Radolicha.
Rakocha.
Rannocha.
Rasungnácha.
Rátáhicha.
Ratocha.
Ringalungcha.
Sahmiongcha.
Sakoramcha.
Sasarkhali.
Saterongcha.
Seralongcha.
Silongcha.
Songdolcha.
Songpang.
Tabre.
Tabrehungcha.
Tamuhácha.
Thunglingyie.
Wálinggricha.
Wátancha.
Yongchen.
Yungcharcha.

## CHAURASIA.

Gaortoke.
Hátáchho.
Mopocho.
Saipâcha.

## CHINAMKHOLE.

Chinamkhole.
Hangchen.
Kamiungka.
Koile.
Siptanka.

## DILPALI.

Bano.
Bokkhim.
Chinámkhole.
Danwáli.
Kengyongma.
Mangbahang.
Mukárám.
Ramangcha.
Rangchin.
Ruchenbun.
Sowâli.

### DUNGMÁLI.

Chángcha.
Charangmule.
Chokhang.
Chuwipang.
Dehatpang.
Dewipang.
Hangbang.
Lungwem.
Nâko.
Pangwa.
Waipang.

### DÚMI.

Hádi.
Hajuru.
Holoksa.
Karbu.
Rángkâsur.
Rátku.
Sátma.
Wolukhpa.

### HÁTUWÁLI.

Bakhsibir.
Chora.
Dhunkhur.
Gaura.
Hangkim.
Harjitar.
Hangsing.
Kamleh.
Lengnuk.
Pangphu.
Sampuktar.
Sángsun.

### HOCHÁTOL.

Hochátol.
Rimuisigang.
Waisúr.
Saimalunggang.

### HENGWA.

Chabungie.
Hengbang.
Ilungbang.

### KÁLING.

Báláling.
Bárálungie.
Beraluch.
Chuchimile.
Dhanragáole.
Dimile.
Hádi.
Halakso.
Hangkula.
Hangkrap.
Jubale.
Jubungie.
Kastawás.
Látos.
Lomarija.
Maikhawas.
Makekra.
Mársoale.
Múlaku.
Pararus.
Páyati.
Phalles.
Puláli.
Rapcha.
Ratdáli.
Teptáli.
Wápcháli.

### KÁPLE.

Mewahang.

### KIMDUNG.

Kimdung.
Sakwa.

### KOWE.

Dherun.
Howadhukku.
Sobopho.
Manchupa.

KULUNG.

Bálákhang.
Bárámis.
Bikhang.
Bokhang.
Chachárlung.
Châmling.
Charipa.
Ghaktalus.
Goduhoj.
Hobermis.
Hochâtol.
Hongelu.

Kálinge.
Kubiti.
Mantaibung.
Mopocho.
Náchiri.
Nágerábung.
Nawápochon.
Pankere.
Pelmangie.
Pidimo.
Pidisái.
Pilámat.
Wálákam.

Pilmonge.
Pupáchos.
Rinhang.
Rubiti.
Rukupa.
Saetis.
Sáji.
Saprung.
Satang.
Sotangie.
Támcha.
Thetos.
Tomnám.

LINGKIM.

Kátwára | Langdappa. | Máringa.
Pákmácha. | Rájbansa.

LINGTEP.

Chiktang. | Lingtep. | Pulung. | Sangwárekeng.

LOHORON.

Álá.
Dehden.
Hedangna.
Kaiasong.

Lamphusong.
Mangdenwa.
Newahang.

Tingwa.
Yangkrong.

NÁCHARING.

Kubitis. | Paitátis. | Rágu.

NECHÁLI.

Deb.
Gelarcha.

Nandesar.
Ralecha.

Randáli.
Sechácha.

NAWÁHANG.

Bahinge.
Chaiahang.
Chalpáchawa.

Degámi.
Dehchang.
Ketra.

Kalchawá.
Lenda
Samewá.

Temonra. | Tenga.

PANGLUN.

Rátkurai.

### PUMÁRHANG.

Gháraja.
Hájiram.
Harirâma.
Mitáhang.
Rorihang.
Tongmalung.
Wáhbuhang.
Yangduhang.

### RÁKHÁLI.

Bangdel.
Náchiring.
Rákháli.

### RALDOCHA.

Namersa.
Raldocha.

### RAPCHÁLI.

Pathoje.

### RUNGDALI.

Bayek.
Dungmácha.

### SAMSONG.

Sáhpáchha.

### SANGPANG.

Báhaluk.
Báli.
Chámling.
Chedapi.
Damrewa.
Dámrung.
Dilpáli.
Dumangcha.
Dumipung.
Dumrebung.
Hachámora.
Hadikung.
Hirahang.
Huwatimtung.
Hungchangmara.
Kártamcha.
Kholapáchha.
Kipatte.
Muluhangcha.
Námnuhangcha.
Newáhang.
Panglunge.
Pittrang.
Pokreli.
Puálang.
Radakosang.
Ráná.
Randocha.
Rawáli.
Rowangkam.
Sámári.
Sámárung.
Sámsagemba.
Takreba.
Tammangcha.
Tonrepubárámúkhi.
Tonrepáchha.
Wakchali.
Wimasing.
Yangkim.

### SAWALI.

Bárálung.
Kimdung.
Sáwali.

### SERALUNGCHA.

Birácha.
Plomácha.

### SIALJONG.

Deosáli.
Tulungia.

### SOTANG.

Náopáchha.

### TULUNG.

Chámtirich.
Charipa.
Chungkúm.
Dámrang.
Demar.
Gariba.
Hadikamcha.
Hangechie.
Hangkechun.
Haopale.
Hasticha.
Horálbu.
Karling.
Langnachio.
Lanna Deosaling.
Lofláli.
Luchir.
Moipa.
Moksumcha.
Námchimichun.
Narchichun.
Paráchi.
Raimut.
Rimdunge.
Semmuche.
Sialjeuchu.
Sieljang.
Tekala.
Wakám.
Wayangcha.

### WALUNG.

Busára.
Kráwáhang.
Siwáhang.

### YAKKA.

Charkhole.
Chiktang.
Eyokhang.
Hengma.
Ilungbang.
Kákim.
Kamenhang.
Koiyungwa.
Kokwáli.
Kongoreng.
Kumcha.
Kumbi.
Kyachung.
Kyakim.
Limbukim.
Lingka.
Makropa.
Oktobhan.
Puiung.
Sámikeng.
Somme.
Somyang.
Sowaren.
Tumpábra.
Yańgkumbhu.
Yoyenghang.
Yungwái.

### YÁMDANG.

Lákchowa.
Lakphewa.
Lenda.
Nukhchilugu.
Rangchháwa.
Tesekhpar.
Yokcharany.

The following are said to be true Ráis, but have not yet been classified either as tribes (swang) or clans :—

Angáli.
Angtipe.
Atábre.
Athpabária.
Babauncha.
Bagbahang.
Bákunga.
Bámleangie.
Bángdele.
Barlos.
Bonom.
Bontharma.
Brankelso.
Buchána.
Chámrási.
Changcha.
Chára.
Chatpahang.
Chaurácha.
Chaurasi.
Chibang.
Chilingia.
Chinamka.
Chokang.
Chongkah.
Damling.
Dikpásungle.
Dingmáh.
Dorpâli.
Dukhim.
Ewokhang.
Gaora.
Girung.
Girungpáchha.
Haidibuthá.
Hangkang.
Hangsang.
Hedangna.
Homodimcha.
Homelung.
Horongpáchha.
Hospucha.
Ichingmewa.
Imole.
Jirung.
Jitsáli.
Jubingeh.
Jubulia.
Kahang.
Karang.
Karmile.
Kási.
Kengyung.
Kesánge.
Kheresáncha.
Khewa.
Khimole.
Khowâli.
Kuasancha.
Kulung.
Kulungpáchha.
Kumbiyákka.
Kuoptong.
Kurdacha.
Lámsong.
Lankawá.
Limruki.
Linkim.
Loṅgaba.
Lulang.
Lungun.
Lungwi.
Machemáre.
Madhehang.
Magrihang.
Maikam.
Makpáli.
Malekumcha.
Malepung.
Maniya.
Manjichao.
Mayáhang.
Mehring.
Mogne.
Moksumcha.
Nabuchor.
Nadung.
Námbocha.
Námdung.
Nardaucha.
Necháli.
Nikun.
Ninámbauncha.
Ninaucha.
Nomahang.
Paderácha.
Palungrátku.
Pangifu.
Pangwi.
Parali.
Phurkeli.
Pilmung.
Plembocha.
Potanga.
Pulunghang.
Rangrisa.
Rapungcha.
Regalauncha.
Rochingacha.
Rokon.
Sábláteng.
Saiyopáchha.
Sakurmi.
Sámsong.
Sangsoi.
Salácho.
Salmáli.
Shopeng.
Sialjong.
Siptangia.
Sotangia.
Sukkim.
Sungdele.
Támring.
Tangahang.
Tangbuah.
Thámmi.
Tuila.
Turchan.
Tuya.
Ulumhang.
Umule.
Utepáchha.
Waidenhang.
Waitpang.
Wálaka.
Yankarung.
Yantambpa.
Yungchár.

# CHAPTER IX.

## OTHER RACES OF EASTERN NEPAL.

*viz.*: { 1. Sunuwárs.
2. Murmis or Lámás.

---

### SUNUWÁRS OR SUNPÁRS, ALSO CALLED MUKIAS.

THE names Sunuwár and Sunpár are said to be derived from the fact of these men residing either to the west or east of Sún Kosi river,—

| | | |
|---|---|---|
| Sunuwár | . . | West of Sún Kosi. |
| Sunpár | . . | East (or across) Sún Kosi. |

Mukia is the name given by the Gurkhá conquerors, and corresponds exactly with Subáh, or Rái, meaning chief.

The habitat of the Sunuwárs is on both banks of the Sún Kosi river, but more especially to the west and north, and they might roughly be described as inhabiting that portion of Népál which lies to the north of the Népál Valley, between the Gurungs on the west and the Ráis on the east, with Thibet as the northern boundary.

In appearance and physique they very much resemble the ordinary Magar and Gurung. They are most undoubtedly of Mongolian descent.

Their traditions state that they originally migrated from Thibet until they reached the basin of the Ganges in India, from whence they worked their way *viâ* Simraghur into Népál.

On reaching the Sún Kosi river they settled on both its banks, but more especially in the Dumja or Duluka district on the western side of the river.

One tradition says they left Thibet and reached India *viâ* Kashmir and the Punjab, whilst another one states that they came from Thibet *viâ* Assam, across the Brahmaputra, and so on.

At the time they reached or left Simraghur they consisted, so tradition says, of three tribes, the descendants of Jetha, Maila, and Khancha—

1. Jetha means eldest brother,
2. Maila means second brother,
3. Khancha means youngest brother.

The Jetha tribe having crossed the Sún Kosi proceeded north until they reached the Jiri and Siri rivers, where they settled down.

From the Jirikhola and Sirikhola are derived the Jiriel and Suriel tribes.

The Jetha branch of the Sunuwár nation was converted to Buddhism by the Lislet Lámás, and to this day, but in a modified and very lax manner, they adhere to Buddhist rites.

Hindu influences, however, are making themselves felt, and no doubt in the course of a few more years their religious belief will consist of a judicious mixture of the least inconvenient precepts of both religions, with an outward show of preference towards the Hindu form.

1. *Jetha.*—The descendants of the Jetha tribe are divided into ten tribes which are collectively called the Das Thare, and are said to consist of the following:—

| | |
|---|---|
| Jetha. | Suinu. |
| Jiriel. | Sunáme. |
| Krelu. | Suriel. |
| Mohria. | Thánu. |
| Pahária. | Wángdi. |

The Das Thare for the sake of convenience may be still called Buddhist, and they are distinctly in the minority now as compared to the Báráh Thare.

This is probably due to conversions brought about owing to the increased privileges which are accorded to the followers of the more favoured religion.

2. *Maila.*—The descendants of Maila remained in the country about the Sún Kosi river, but mostly on its eastern bank.

This branch of the Sunuwárs was converted by Brahmans to the Hindu religion which they to this day more or less profess.

They were, however, denied the sacred thread.—(*Jenái.*)

Their birth and death ceremonies are conducted by Opadhia Brahmans.

Collectively the Maila branch are called the Báráh Thare, and are said to have the same habits, customs, etc., as the Magars and Gurungs.

In the Népál army are to be found a number of Sunuwár soldiers, but they mostly belong to the Báráh Thare branch.

The Magars, Gurungs, and Sunuwárs are often called in Népál "Duwál bandi," "two bound together," and sometimes "Okhar Pangro," *viz.*, "Walnut and chestnut," the intention being to convey thereby that they are as closely related as one nut to another.

The Báráh Thare Sunuwárs' birth ceremony is carried out as follows:—

For the first eleven days after birth of child the mother is called Sutikah, and, being considered unclean, she is forbidden to eat or drink with any one else.

On the eleventh day a ceremony called "Nawáran" corresponding with our christening takes place; and the Opadhia Brahman gives a name to the child.

Five or six months later another ceremony takes place, which is called "Pásmi" or "Bhát khuwai," which means to "feed with rice." This is exactly the same as is carried out by Gurkhás as described at Chapter V, page 64.

The marriage ceremonies of the Báráh Thare Sunuwárs is again the same as that of Magars and Gurungs, and is called "Bhartmán" or "Karn Chalannu."

No Báráh Thare Sunuwár can marry a Das Thare Sunuwár or *vice versâ*.

2. *Khancha.*—The descendants of the Khancha branch set off to the south-east and are said to have assimilated themselves to such a degree with the Rais that they have practically been absorbed into and form a portion of the same.

It should be noticed that whilst the Das Thare tribes are still only ten in number, owing to the absence of caste in Buddhist religion, those of the Báráh Thare are very numerous.

For the sake of convenience the tribes of each division are now shown, with such few clans as I have found out after much trouble.

The Sunuwárs have very few prejudices, and until married will eat and drink equally with Magars, Gurungs, Limbús, and Ráis.

After marriage even they only draw the line at "dhál bhát" (see chapter on Gurkhás at page 72).

The Sunuwárs in appearance greatly resemble the ordinary Magar or Gurung as already mentioned, and would seem very desirable lads to enlist.

From personal observations I am led to believe that Sunuwárs are closely allied to Magars, Gurungs, and Ráis, with a touch of the Thibetan.

In the following list no doubt several clans are shown as tribes, and many tribes are also shown twice, once under their Khaskúra name and once in Súnkura.

The whole list is very incomplete and probably very inaccurate, but I have had very few opportunities of verifying the same, and only experience can give a more complete and accurate classification:—

*Báráh Thare Sunuwárs.*

Angwáchhá.
Bagalekiába.
Bámnayáta.
Barácha.
Báráh Thare.
Barmachha.
Bigia.
Boásuchha.
Bráhmilichha.
Bromlichho.
Bujichha.
Chappátichha.
Chár Thare.
Chhopatti.
Chiaba.
Chuichha.
Chuitichha
Chungpatti.
Darkháli.
Dasúchha.
Debbáchha.
Digercha.
Dinechha.
Durbichha.
Garachha.
Gnáwáchha.
Gutichha.
Haláwálichháwa.
Halwáchha.
Hamáli.
Howáli.
Jaspuchha.
Jenti.
Jespuchha.
Jitichha.
Karmach.
Katichha.
Katilich.
Kiába.
Kijowár.
Kintichha.
Kiúduchha.
Kormochha.
Kyahbochha.
Kyongpotichha.
Lachpáli.
Lákach.
Lákácháwa.
Laspáchha.
Liiámi.
Linhochha.
Liokichha.
Lokke.
Longku.
Lungkuchha.
Nahási.
Namfelich.
Náochha.
Noplichhá.
Ohndé.
Párgachha.
Párgháli.
Phatich.
Phewalichha.
Pirtiwál.
Prágáchha.
Prápchap.
Pritichha.
Rápichha.
Ráráchába.
Ráwáchha.
Risich.
Rudichha.
Rupáchha.
Sahpráli.
Sabrachha.
Saipulie.
Sanpráchha.
Shushichha.
Siochul.
Suchha.
Sutichha.
Súyúchulung.
Tangkercha.
Tapaj.
Taruch.
Thokláchha.
Tholochha.
Thumuchha.
Tokuchha.
Tungkuchha.
Tungruch.
Tusuchha.
Yaktachha.
Yátá.
Yeti.

Liiámi Khaskura for Linnocha Sunkúr
Sápráli do. Sahprachha do.
Pirtiwál do. Pargá ha do.

*Das Thare Sunuwárs.*

| | |
|---|---|
| Jetha. | Suinu. |
| Jiriel. | Sunáme. |
| Krelu. | Surel. |
| Mohria. | Thánu. |
| Pahária. | Wangdi. |

BÁRÁHTHARE CLANS.

*ujichcha (Clans).*

| | |
|---|---|
| Goruphile. | Makephite. |
| Jetburaphile. | Nahasojphite. |

*Jenti (Clans).*

| | | |
|---|---|---|
| Chich. | Nahaphilich. | Tankunch. |
| Jobo. | Nawachha. | Turasuch. |
| Karmachha. | Pritichha. | Wachpoli. |
| Láwá. | Rupa. | |
| Maolichha. | Sáwachha. | |

*Linhochha or Lilámi (Clans).*

| | |
|---|---|
| Baibungie. | Tinbungie. |

*Yátá (Clans).*

| | | |
|---|---|---|
| Bakali. | Grámsing. | Pakále. |
| Bame. | Homáli. | Piwaklite. |
| Bámans. | Khása. | Surkeli. |
| Chitowli. | Namárech. | |
| Garshi. | Pacheibaki. | |

## MURMIS, ALSO CALLED LÁMÁS OR TAMANGS, ISHÁNGS OR SAINGS.

The Murmis have the following tradition regarding their origin. Once upon a time three brothers, by name Brahma, Vishnu, and Mahesur, went out shooting. All day long they wandered about the jungle, but saw no deer nor game of any kind, until they suddenly came across a "Gauri Gai" or cow bison.

Vishnu killed the same with an arrow, and all three being tired and hungry they prepared to get the carcase ready for food. Having skinned the animal, and having extracted the bowels, Mahesur as the youngest brother was given the latter to wash in a stream which ran close by. Whilst Mahesur was washing the bowels in the stream, Brahma and Vishnu cooked the meat on a fire and prepared it for food, with salt and spices, and then divided it into three equal portions, one for each of them.

When the meat was ready to eat Brahma said to Vishnu: "Oh, brother, this is cow's meat and we cannot therefore partake of it."

Thereupon Brahma and Vishnu each hid his share.

When Mahesur returned from having washed and cleaned the intestines, Brahma and Vishnu both said: "We have eaten our own shares of meat, being very hungry, but here is yours all ready, so eat it now and be strong."

Mahesur thereupon eat his share in front of them, after which Brahma and Vishnu showed their concealed shares, and abused Mahesur for having partaken of cow's meat.

Mahesur thereupon became very angry and struck both his brothers with the intestines, some of which clung round the shoulders of Brahma and Vishnu, and which accounts for the wearing of the sacred thread.

From having eaten cow's meat Mahesur was degraded socially, and hence cow-eaters like the Murmis are followers of his. The Murmis say that "Narayan," "Bhaguwán," that is, God, created the three brothers: Brahma the eldest, Vishnu the second, and Mahesur the youngest, and that from Mahesur are descended the present race called Murmis or Lámás.

Mahesur intercedes to God for the Lámás and is therefore their patron saint.

Hamilton writing in 1819 says:—

" The Murmis or Lámás are by many considered a branch of Bhutias.

" They have such an appetite for beef that they cannot abstain from oxen that die a natural death, as they are not now permitted to kill the sacred animal.

" The Gurkháli by way of ridicule call the Murmis 'Siyena Bhutias,' or 'Bhutias who eat carrion.'

" They follow the profession of agriculture, and of carrying loads, being a people uncommonly robust."

Most of Sir Bir Sham Sher's coolies on shooting trips are Murmis.

The Murmis or Lámás are divided into two great divisions :—

1. Báráthamang.
2. Atháráját.

The Báráthamang are the pure Murmis and they claim descent direct from Mahesur, and are considered socially superior to the Atháráját, but only slightly so, and only amongst themselves.

The Murmis show in a marked manner that they come of Mongolian stock. In fact they probably are nothing more or less than a Thibetan tribe whose ancestors wandered into Népál. Ancient history would seem to point out that they were the original inhabitants of the Népál Valley, but that after a certain lapse of time they were conquered by some other races who subjected them to many indignities, and made practically slaves of them, forcing them do all the hard labour, such as tilling fields, carrying loads, hewing wood, etc., etc.

To escape this, numbers wandered away into Eastern Népál, and settled there.

Intermarriage, or anyhow connection with other races for ages, has had the natural effect of giving to what was probably a pure Thibetan tribe, a certain foreign strain which can be traced in the appearance of almost every Murmi nowadays.

To this day other races in Népál look upon Murmis as Bhutiás, and I have myself heard a recruit return himself as a Bhutiá Murmi.

There is no doubt that many Thibetans and Lepchas have been admitted into the Murmi nation as members of the same.

Being merely Thibetans there was no such thing as caste

amongst the Murmis in olden days, and although prior to the Gurkhá conquest the Murmis were divided into Báráthamang and Atháráját, nevertheless there was no social difference between them.

Prior to the Gurkhá conquest the Báráthamangs and Athárájat eat and drank together and intermarried.

The term Athárájat was given in those days to the progeny of a Murmi with any foreigner, merely as a distinctive name for a mixed breed, but it in no ways caused any social superiority or inferiority. This breed, although of mixed blood, was accepted into the Murmi nationality without question and enjoyed all the privileges of any other Murmi.

But with the Gurkhá conquest and the consequent influences brought to bear, many changes have taken place, and are doing so more and more, and the line drawn between the Báráthamang and the Athárájat is much more strongly defined now, and no doubt fifty years hence the rules which exist at present regarding social customs, marriages, etc., will have undergone still greater modifications.

In this book the peculiarities of the Murmis will be discussed as they actually exist now.

The national name is Murmi or Lámá or Thamang. Questioning men of the race would be as follows:—

| | | |
|---|---|---|
| What is your name? | . | Narbir. |
| What are you? | . | Murmi, Lámá, or Thamang. |
| What Thamang? | . | Báráthamang or Athárájat. |
| What Báráthamang? | . | Ghising. |
| What is your kipat? | . | Taljun. |

The Báráthamang is divided into a large number of tribes. The Athárájat into three only, *viz.*, (1) Gothar, (2) Narba, (3) Sangri.

A Báráthamang cannot marry any of the Athárájat except the Narba, and then only if the Narba's ancestors have been pure Narbas for three generations.

Báráthamangs can eat all and every kind of food with Narbas. They can also eat all kinds of food with Gothar and Sángri, but with the one exception of dhál and rice.

Before the Gurkhá conquest there were no restrictions of any kind, and Báráthamangs and Athárájats could eat all and every kind of food together.

In certain cases the illegitimate progeny of Báráthamangs

with Athárájáts have been and are promoted into the former, but in most they remain in the lower grade, namely, Athárájáts.

No Báráthamang can marry into his own tribe, but with a few exceptions he can marry into any of the other tribes of the Báráthamang.

A Ghising, for instance, can marry any Báráthamang, except Ghisings, Giábás, Los, and Lopchans.

A Mokthan can marry any Báráthamáng, except Mokthans, Mikchans, Siángdans, and Thokars.

Originally the Báráthamangs were divided into twelve tribes only. The following are said to be the original ones :—

| | | |
|---|---|---|
| Baju. | Giábá. | Pákrim. |
| Bal. | Gole. | Siángdan. |
| Dumjan. | Mikchan. | Thing. |
| Ghising. | Mokthan. | Yonjan. |

Nowadays there are a very much larger number, a list of which is given further on.

A curious point about Murmis, whether of the Báráthamang or of the Athárájat, is that there are no clans. Each man can only give his tribe. Thus, Ghisings and their lawful progeny remain always Ghisings, and Ghisings only.

There are no clans of Ghisings.

Some of the Báráthamang tribes, however, have what thay call "kipats," *viz.*, "original homes.'

The first and original home of the Ghisings is said to be Taljun, but as they increased in numbers, the Ghisings spread out and formed other homes ; thus we find the Modi, Tilbung, etc. These again formed fresh homes for themselves as they increased in numbers, but they are not to be considered as subdivisions or clans of the Ghisings, but merely "kipats" or places of residence.

Thus a Taljun Ghising is merely a Ghising residing in Taljun, or descended from a Ghising resident of Taljun, and he is in every respect neither more nor less than any other Ghising, whether a resident of Modi, Mirgie, Tilbung, or any other "kipat," and he therefore cannot marry any other Ghising.

A pure-bred Báráthamang will always be able to give his "kipat," and hence to find out whether any man really is what he represents himself to be, I give further on all such "kipats" as I have been able to find.

The Athárájat, as already mentioned, are divided into three great tribes:—

1. Gothar. 2. Narba. 3. Sángri.

There are no subdivisions to these.

1. *Gothar.*—The Gothars are the progeny of Murmis with Brahmans, Chettries, or Thákurs. As long as one of the parents, either the father or the mother, was a Murmi, and the other a Brahman, Chettri, or Thákur, the progeny becomes a Gothar.

In olden days (prior to Gurkhá conquest) the progeny of Murmis with Khas became Gothars, but since the conquest they are called Khattris.

A Narba is the progeny born of intercourse between Murmis and Newárs. As long as one of the parents was a Murmi and the other a Newár, the progeny becomes a Narba.

A Narba who can prove his descent for three generations from pure Narbas can marry into the Bárátham ang.

A Sángri is the progeny of a Murmi with Magar, Gurung, Limbú, Rái, or Sunuwár.

As long as one of the parents was a Murmi and the other one of the five classes mentioned, the progeny becomes a Sángri.

The Narba has the highest social standing amongst the Athárájат, and ranks nearly equal to the Báráthamang.

Very good recruits can be obtained from the Murmis as far as physique goes. The Báráthamangs are much the most numerous.

*Athárájat Murmis.*

| 1. Gothar. | 2. Narba. | 3. Sángri. |
|---|---|---|

*Báráthamang Murmis.*

Baju.
Bal.
Baltong (promoted from Atháráját).
Blan.*
Bomjan.
Chapenkor (promoted from Bhotia).
Chumi (probably Jumi).
Dáon.
Dongba.
Dúmjan.
Gámdem (promoted from Athárájat).
Ghising.
Giábá.
Glan.
Gole.
Gomden.
Gongbá.
Grandan.

Hopthen.
Jimba.
Jongan (promoted from Athá-ráját).
Juni.
Khanikor (promoted from Bhotia).
Khiungbá.
Kitung.
Kulden.
Lámágonju.
Lámákhor.
Lo.
Lopchan.
Lungba.
Márnumba.
Mekchan.
Moktang.
Neki } promoted from Athá-ráját.
Nesur }
Pakrim.
Palchoke.
Rumbha.
Sharbakhor (promoted from Bhotia).
Siándan.
Singar.
Singdan.
Songden.
Siangbo.
Tonwaira } promoted from Athá-ráját.
Toisien }
Thing.
Thokar.
Titung.
Tunbahr (promoted from Bhotia).
Waiva.
Yonjan.

The following are the few "kipats" I have been able to find :—

*Bhomjan Kipats.*

Hebung.
Námlang.

*Ghising Kipats.*

Bhisil.
Karju.
Mirgie.
Modi.
Náhja.
Phetali.
Tálju.
Tilbung.

*Moktang Kipats.*

Barkháni.
Bhoja.
Jegún.
Káman.
Márga.
Márkháni.
Phasku.
Popti.
Rite.
Thapkan.

*Yonjan Kipats.*

Dáhding.
Dáwú.
Púlbung
Risángu.

*Palchoka Kipat.*

Siangbo.

# CHAPTER X.

## LIST OF TEHSILS AND VILLAGES OF CENTRAL NÉPÁL.

### BÁGLUNG.

*Villages belonging to Báglung Tehsil.*

Báchigáon.
Bágbing.
Balewá.
Balkot.
Ballia.
Bángá.
Bángdúk.
Bankewá.
Bánskhark.
Bánskhola.
Banung.
Bárah.
Bátale.
Bátchigáon.
Bhágkemiti.
Bhalkot.
Bháonkholá.
Bhimpokhrá.
Bhimá.
Bimákot.
Birkot.
Bitreni.
Bokharni.
Bokiámdi.
Boksing.
Brangja.
Burákot.
Buráthok.
Chakchake.
Cháhare.
Chanderkot.
Chimkhola.
Chioribot.
Chouban.
Choras.
Chúniamurá.
Chunkholá.
Chupkholá.
Chusúkholá.
Damek.
Dajman.
Dángnám.
Dángsing.
Dárbing.
Dármijá.
Deorali.
Dhaduwa.
Dhárápáni.
Dharm.
Dhobá.
Dhottham.
Drabdi.
Drámkháni.
Fagám.
Gairágáon.
Gajuri.
Galkot.
Ghanrung.
Ghára.
Ghi.
Ghiring.
Goáran.
Goera.
Gurjá.
Gurungdi.
Halwa.
Hile.
Histáng.
Husláng.
Iming.
Istám.
Jhulbáng.
Jingkani.
Jinia.
Jumla.
Kahare and Kaigiá.
Kakre.
Kaleri.
Kamire.
Karadi.
Karagaon.
Kebáng.
Khabre.
Khárákáni.
Kiángsi.
Kimle.
Kitini.
Kordánrá.
Kotgáon.
Kujibáng.
Kunákánrá.
Kuudle.
Kurjá.
Lakáni.
Lame.
Lámágáon.
Lebáng.
Lespár.
Logum.
Lopre.
Lúghon.
Mahata.
Majakuruwa.
Májkot.
Malja.
Malkábáng.
Maráng.
Modi.

BAGLUNG—*continued.*

Mohato.
Moring
Múná.
Muru.
Nayagaon.
Nepáni.
Nigálpáni.
Nimtol.
Nindechaur.
Niskot.
Niskun.
Nisi.
Ouákot.
Padámi.
Pagdár.
Pakdowár.
Palkú.
Pálpálichháp.
Parábáng.
Páodánrá.
Patár.
Patlekhet
Páticham..
Phángá.

Piung.
Purtibang.
Ráikhani.
Ráipur.
Rákhu.
Ranche.
Rangsing.
Rasa.
Rasdáng.
Rastál.
Ratnechaur.
Rego.
Resi.
Rukum.
Runmá.
Sabit.
Sákindánrá.
Salisa.
Sángekot.
Sarbudánrá.
Sarntár.
Sherá.
Sidedkot.

Sikdi.
Sikha.
Silkot.
Siltumg.
Simáherá.
Sirukhark.
Sirseni.
Táka.
Tamán.
Tamrán
Tangli
Tánkot
Tevási.
Thák.
Thalkot.
Thálung.
Thantháp.
Tilahar.
Titeni.
Titing.
Torikhola.
Úndá.
Wakli.

BANDIPUR.

Aletár.
Ámdánrá.
Árkhole.
Bachhaitar.
Bálihok.
Bánspani.
Bhausar.
Bhirkuná.
Binikot.
Bising.
Chanchil.
Chandoli.
Chápthar.
Chhanung.
Dánrágaon.
Dhanung.
Dharampáni.
Dhenri.
Dhor.

Doriámá.
Drungchung.
Gamrá.
Gargáon.
Gázátári.
Gihásthok.
Gisithok.
Giring.
Hilekhark.
Huslang.
Jahargáon.
Jalwáng.
Kacháp.
Kálche.
Kaleri.
Kartop.
Kolakáni.
Kunúng.
Lámágáon.

Máirá.
Mirlung.
Mohore.
Muchák.
Nábájú.
Naiágáon.
Naram.
Nibúapari
Páchthar.
Pákáthok.
Palteng.
Perung.
Pipalnálá.
Rámkot.
Sebring.
Simpáni.
Sunákot.
Táruká.
Thapre.

BANDIPUR—*continued.*

Tinang.
Ting.
Úmchok.
Wákle.
Yamchok.

BHIRKOT.

Amildung.
Artal.
Arukhark.
Atthar.
Bájdái.
Baleo.
Banáre.
Barágáon.
Bardánrá.
Bárle.
Bhaluadánrá.
Budipur.
Cháháre.
Chaigmi.
Chainpur.
Chángsing.
Jháp.
Chapte.
Chépung
Chiária.
Chibung.
Chitra.
Dánrágáon.
Dánrákot.
Dharampáni.
Dháring.
Dháp.
Dhápu.
Durchung.
Gahate.
Gáondánrá.
Gáonka.
Giámisowárá.
Gainsing.
Girchat.
Gobrehota.
Guárdi.
Gurbal.
Gurdánrá.
Hukádánrá.
Járpandánrá.
Jepúndánrá.
Jélong.
Jháuri.
Jogithum.
Kálche.
Káfaldánrá.
Kalku.
Kánre.
Karon Sowárá.
Kawári.
Kebang.
Kekmi.
Khairekot.
Kiágmi.
Kihung.
Kighá.
Kijinás.
Kilung.
Kohidim.
Kohúng.
Kokhiá.
Kumirjung.
Kutamso.
Lámdánrá.
Magem.
Málágiri.
Malingkot.
Mohore.
Mugrani.
Námjákot.
Nayagaon.
Pánglúng.
Patrá.
Rángbháng.
Rágná.
Rahu.
Rapakot.
Rastal.
Rayále.
Sákhar.
Sakhep.
Sámákot.
Samris.
Samús.
Sankar.
Sápangdi.
Sallián.
Sarbor.
Sekám.
Sildánrá.
Sirukhark.
Surung.
Tarke.
Totke.
Udcssi.
Umlungá.

DAILAKH.

Balwádánrá.
Bhirkona.
Biánsi.
Charkule.
Chátikot.
Chitarkot.
Cholpa.
Dabra.
Dánrágáon.
Githákot.
Guari.
Kábrechaur.
Kálimati.
Kálitáker.
Kara.
Khárigáirá.
Pákhápáni.
Pinchaur.

## DAILAKH—*continued.*

Rákmiá.
Ránikot.
Ratikhola.
Ráto.
Ritedánrá.
Simtá.
Sirpa.
Tárápáni.
Toli.
Weri.

## GALKOT.

Hil.
Riga.
Ruma.
Tanter.

## GARHUNG.

Andhigáon.
Ándhikholá.
Aonle.
Arghá.
Arjewá.
Arungkot.
Bajáhkot.
Bajangkot.
Balám.
Balthung.
Bangráti.
Banjáng.
Bankatta.
Bardanra.
Barki.
Barlálung.
Beleha.
Belkákot.
Bhounriá.
Birgá.
Bohre.
Chap.
Chapkot.
Chárkot.
Chiruwa.
Dángsing.
Dhore.
Gahatia.
Gajuri.
Galkot.
Garángdi.
Giája.
Gijantis.
Gurungdi.
Gurunggáon.
Jimuwa.
Káchikot.
Kaleri.
Kaphaldánra.
Kapurdi.
Kárkikot.
Kátákot.
Limdánra.
Madái.
Mahundánrá.
Májkot.
Majmare.
Minamkot.
Nayakark.
Pakbádi.
Peku.
Pelákot.
Pitle.
Pokwádi.
Rangdang.
Rasikholá.
Salángkot.
Siálkot.
Sirkot.
Sirsekot.
Sorel.
Tari.
Telákot.
Tevási.
Thánidánrá.
Thanthháp.
Thápke.
Turkot.
Weghá.

## GURHKA.

Abri.
Ámdánrá.
Ajirkot.
Áru.
Arwat.
Aunle.
Bagepáni.
Balsohorá.
Bángábári.
Barbáh.
Bardánrá.
Barpák.
Baseri.
Batáse.
Betáni.
Bhábre.
Bhiáguti.
Bhounrábári.
Birsing.
Bubre.
Bunkot.
Champáni.
Chautrá.
Chengle.
Chiápsá.
Chilang.
Chipliati.
Dánrágáon.
Dánrápáni.
Darbhú.

GURKHÁ—*continued.*

Darling.
Deoráli.
Dhansiorá.
Dhárapáni.
Dibling.
Dúánkot.
Finám.
Gáikhur.
Gáirun.
Gajuri.
Gandrá.
Garung.
Gegrichhap.
Genchok.
Gharung.
Gumdi.
Harme.
Harpia.
Hirkot.
Jánrung.
Járang.
Jhár.
Jiori.
Kaijalpáni.
Kaleri.
Kamchok.
Katunje.
Khanchok.
Khari.
Kharkkot.
Khopláng.
Kokeá.
Kumpur.
Kushene.
Laguwa.
Láku.
Lámachástará.
Láme.
Liglig.
Limi.
Machel.
Makaipur.
Makesing.
Manokámná.
Máte.
Meláng.
Mengbu.
Millim.
Mirkot.
Mukásing.
Mulábári.
Nawakot.
Nayagaon.
Nepáni.
Ochreni.
Pairia.
Palba.
Pákhuria.
Pám.
Pásláng.
Pausra.
Phenám.
Pipalthok.
Pirájung.
Pokhrithok.
Ponjai.
Purkot.
Ráinás.
Ránágaon.
Saláng.
Sallian.
Sekám.
Siártung.
Siláng kot.
Sinachor.
Siranchok.
Sirjor.
Sunjung
Táklung.
Taksar.
Tákur.
Tanchok.
Taulechauk.
Tunnáne.
Udaipur.
Waihak.

GULMI.

Ápun.
Ámbote.
Ámchaur.
Arbhákot.
Archanwás.
Ardewá.
Arghá.
Arghathok.
Arkhole.
Badánrá.
Balkot.
Balthum.
Banga.
Báraghare.
Bárlebás.
Barsiah.
Bátechaur.
Bátlechaur.
Bhárse.
Bhátgáon.
Bhorel.
Bhutuka
Birkot.
Biskhark.
Bokeni.
Bomghá.
Bud.
Buchipúr.
Burathok.
Chahare.
Chaidpáni.
Chandarkot.
Chháp.
Chiápáni.
Chidi.
Chiúrgaha.
Chirigha.
Chitpur.
Choegá.
Dagunkháni.
Dáhá.
Dajákot.

GULMI—*continued.*

Darámkháni.
Darbam.
Dhaireni.
Dharampáni.
Dhamsikot.
Dháp.
Dhát.
Digám.
Digáro.
Dhongá.
Dowlejil.
Durlám.
Gabatdánra.
Giausing.
Ghorle.
Gurbakote.
Gwádi.
Hile.
Hungá.
Jabung.
Jagun.
Jamad.
Jogithum.
Johang.
Jnnia.
Kabrebhat.
Kálidánrá.
Kánichor,
Kariul.
Karkikot.
Káwole.
Kerúngá.
Kidim.
Kongdi.
Lámkánrá.
Limghá.
Litung.
Lumpek.
Májkot.
Manhare.
Mánkot.
Matukáni.
Máyágáon.
Minamkot.
Mohane.
Mohore.
Motuka.
Misughá.
Múru.
Náitál.
Nayágáon.
Nayákoni.
Náykot.
Nidur.
Okhaldhungá.
Oliháng.
Pálpáthok.
Pálung.
Parálmi.
Palmi.
Phoksing.
Púnkhá.
Ráili.
Rájá.
Rami.
Ramichháp.
Rámkani.
Rángbás.
Rátámati.
Ránisowárá.
Runkhá.
Rupákot.
Ságdi.
Sakh.
Sardi.
Sáyá.
Setung.
Simichaur.
Sukorá.
Tamári.
Tárábáng.
Thanthάp.
Thansing.
Tin Gharia.
Torga.
Tulakot.
Tunga.
Tutáng.
Ulibáng.
Urlemi.

GURBAKOT.

Checherai.
Julpila.

ISMA.

Arewá.
Baiskhani.
Bhimkholá.
Chháp.
Darbáng.
Gamir.
Gayábári.
Holá.
Kábre.
Kaleri.
Karnkot.
Kateri.
Mehlá.
Morgáng.
Nelágáon.
Netádárling.
Powá.
Purkot.

KÁSKI.

Bumdi.
Lunghi.
Naganpur.
Ribang.

## KHANCHI.

Ámdánrá.
Argha.
Arjan.
Awál.
Bámruk.
Bánskhark.
Budank.
Buranmára.
Dánrágáon.
Dánrápáni.
Dekhoro.
Dhanrákedim.
Dhor.
Durkota.
Gorlundá.
Halde.
Hansápur.
Indrek.
Janni.
Jukiáná.
Jura.
Kimdánrá.
Jámátol.
Maubág.
Pátandánrá.
Pátle.
Pokhardánrá.
Sákindhánrá.
Samáni.
Shidánrá.
Sihár.
Surkholá.

## KUSMÁ.

Bájung.
Balkot.
Durláng.
Gendi.
Ghánruk.
Kenga.
Kuphilchám.
Lángdi.
Lesbor.
Sábit.

## KUT.

Arka.
Bahálkot.
Bángá.
Bitreni.
Chirbáng.
Harpe.
Khâre.
Kholsebáng.
Kudámkholá.
Lebáng.
Nâlesbáng.
Puja.
Sirbáng.
Thamán.

## LAJUNG.

Narinchor.
Nayagaon.

## MUSHIKOT.

Daha.
Daza.
Dazakot.
Kudri.
Sakul.

## NEPÁL.

Abri.
Argádim.
Assare.
Bakrá.
Baljin.
Bárámulá.
Bhim.
Burán.
Chanchil.
Chando.
Dawáchok.
Dhonkâthâ.
Dhychhâp.
Dumja.
Durâsá.
Durmijá.
Fedáp.
Gairúgn.
Gajuriperá.
Garangdi.
Guâng.
Hánsidol.
Hátipáilá.
Jamiria.
Jhálkelari.
Jhargáon.
Kibáng.
Korku.
Koyâpáni.
Lungle.
Maidi.
Majigaon.

NEPAL—*continued.*

Manárâ.
Maráng.
Nadkot.
Rájbárá.
Siártúng.
Siburi.
Sika.
Sikhári.
Thelá.
Tishtung.

## NUWAKOT.

Arthar.
Báglung.
Baldánrá.
Bardánra.
Bárrá.
Básen.
Basnapúr.
Bástar.
Bhalthung.
Bhangara.
Busnápur.
Chápre.
Chepár.
Dáding.
Dánragaonra.
Dánráthok.
Deoráli.
Dháur.
Dopahare.
Gaira.
Gayá.
Gerku.
Gurjá.
Jamunia.
Kabilás.
Kahare.
Káhule.
Kakmi.
Kalianpur.
Kálku.
Kaonli.
Karkigaon.
Kinchit.
Kiristi.
Kodánra.
Kolmá.
Lajiáng.
Lámchháp.
Lámichor.
Lanchiá.
Limia.
Limitâr.
Magarnás.
Maidi.
Maidision.
Matikháni.
Namcheu.
Nayagáon.
Páku.
Pátchok.
Pokhrá.
Poye.
Pulkachor.
Putlikhat.
Rájwára.
Rámkot.
Rátámáti.
Sandhikholá.
Satikot.
Sirkot.
Sisápáni.
Sisneri.
Taksâr.
Tarle.
Tháná.
Totke.

## PÁLPÁ.*

Adámára.
Aglung.
Akhárthok.
Altong.
Amdánrá.
Amile.
Andhiárákholá.
Arehate.
Arewá.
Argáli.
Arghá.
Arghásing.
Árkhole.
Asssáre.
Bádarpur.
Bagáliá.
Bagnás.
Báhádurpur.
Baldenggari.
Balgá.
Balthúng.
Bandrikánrá.
Bángláng.
Bangung.
Bánká.
Bansidáurá.
Baráchuli.
Barákot.
Barángdi.
Bardánrá.
Barektung.
Bárikot.
Barkul.
Basnápur.
Bátásár.
Batáse.
Bayám.
Beldáurá.
Beluá.
Besagá.
Bhajári.
Bhangi.
Bharek.
Bháronsio.
Bháwgá.

* Tansen is practically the same as Pálpá, and hence all villages of the former is included under heading of Pálpá.

PÁLPÁ—*continued.*

Bhirpáni.
Bhustung.
Bhutuko.
Birkot.
Bisundánrá.
Boighá.
Bolanje.
Bolipokhrá.
Borsiá.
Botákuná.
Boza.
Bujúng.
Bulbúle.
Bumgas.
Burathok.
Burikot.
Chábáre.
Chálku.
Changále.
Chapthok.
Chárghare.
Chidipáni.
Chilángdi.
Chistung.
Choraku.
Chorkot.
Dánrádum.
Dánrágáon.
Dánráthok.
Dánsing.
Darámpaud.
Dargá.
Darkasing.
Dawári.
Dáyá.
Deochuliboiá.
Deoghir.
Deoráli.
Deorálithok.
Dhabitang.
Dilungá.
Dhirkhark.
Dhobádi.
Dholimorá.
Dhiajú.
Dhustung.
Durcha.
Durdung.
Galdo.
Ganrakot.
Garkani.
Gayáthok.
Gensingchháp.
Ghamire.
Ghanpokhrá.
Gherdi.
Ghotási.
Giájá.
Goithán.
Gokhungá.
Golipátan.
Gopálchháp.
Gorlikhark.
Gothádi.
Grángdi.
Gumbá.
Gumrá.
Gurbhákot.
Gurungjung.
Hanjiabári.
Harpiákhark.
Hátigonnrá.
Hekláng.
Honsák.
Huksiákot.
Humin.
Hunga.
Hungi.
Huwádi.
Jabhung.
Jabkári.
Jamire.
Jarbáns.
Jarlángdi.
Jehungi.
Jhamrang.
Jherdi.
Jhirrá.
Kadhár.
Káfalbensi.
Kahare.
Kahseni.
Kaleri.
Kángrung.
Kánibás.
Karamdi.
Karamkot.
Karanghá.
Karbung.
Karikot.
Kehádánrá.
Kekláng.
Kenarung.
Kernedánrá.
Kertung.
Kiámrung.
Kiodánrá.
Kiun.
Kobári.
Koká.
Kokalchháp.
Koldánrá.
Konádánrá.
Koplák.
Kotla.
Kuákot.
Kudánr..
Kunápáni.
Kurgá.
Kurjáng.
Kuslang.
Lánkhuri.
Lápe.
Limdem.
Limpáta.
Limtáng.
Loreng.
Lumbás.
Mádi.
Máhákál.
Majkot.
Málágachi.
Mangare.
Manwá.
Maráng.
Marángkot.
Mársidánrá.
Masem.

PÁLPÁ—*continued.*

Máthá.
Mehildháp.
Mewábári.
Mitel.
Mohadánrá.
Mohore.
Morung.
Mothábári.
Mujung.
Musikot.
Nachuni.
Naher.
Naitola.
Namidánrá.
Namta.
Naram.
Naramchháp.
Nayagaon.
Nayágari.
Nayápáti.
Nayár.
Nuwákot.
Okhlia.
Pabáng.
Paklua.
Páktung.
Palasardanra.
Páligbá.
Páltung.
Pálung.
Pangria.
Pánikot.
Párakthok.
Pátan.
Pátle.
Páundi.
Pihaldánrá.
Piluá.
Pipalchháp.
Pipaldánrá.
Pokhri.
Porkáni.
Postádikholá.
Pototi.
Púngá.
Rabás.
Ralábas.
Ramchia.
Rámpur.
Rátámáti.
Rimghá.
Roiá.
Rucháng.
Rukse.
Rulbáns.
Rumsi.
Sákine.
Sálbás.
Saleot.
Saliánthan.
Samánchi.
Samangkot.
Samot.
Samúngá.
Sanáhúngi.
Sáone.
Satbáh.
Sateoti.
Satigarhi.
Satukol.
Shikarkot.
Siahju.
Siándánrá.
Sidhipáni.
Sikár.
Sikárdánrá.
Sildung.
Silingi.
Silna.
Siluwá.
Simaldánra.
Sinchás.
Sindánrá.
Singehás.
Sirtúng.
Siún.
Somre.
Somerdi.
Sungdi.
Tahnu.
Tálájerdi.
Táltung.
Tamás.
Tamasdánrá.
Tánsing.
Táprek.
Táre.
Tátam.
Tekjor.
Thánsil.
Thápákot.
Tinghére.
Uládi.
Wángsijung.
Wotáng.

PARWADANRA.

Aruchor.
Báchok.
Balkot.
Balewá.
Bánglichok.
Baráng.
Bárapá.
Barigaon.
Bansiá.
Bánspáni.
Bateri.
Bátichour.
Bazarkot.
Bidiáni.
Bumlichok.
Cháinpur.
Chámlilá.
Chaotán.
Chárthar.
Chindekhark.
Chisungá.
Choudelá.
Dailung.
Dakapludi.
Dángsáng.
Darawá.
Deoráli.

PARWADANRA—*continued.*

Dhanrákátin.
Dhur.
Durá.
Durshá.
Gamárchok.
Gásepateá.
Gemi.
Ghanpokhrá.
Ghote.
Gobre.
Ghousi.
Hárigáon.
Jarkhán.
Jitá.
Jitákot.
Káfaldánra.
Kalki.
Kareli.
Karni.
Káski.
Keraonbote.
Kubli.
Kúnchha.
Lákájung.
Lámágáon.
Lamelung.
Lamjúng.
Lamtong.
Lubhung.
Lumgá.
Lumpex.
Máling.
Májkhark.
Mirlung.
Naotár.
Narwál.
Nawáthár.
Páchok.
Pasrikos.
Pándánrá.
Páninúnkháni.
Pátle.
Pátlighárá.
Pirajung.
Porthok.
Punia.
Puránkot.
Ráinás.
Pámchok.
Ramgá.
Ratanpur.
Sálburu.
Sámakot.
Sángdi.
Sangapo.
Sanjao.
Silánchour.
Simle.
Sirápáni.
Siringchok.
Sirseni.
Sukiakot.
Tákkia.
Tákoun.
Tándráng.
Tápákot.
Thánsing.
Tilár.
Titákot.
Toksa.
Ukári.

PIÚTHAN.

Amáre.
Amili.
Aoútkot.
Arghám.
Arjan.
Arkha.
Árkul.
Asurkot.
Áwá.
Báche.
Bádam.
Bágcháre.
Bajang.
Balkot.
Bánchkot.
Bandikot.
Bánskoh.
Bardánrá.
Báring.
Belbás.
Beteni.
Bhángbari.
Bhansár.
Biansi.
Bijuar.
Bijúli.
Birimkot.
Bithrikot.
Bitrá.
Budúmárá.
Búichipe.
Bukeni.
Bunari.
Buronlá.
Chaiba.
Cháklághát.
Chálbáng.
Chháton.
Chidikhola.
Chidipáni.
Chungjá.
Dákákot.
Damri.
Dángmáng.
Dángsár.
Dárlim.
Dhanrechor.
Dhanúbáns.
Dhungá.
Dhairkhark.
Dhandu.
Dharampáni.
Dhobing.
Dhungárkot.
Dhungegari.
Dobichor.
Fagám.

PIÚTHAN—*continued.*

Faľámkhilli.
Gájákhark.
Gámo.
Ghám.
Gowánpáni.
Goulkot.
Gumchál.
Hámrikot.
Harám.
Harchang.
Harmaki.
Hobing.
Hogám.
Jalbang.
Jaljaláh.
Jamán.
Jaspur.
Jimi.
Jogikhark.
Jumrikánrá.
Kabrechour.
Kairan.
Karáh.
Karakhola.
Káte.
Khabáng.
Kharin.
Khung.
Kigi.
Kole.
Koligáon.
Kuchibáng.
Kuta.
Kutichor.
Lápál.
Libang.
Lighá.
Lukurbang.
Mabhár.
Machiná.
Madhári.
Majkot.
Mándre.
Mándrechháp.
Mándrechour.
Marántháná.
Márkhábáng.
Mirlúng.
Moráng.
Mundanra.
Nagar.
Narikot.
Nassa.
Nayakot.
Nimkhark.
Pakhádi.
Pángi.
Pángre.
Parikánra.
Pátlopáni.
Phalánto.
Phátá.
Pong.
Pupli.
Purkot.
Purtibang.
Rajuni.
Rámli.
Rámlikánrá.
Rángse.
Ranikot.
Ráspur.
Riji.
Rángá.
Sagin.
Sájekot.
Sákia.
Saktuma.
Sánghú.
Sari.
Simaldánra.
Siole.
Siripáni.
Sirpu.
Sirni.
Sirpá.
Sirpár.
Sirseni.
Siúlibáng.
Siúre.
Tápá.
Tarátúng.
Tuni.
Udiapur.
Uma.
Uwagáon.

PIWANGMI.

Báchá.
Badsháh.
Bálákot.
Damárgáon.
Dánsing.
Deoráli.
Dewánkot.
Duráthok.
Ganespur.
Hasrángi.
Hatiá.
Lunkú.
Narkot.
Nawákhark.
Páyunbátchá.
Rabáj.

POKHRA.

Alkátár.
Anpádu.
Apu.
Arghá.
Arghúm.
Armol.

POKHRA—*continued*.

Armoládánrá.
Arwa.
Astáum.
Badon.
Baghiá.
Báhákot.
Baidirsing.
Baidúng.
Bajádi.
Balámdi.
Barba.
Bátale.
Bátechour.
Bhainsigounrá.
Bhuk.
Bijepur.
Bircho.
Birkot.
Bispur.
Boli.
Branja.
Chárble.
Chángle.
Chánglung.
Chankpur.
Chárgáon.
Chetle.
Chipli.
Chisápáni.
Chitre.
Dabúng.
Dágu.
Dampus.
Dangsing.
Dánpos.
Danra.
Daruwá.
Déoráli.
Dháni.
Dhárágáon.
Dharsing.
Dhor.
Dhuánkot.
Ditarli.
Dobahare.
Durungchung.
Eikáng.
Fuinchok.
Gardigáon.
Gayáchok.
Ghable.
Ghráchok.
Ghalel.
Ghánrúng.
Giabrán.
Gilung.
Harpan.
Hásúpur.
Hile.
Hinjákot.
Jaithung.
Jamire.
Janjerori.
Jhúlákot.
Kábre.
Kafulbot.
Kaire.
Kájaldanrá.
Kálábáng.
Kánágáon.
Kárágáon.
Kardi.
Karina.
Karpu.
Karputár.
Káshki.
Khádirjung.
Khayadurjang.
Khillung.
Khinja.
Kiristi.
Koiripáni.
Kolmá.
Kordánrá.
Kowli.
Kulki.
Kúnákanrá.
Kundandanra.
Kurá.
Lále.
Lámachaur.
Lámágáon.
Lámásunwárá.
Lángle.
Lespal.
Limi.
Loang.
Máj.
Makánpur.
Málágiri.
Mandanra.
Manja.
Mánung.
Mánungkot.
Márghi.
Máringsár.
Mohore.
Nawakot.
Nayádánrá.
Nayágáon.
Nindiáchaur.
Okdi.
Okharia.
Painchok.
Pakdhar.
Paljungtar.
Pálpálichhháp.
Pángdur.
Panthdánrá.
Párliá.
Phuleras.
Piárjung.
Pilang.
Pokhrá Bazár.
Pondhar.
Punjia.
Purankot.
Pustum.
Ráinás.
Ráipur.
Ránisuwárá.
Ranjá.
Ranpu.
Rastál.
Remau.

POKHRA—*continued.*

Ribang.
Rijikur.
Rupákot.
Ruse.
Sábit.
Salángkot.
Saldánrá.
Sallián.
Sami.
Sandhikholá.
Samris.
Sánkhu.
Sare.
Shengi.
Shiáklung.
Sidáne.
Siká.
Sidklung.
Siklish.
Sirkot.
Sisapáni.
Sisne.
Sungle.
Ták.
Tákle.
Tákur.
Tamráng.
Tánchok.
Tanjoli.
Tanúng.
Tánsing.
Tántin.
Táondio.
Tárle.
Táprung.
Tulákot.
Uleri.
Wámuna.
Yánjákot.

PYUNG.

Birlung.
Chishapáni.
Lawthung.

RISING.

Amdánrá.
Archald.
Baidi.
Bajágaráh.
Chanchil.
Cherangá.
Chokdánrá.
Danrakhori.
Dánrákthok.
Dená.
Deorali.
Dúmkot.
Gharnng.
Ghiring.
Gongolákh.
Ghothání.
Guáslúm.
Gumántele.
Huka-Huka.
Kakúng.
Khoke.
Kilá.
Kondi.
Kotaidi.
Newápáni.
Paltang.
Panerthok.
Pirung.
Ringkái.
Sabándgi.
Sallián.
Sising.

RUKHAM.

Báchi.
Báchigáon.
Bardákot.
Dhanká.
Dúgúm.
Gorlechháp.
Júlbáng.
Káfaldánrá.
Kálche.
Kánkri.
Kántikot.
Kinushi.
Kurjá.
Magarkot.
Námláng.
Niápáni.
Nigálpáni.
Nisi.
Páchi.
Padámi.
Palentáti.
Rángsing.
Rinke.
Rukam.
Sapángdi.
Sowálá.
Ták.
Tabáng.
Tamán.

## SALLIAN.

Amápur.
Aneri.
Arruah.
Aththar.
Báphi.
Baráchok.
Barágáon.
Dáding.
Dajia.
Dámáchaur.
Dáng.
Dhortá.
Dubring.
Garáhá.
Gorákot.
Hánspur.
Haumuan.
Heng.
Ichok.
Jajarkot.
Jaljalá.
Jamunia.
Jaspur.
Khumkháni.
Kimlang.
Korbáng.
Kotjhári.
Kowlia.
Lachimipur.
Lámtúng.
Madankánrá.
Marpes.
Musikot.
Phándá.
Phártá.
Phidáp.
Rámikánrá.
Rolpakot.
Saipur.
Sakki.
Sákne.
Sallián Bazár.
Sanbás.
Sanká.
Sarbang.
Sirukhark.
Timilkáurá.
Totábás.

## SIANJA.

Adi.
Aigámbi.
Árchaur.
Artha.
Asáre.
Aththar.
Bagnung.
Bálákot.
Bale.
Balgá.
Balkot.
Bangárá.
Batichor.
Bhaderpátá.
Bhaisagaonra.
Binaogkot.
Chábáre.
Chepti.
Chiruwá.
Dádre.
Dángling.
Dánrákot
Deoráli.
Dewánkot.
Dhankot.
Dhunakot.
Gaindi.
Galdo.
Garángdi.
Garúng.
Gemi.
Guáng.
Guliáng.
Gurunj.
Gurungsing.
Hingi.
Jiláng.
Kabre.
Kádámi.
Kaliari.
Kamti.
Karansurá.
Kegmi.
Khaltia.
Kilúng.
Kimudánrá.
Kiristi.
Kolmá.
Láme.
Lápuli.
Limdánrá.
Malángkot.
Nayákark.
Orgádim.
Pakdár.
Pátlepáni.
Pipaltár.
Pokhrichháp.
Ránbáng.
Rapu.
Riserdánrá.
Risinge.
Rugwa.
Sallián.
Sikam.
Singárkot.
Sirbári.
Sirúkhárk.
Siungdi.
Talakot.
Tángráng.
Thela.

## TANUNG

Báhádurpur.
Baisikarka.
Bandipur.
Bankattá.
Bánkewá.
Basnápur.

TANUNG—*continued.*

Bazarkot.
Biáhguti.
Boribot.
Chámákhark.
Chandrá.
Cháng.
Chanoutia.
Chhápthok.
Chisápáni.
Chunemurá.
Dagun.
Darwa.
Deoráli.
Dharampáni.
Doke.
Dordor.
Faruká.
Gajarkot.
Galikhám.
Gehri.
Gunga.
Harkpur.
Jamrung.
Jarbáns.
Jaspur.
Jhár.
Jita.
Jowbári.
Káfalsom.
Katunjia.
Kianing.
Máunng.
Manur.
Marángkot.
Mayakhu.
Mewábari.
Moria.
Nagráon.
Naidar.
Nayágáon.
Okhaldi.
Pachem.
Púlimárung.
Ramkot.
Rátamáta.
Ráwaldanra.
Salbájung.
Sanjá.
Simle.
Sirangá.
Sunder.
Syáno.
Tankot.
Tránka.
Tulsárá.

THANTHAP.

Bokenthan.
Cholomikark.

# CHAPTER XI.

## EASTERN NÉPÁL.

I am told that Eastern Népál is divided into twelve districts; but, notwithstanding my utmost endeavours, I have been unable so far to obtain a correct list of the same.

The following, I feel pretty positive, are true tehsils:—

| | |
|---|---|
| Bhojpur. | Ilam. |
| Dhankota. | Okaldunga. |

I also believe the following to be tehsils:—

Aisal-Kharka, Charikot, Dinglah, Dulkhel, and Chainpur.

I have also heard the following called tehsils:—

Rangeli, Melung, Ramechap.

As a matter of fact, it would seem that any town in which troops are quartered, under the command of an officer, generally not under the rank of Captain, becomes the chief town of the district during such time as the troops are there.

Now, in certain towns troops only remain during the cold weather, like Rangeli.

Numbers of villages would therefore be returned during the cold weather as belonging to the Rangeli district, but on the advent of the hot weather, and consequent departure of the troops to some cooler place, these very villages would no longer be described as belonging to the Rangeli district, but to the town to which the troops have been moved.

A district, therefore, is generally called after the name of the town in which the troops are quartered.

Now, in certain towns, troops remain permanently, such as Dhankota, Ilam, etc., and therefore these are undoubted districts and called Dhankota, Ilam, etc. As a result of the effect that the climate has in the names of certain districts, I may mention that I have often had villages given to me during the hot weather in Darjeeling as belonging to a certain district, whilst in the cold weather at Purneah these same villages have been returned under a different tehsil.

To this custom, therefore, is probably due the confusion which seems to exist regarding the names of the districts into which Eastern Népál is divided, and my difficulty in obtaining a correct list.

I may here mention that the districts of Eastern Népál were originally numbered, and to this day even Bhojpur and Okaldunga are spoken of as "Char number" and "Tín number," respectively.

The adoption of the English word "number" would seem to indicate that the dividing Eastern Népál into districts took place after our war with Népál.

Ilam is just as often called "Kalunga" (*fort*) or "Ilam Kalung."

In the following list no doubt a number of villages appear under two or more tehsils, and I am very fully conscious how very inaccurate my classification probably is, but I think perhaps it is best to submit it as it stands, as it will facilitate the researches of anybody else who undertakes this work after me.

## AISAL-KHARKA.

Badeal.
Baksila.
Bamti.
Bangdeal.
Banspáni.
Bawlia.
Begtaksar.
Bhirkharka.
Bhupsa.
Buigati.
Bung.
Butho.
Charikot.
Chaskori.
Chaukeni.
Chekuwa.
Chibrung.
Chillankar.
Chochmi.
Chonku.
Dimla.
Dimma.
Dipsong.
Dolaka.
Dumko.
Dumria.
Durmadunga.
Ghoti.
Gumdung.
Gumtar.
Hargkhola.
Hungcha.
Ikang.
Jemrire.
Jingu.
Jobin.
Jubo.
Karmi.
Kartamcha.
Kartangchap.
Kewachap.
Khaleri.
Khaple.
Khemti.
Khorada.
Khuabung.
Kolbotia.
Kumdel.
Laduptaksar.
Lamidanah.
Likkukhola.
Lukhim.
Mahabirkhani.
Majuwa.
Makpa.
Mamatim.
Mangtawa.
Nebharia.
Okhre.
Pahare.
Paleka.
Papunga.
Para.
Paspo.
Patel.
Phaliadingle.
Pulchoke.
Rakha.
Ramchap.
Ranikhola.
Rasnalu.
Rawadumba.

AISAL-KHARKA—*continued*.

Rawakhola.
Ribdung.
Salli.
Salpa.
Songdeal.
Sunkhani.
Taothali.
Tintala.
Torikheti.
Tosikhani.
Ulak.
Waoha.
Wakum.
Wapsu.
Wayong.
Yasa.

BHOJPUR.

Ajawa.
Amchoke.
Angtep.
Argolah.
Bágsllanka.
Baiparbasiri.
Biramcho.
Baksila.
Balakharka.
Balumtar.
Bangdel.
Banspani.
Barta.
Rawáni.
Bechuncha.
Begamcha.
Bekomcha.
Bhojkharka.
Bhojpur.
Botla.
Boianamkila.
Bokkim.
Boktan.
Boktar.
Boiabuipa.
Buipar.
Chichile.
Chichumba.
Chiuamkhola.
Chinamku.
Chinamoka.
Chipleti.
Chisnery.
Choladhan.
Chowleny.
Chuichumba.
Dagma.
Danrabakkim.
Danrigunra.
Deosala.
Dhanrakarka.
Dhanwa.
Dibling.
Dikhtel.
Dilpa.
Dinglapa.
Diprung.
Disangwa.
Durpa.
Gairigaon.
Ghunransi.
Ghut.
Goganni.
Gurdum.
Gurrassi.
Hatuwa.
Helungbhon.
Hilongcha.
Hulum.
Immekim.
Jariotar.
Jubung.
Kaberi.
Kanare.
Karlamcha.
Karmi.
Katti.
Kattibamrang.
Kesankur.
Khesungba.
Khikamacha.
Khatoje.
Khukamacha.
Koksik.
Kokombu.
Kotang.
Kumdaling.
Kutung.
Kutta.
Lámakhu.
Likuwa.
Lomdhu.
Lungkuwa.
Lungtung.
Magneh.
Majkharka.
Majkirat.
Majna.
Majuwa.
Makaibari.
Mákpar.
Malbasi.
Malubansi.
Manding.
Matim.
Menpur.
Namanta.
Nigabas.
Norrong.
Pangta.
Phalidingla.
Phalikot.
Pokhre.
Photung.
Powakhesang.
Rakha.
Rasuwa.
Ratuncha.
Rawakhola.
Reeng.
Rimchin.
Rumbna.
Rumjatar.
Salatem.

BHOJPUR—*continued.*

Sangpang.
Sangrang.
Sawa.
Sikayo.
Siktel.
Siktelwerung.
Siltal.
Simpani.
Sindran.
Sisnari.
Solliah.
Soring.
Soraka.
Sotang.
Sungdel.
Tallegaon.
Tamlicha.
Tangbang.
Timba.
Wacha.
Yamdang.
Yámdang.
Yaphu.

CHAINPUR.

Ambote.
Arjale.
Bagha.
Batase.
Chanwa.
Chapabhain.
Chitlang.
Chongkurung.
Damara.
Danragaon.
Dhubbu.
Eba.
Hangpang.
Hatisuni.
Kambara.
Karangdanra.
Kherabari.
Kuigiring.
Kusuwa.
Langlingkhane.
Madin.
Maidane.
Malbanse.
Mamling.
Mowaden.
Nandhaki.
Paka.
Pakribas.
Phabin.
Phadem.
Pitala.
Pokribas.
Sidipur.
Simphua.
Singlagarri.
Sunajik.
Tumling.
Wana.
Wabung.
Yangsango.

CHARIKOT.

Bamti.
Bangdali.
Begutaksar.
Bhanda.
Bingati.
Bulung.
Butho.
Changkhu.
Charikot.
Chillankai.
Chougku.
Damara.
Dolaka.
Dula.
Ghoti.
Gumdung.
Gumtar.
Hambu.
Haskhu.
Ikaung.
Jangu.
Jemire.
Kabre.
Kaleri.
Khapli.
Khemti.
Laduptaksar.
Likkukhola.
Mahabirkhani.
Mangtawa.
Melung.
Mukiabári.
Namdung.
Ningalia.
Okre.
Pákár.
Pobott.
Puhare.
Puspo.
Ranichap.
Ranikhola.
Rasnala.
Sulpa.
Sunkhani.
Taotale.
Torikhet.
Tosikhani.
Ulak.
Yasa.

DHANKOTA.

Ahalia.
Akhisalla.
Akhoboi.
Ambalung.
Ambhotia.
Ambole.
Andhiri.
Angho.
Angna.
Angsrang.
Argale.
Arubhotia.
Atbrai.
Bagha.
Bagunga.

DHANKOTA—*continued.*

Báldunga.
Bálukhop.
Baniagharu.
Banspani.
Barabase.
Barjam.
Batasse.
Bejambo.
Belárá.
Beugna.
Bettara.
Bhalukote.
Bharapar.
Bhittria.
Bhode.
Bhodok.
Bokkim.
Buddia.
Budhekarle.
Budhok.
Bunchania.
Burimorong.
Chainpu.
Chaintimba.
Chaluwa.
Chamtapu.
Chandani.
Changia.
Chanowa.
Chantápu.
Chaodanda.
Chapabhain.
Cheruwa.
Chiabre.
Chikroba.
Chimpakot.
Chintang.
Chitloug.
Chityok.
Chokmago.
Chougkurang.
Chowdanna.
Chowria.
Chuhandanra.
Chummangdangsi.
Chumpakota.
Chungbang.
Churman.
Damara.
Damresi.
Dangdange.
Danragaon.
Darlámi.
Dembi.
Dengápá.
Dhaukota.
Dhoku.
Dhoraj.
Dhubbe.
Didima.
Dingla.
Dorumba.
Duseni.
Eba.
Fakuma.
Fauguwa.
Gairi.
Garrigaon.
Gasuwa.
Gomanipata.
Gosuwa.
Guranse.
Gurhumba.
Halliasi.
Hallikarki.
Hamarjang.
Hamlalung.
Hangdewa.
Hangdem.
Hangghum.
Hangmara.
Haugpabung.
Hangpang.
Hangsimba.
Hangthawa.
Hanjoun.
Hastapur.
Háthimárá.
Hatikarkarka.
Hatisunre.
Hellia.
Hewako.
Hora.
Hunga.
Imbong.
Inchimári.
Isbo.
Jagamágu.
Jagdabari.
Jelahar.
Jinjuwa.
Jongia.
Kamba.
Kambare.
Kamlalung.
Kanjabar.
Kauniabar.
Kaphrebás.
Kaphrebote.
Kartike.
Karangdanra.
Kasirah.
Keharapua.
Kepek.
Keplabung.
Karinim.
Kewaring.
Kheoren.
Khesirata.
Khesita.
Khewabari.
Khikamacha.
Khodambu.
Khokse.
Khopchia.
Khopek.
Khowaphuk
Khuuwa.
Kibaug.
Kingring.
Kogling.
Kopchia.
Koyakhola.
Kumdaug.
Kurle.
Kurungbang.
Kusuwa.
Labre.

DHANKOTA—*continued.*

Laktapa.
Lálikarka.
Lámátár.
Langlingkani.
Lanjakor.
Lasunia.
Lebong.
Libang.
Lingdep.
Lingdim.
Lingkim.
Loapho.
Loungphabang.
Lumluk.
Lungwdi.
Lysingbang.
Madi.
Madamsing.
Máhabangkhu.
Mahang.
Mahangbelara.
Mahden.
Mahwa.
Maidane.
Majtola.
Makluba.
Maklung.
Malabasi.
Malabari.
Malgaon.
Malna.
Mamling.
Manaljong.
Manebung.
Mandrewa.
Mare.
Mehalbotia.
Mehale.
Mewakhola.
Mewaraja.
Moga.
Mongsari.
Morhangsurki.
Morongabang.
Mulgaon.
Munaljong.
Murtidunga.
Muwaden.
Nage.
Namdaki.
Namdukhola.
Namja.
Namjong.
Nampua.
Nangin.
Nankhola.
Naongia.
Nasawa.
Nembang.
Nenadin.
Newradin.
Nigalia.
Nihili.
Nimba.
Ningáli.
Nirpa.
Nohwa.
Nungia.
Oba.
Okri.
Oplabung.
Orok.
Oyem.
Paka.
Pákungwa.
Pakribas.
Pále.
Palthen.
Panthar.
Parjong.
Parriadin.
Parti.
Patigaon.
Patlia.
Pawakhola.
Pehwa.
Perwaden.
Petala.
Phabin.
Phakchowa.
Phakdag.
Phákuma.
Phámtung.
Phedap.
Phedayo.
Phedapjung.
Phedim.
Phejongyok.
Phembia.
Pheodim.
Phewa.
Phijung.
Phokribas.
Phoglung.
Phondara.
Phugong.
Phundwa.
Phurpa.
Pithungba.
Pitlap.
Poklabung.
Pokri.
Puldung.
Pulkia.
Purjan.
Rakha.
Rámpur.
Ranigaon.
Rasna.
Rawakhola.
Rinchim.
Safinwa.
Sajingwa.
Sakayajong.
Salerí.
Salungwa.
Samangku.
Samba.
Sambiyok.
Samdorok.
Sandu.
Sangabho.
Sangakar.
Sanguam.
Sangu.
Sánsingwa.
Santas.
Santhakra.

DHANKOTA—*continued.*

Saplaku.
Sárán.
Sartap.
Saungbang.
Sawaden.
Sawreni.
Seabrung.
Selajung.
Sendowa.
Serung.
Shaungia.
Sheabrumba.
Shubhong.
Siawa.
Sindua.
Sikhtem.
Sikkarpur.
Silijung.
Simle.
Simphua.
Simra.
Sinam.
Singdeal.
Singiti.
Sirahe.
Sirjaon.
Sirpong.
Siwakhola.
Solaháni.
Solma.
Sowriani.
Subhang.
Subna.
Sundanre.
Sumdhu.
Sudáp.
Sungnam.
Suwara.
Tábibhung.
Tablijung.
Tamakia.
Tamaphuk.
Tambarkholu.
Támkhu.
Tamrang.
Tamsang.
Tamtung.
Tangkna.
Tángphu.
Tangsua.
Taprung.
Tapliajung.
Tárid.
Taungaba.
Taunkowa.
Taunyma.
Tekunala.
Tellang.
Tellok.
Tembhe.
Thamthum.
Tharpu.
Thechomba.
Thinglabo.
Thobibung.
Thoppi.
Thorke.
Thouglong.
Thougseling.
Thotni.
Thukima.
Thungkaling.
Thunglabang.
Thungsaling.
Tilkani.
Tilluk.
Tinsale.
Tiringia.
Titima.
Torke.
Tua.
Tumling.
Tungka.
Tunglabong.
Tungrungwa.
Tungsumma.
Tunlung.
Umlabong.
Umling.
Unglabary.
Ungsaon.
Wadin.
Wajong.
Waneni.
Waredin.
Warephung.
Werakot.
Whaku.
Woroka.
Woroklámá.
Woyom.
Yangmang.
Yangrup.
Yangsingjong.
Yasok.
Yeawah.
Yeogumba.
Yesabu.
Yoem.
Yumbung.
Yuwa.

DINGLA.

Angola.
Begamcha.
Boya.
Chichila.
Dinglah.
Hálhbári.
Kartamcha.
Kumdalung.
Mojuwa.
Palisangpang.
Phedi.
Salio.
Salwa.
Sangpang.
Sangrang.
Siktel.
Sishneri.
Wacha.

## ILAM.

Ahle.
Amchok.
Angdang.
Angklibuin.
Arubote.
Balang.
Bangin.
Bárápání.
Barbote.
Bardu.
Basthala.
Batasse.
Bhirhe.
Bhite.
Bilandu.
Budhok.
Chainpur.
Chamaita.
Charkhola.
Chetok.
Chipchongba.
Chirbong.
Chisopani.
Chitre.
Chombang.
Chuichumba.
Churighatta.
Ebang.
Ekatapa.
Fudnk.
Guiri.
Geabang.
Godak.
Godop.
Gogune.
Golakharka.
Gorkhia.
Gorkhiajagat.
Guling.
Gupta.
Hangsarumba.
Ibaung.
Ilam.
Ingla.
Jamuna.
Jaobari.
Jil.
Jitpur.
Jogmai.
Jumbling.
Kagatpani.
Kakchumbung.
Kalumsing.
Kannia.
Karbirtár.
Katebung.
Keangbung.
Kerabari.
Kerbok.
Kewabung.
Khámáng.
Khanibanjan.
Kholme.
Kolbote.
Kurplok.
Laohetár.
Langrup.
Lingden.
Lodia.
Lodiajagat.
Longrapa.
Lumbeh.
Lumde.
Madebung.
Madu.
Maglapa.
Mahbo.
Maidane.
Maimajuwa.
Mainrapnr.
Majowa.
Mallate.
Maltu.
Mánglabári.
Márluba.
Marse.
Meamkhola.
Mechi.
Mehalbote.
Moyangkhola.
Nagrung.
Namsaling.
Namthala.
Nindaka.
Okri.
Pangdola.
Pangnam.
Panghung.
Pangkha.
Pawana.
Peang.
Pengpatal.
Permighari.
Phajebung.
Phajiphekal.
Phakphok.
Phekal.
Phuantapa.
Phudap.
Phudok.
Phudokshiswa.
Pongkom.
Pungpung.
Rabbi.
Rangapang.
Ratmáti.
Rungsung.
Sabri.
Saffia.
Sakanamba
Sakhejung.
Sakia.
Samalbung.
Sambek.
Sangromba.
Saunlungba.
Sidhikhola.
Sinam.
Singlapa.
Singphering.
Sirbong.
Sirrisse.
Soyang.
Sulubung.
Sumbhiyok.
Suntalli.
Surkia.

ILAM—*continued.*

Tági.
Takpare.
Talkharka.
Targaon.
Tawaung.
Telpani.
Thaungalungma.
Tingiapani.
Tobang.
Tumling.
Tungphung.
Ulákdhanra.
Untu.
Walfrung.
Yabadeppa.
Yektapa.

OKALDUNGA.

Aisalkarka.
Amsownar.
Arkhowli.
Bagutaksar.
Baksila.
Bámráng.
Bansbhotea.
Bedesi.
Betali.
Beteui.
Bilinde.
Bodia.
Botachap.
Boungnam.
Buipar.
Buiparuleui.
Bunga.
Bunpha.
Burdung.
Chainpur.
Charku.
Charnsing.
Cheskam.
Chimpi.
Chinam.
Chisopani.
Chisungu.
Chisunpha.
Chochima.
Chowtara.
Chumako.
Chuple.
Danrugaon.
Dariatar.
Deorali.
Deosur.
Dhulkia.
Dimma.
Dipsing.
Dropuge.
Drosa.
Durpat.
Gairigaon.
Gudeh.
Hakola.
Halesi.
Hanchur.
Iname.
Jangjong.
Jantarkhaui.
Jarugi.
Jubling.
Jubung.
Jupa.
Kalpa.
Kanggial.
Kangkhu.
Kanjel.
Kanka.
Katiki.
Katonjia.
Kerung.
Kewangia.
Khaleling.
Kikamacha.
Kisanku.
Kuibir.
Kumaltar.
Likhukhola.
Limitar.
Madapur.
Maideal.
Majkharka.
Majuwa.
Makha.
Makpha.
Mame.
Manibharjan.
Mukle.
Náme.
Namsaling.
Nawalpur.
Necha.
Nerpa.
Oksachowrasi.
Parapenha.
Phedi.
Phuksia.
Phuliali.
Pilma.
Ramechap.
Ranadip.
Rapcha.
Rassim.
Ratamate.
Rawakhola.
Rippa.
Rumjadhanra.
Rumjatar.
Saddi.
Salla.
Sarreh.
Sirna.
Solamani.
Sotang.
Sungnam.
Taluwa.
Tari.
Tekanpur.
Tilpung.
Tinglah.
Urlane.
Waku.
Waksikang.
Watcha.
Woksar.
Yesiong.
Yesom.